Religion,
Postcolonialism,
and Globalization

ALSO AVAILABLE FROM BLOOMSBURY

The Study of Religion, George Chryssides and Benjamin Zeller
Religions and Environments, Richard Bohannon
The Daoist Tradition, Louis Komjathy

Religion, Postcolonialism, and Globalization

A Sourcebook

JENNIFER REID

Bloomsbury Academic
An imprint of Bloomsbury Publishing Plc

B L O O M S B U R Y
LONDON • NEW DELHI • NEW YORK • SYDNEY

Bloomsbury Academic

An imprint of Bloomsbury Publishing Plc

50 Bedford Square	1385 Broadway
London	New York
WC1B 3DP	NY 10018
UK	USA

www.bloomsbury.com

BLOOMSBURY and the Diana logo are trademarks of Bloomsbury Publishing Plc

First published 2015

British Library Cataloguing-in-Publication Data

A catalogue record for this book is available from the British Library.

ISBN: HB: 978-1-4725-8608-7
PB: 978-1-4725-8609-4
ePDF: 978-1-4725-8610-0
ePub: 978-1-4725-8611-7

Library of Congress Cataloging-in-Publication Data

Religion, postcolonialism, and globalization : a sourcebook / [edited by] Jennifer Reid.
pages cm
Includes bibliographical references.
ISBN 978-1-4725-8608-7 (hardback)– ISBN 978-1-4725-8609-4 (paperback) 1. Globalization–Religious aspects. 2. Postcolonialism–Religious aspects I. Reid, Jennifer, 1962- editor.
BL65.G55R425 2015
201'.7–dc23
2014032531

Typeset by Fakenham Prepress Solutions, Fakenham, Norfolk NR21 8NN
Printed and bound in Great Britain

For my students

Contents

CONTENTS

Permission information

The following extracts were reproduced with kind permission. The publishers have made every effort to trace copyright holders and to obtain permission to reproduce extracts. Any omissions brought to our attention will be remedied on future editions.

Section I

1.1 "Inter Caetera," in Frances Gardiner Davenport (ed.), *European Treaties Bearing on the History of the United States and Its Dependencies to 1648* (1917) reproduced by permission of the Carnegie Institution for Science.

1.2 Copy of Letters Patent granted by Henry VII to John Cabot (March 5, 1496). Source: Library and Archives Canada/The precursors of Jacques Cartier, 1497–1534: A collection of documents relating to the early history of the Dominion of Canada/AMICUS 4479920 / pp. 8–10. This text is in the public domain.

1.3 "An Act for Continuing in The East India Company, for a further Term, The Possession of the British Territories in India, together with certain exclusive Privileges for establishing further Regulations for the Government of the said Territories, and the better Administration of Justice within the same; and for regulating the Trade to, and from, the Places within the Limits of the said Company's Charter" (July 21, 1813). © The British Library Board, IOL.1947.b.325(a).

1.4 "Military Globalization is Nothing New," by Tarak Barkawi (June 11, 2011), reproduced by permission of *Aljazeera America* online (AJE).

1.5 Immanuel Wallerstein, *The Modern World System I: Capitalist Agriculture and the Origins of the European World Economy in the Sixteenth Century*, © 2011 by the Regents of the University of California. Published by the University of California Press.

1.6 Max Weber, *Protestant Ethic and the Spirit of Capitalism*, first edn, © 1977, pp. 90–97. Reprinted by permission of Pearson Education, Inc., Upper Saddle River, NJ.

Section II

2.1 "The Clash of Civilizations," by Samuel P. Huntington, abridged from *Foreign Affairs* (1993), reprinted by permission of *Foreign Affairs*, 72, no. 3, summer 1993, © 1993 by the Council on Foreign Relations, Inc. www. ForeignAffairs.com.

2.2 "Jihad vs. McWorld," by Benjamin Barber, abridged from *The Atlantic* (1992). Published originally in "Jihad vs. McWorld," Benjamin R. Barber, *The Atlantic*, 269, March 3, 1992, pp. 53–65.

Benjamin R. Barber is president of the international NGO CivWorld and of the Interdependence Movement, Walt Whitman Professor Emeritus at Rutgers University, and the author of 19 books, including the classic Strong Democracy, the international best-seller *Jihad vs. McWorld*, and, forthcoming from Yale University Press, *If Mayors Ruled the World*.

2.3 "Ethics Must be Global, Not Local," by Bill George, *Business Week* (February 12, 2008), reproduced by permission of *Business Week*.

2.4 "The Clash of Ignorance," by Edward W. Said, from *The Nation* (October 4, 2001), reproduced by permission of *The Nation*.

2.5 "Disjuncture and Difference in the Global Cultural Economy," by Arjun Appadurai, abridged from *Public Culture*, 2, no. 4, 1990, pp. 1–24, © 1990, Duke University Press. All rights reserved. Republished by permission of the copyright holder, Duke University Press. www.dukeupress.edu.

2.6 "What Clash of Civilization? Why Religious Identity Isn't Destiny," by Amartya Sen, from *Slate* (March 29, 2006), reproduced by permission of Amartya Sen.

2.7 "Doing Cross-Cultural Religious Business: Globalization, Americanization, Cocacolonization, McDonaldization, Disneyization, Tupperization, and other Local Dilemmas of Global Signification in the Study of Religion," by David Chidester, abridged from *Religion and Global Culture* (2003), reproduced by permission of Lexington Books.

Section III

3.1 "Perpetual Peace: A Philosophical Essay," by Immanuel Kant [1795], The Macmillan Company, (1917). This text is in the public domain.

3.2 "The Kantian Project of the Constitutionalization of International Law: Does it Still Have a Chance?," by Jürgen Habermas, abridged from *Multiculturalism and Law: A Critical Debate* (2007), reproduced by permission of University of Wales Press.

3.3 "Patriotism and Cosmopolitanism," by Martha Nussbaum, © 1996 by Martha Nussbaum and Joshua Cohen. Reprinted by permission of Beacon Press, Boston.

3.4 "Cosmopolitan Democracy and the Global Order: A New Agenda," by David Held. James Bohman and Matthias Lutz-Bachman (eds), *Perpetual Peace: Essays on Kant's Cosmopolitan Ideal*, pp. up to 4,000 words, © 1997 Massachusetts Institute of Technology, by permission of The MIT Press.

3.5 "The Case for Contamination," by Kwame Anthony Appiah, *New York Times* (January 1, 2006), reproduced by permission of Kwame Anthony Appiah.

3.6 "Cosmopolitanism and Nationalism," by Craig Calhoun, abridged from "Cosmopolitanism and Nationalism," *Nations and Nationalism*, 14, no. 3, 2008, pp. 427–48, reproduced by permission of Wiley.

3.7 "Defining a New Cosmopolitanism: Towards a Dialogue of Asian Civilizations," by Ashis Nandy. Kuan-Hsing Chen (ed), *Trajectories: Inter-Asia Cultural Studies*, © 1998 and Routledge. Reproduced by permission of Taylor & Francis Books UK.

3.8 Srinivas Aravamudan, "Guru English," in *Social Text*, 66, no. 1, 2001, pp. 19–44, © 2001, Duke University Press. All rights reserved. Republished by permission of the copyright holder, Duke University Press. www.dukeupress. edu.

Section IV

4.1 "Royal Commentaries of the Incas and General History of Peru, Part One," by Garcilaso de la Vega, translated by Harold V. Livermore, © 1966. Reproduced by permission of University of Texas Press.

4.2 "Manifesto of the Second Pan-African Congress," *The Crisis*, 23 (November 1921). This text is in the public domain.

4.3 "The Fourth World: Nations without a State," by Bernard O. Nietschmann (1985), reproduced by permission of the Center for World Indigenous Studies.

4.4 "United League of Indigenous Nations Treaty, 2007," reproduced by permission of the United League of Indigenous Nations.

4.5 "Economic Globalization, Indigenous Peoples, and the Role of Indigenous Women," by Makere Harawira, presentation at The Hague Appeal for Peace Conference (May 1999), reproduced by permission of Makere Harawira.

4.6 "In Living Memory," by Pedro Pérez Sarduy, translated by Jean Stubbs (2001), reproduced by permission of Pedro Pérez Sarduy.

4.7 "EarthChild," by Kofi Anyidoho, from *Ancestrallogic and Caribbean Blues* (1993), reproduced by permission of Africa World Press & The Red Sea Press.

4.8 "My Kind of Exile," by Tenzin Tsundue, reproduced with the author's permission from *KORA: Stories and Poems*, eighth edn, 2012, published by TibetWrites. ISBN number: 81-904174-5-2.

Acknowledgments

In compiling this sourcebook I received assistance from a number of people. In my attempt to track down certain sources I was helped by Randal Cummings, Jualynne Dodson, Marisela Funes, and Casey Koons. Thank you to each of you. I must also thank Kristin McLaren for her willingness to hash through questions for discussion with me; and Sarah Otley, Debra Kinney, and Shari Witham for their tireless support of my research. My thanks also to Charles H. Long for his patience in discussing the ideas underlying this sourcebook, and for years of conversation without which the book could not have materialized. Finally my thanks to Lalle Pursglove for her unflagging faith in the project.

Introduction

[handwritten annotations at top:]
- Fundamentalism → self-description of Christian movement (1910s–
There is a core to the belief (literal biblical reading) 1920s)
* when globalization happens, fundamentalist get angry & want to defend religion

While the subject of globalization has inspired a mind-boggling number of academic and popular books over the past few decades, the relationship between globalization and religion has received comparatively scant attention. Moreover when the subject has been broached it has generally entered into our field of vision in one of three ways. First, the discussion of religion and globalization often constellates around the rise of fundamentalism, especially Islamic fundamentalism but, by extension, fundamentalisms elsewhere (for example, Christian evangelicalism in the United States). In this camp we find a spate of books published in the last decade or so with titles like *Fundamentalism in the Modern World*; *The Battle for God*; *Unholy War: Terror in the Name of Islam*; *Terror in the Mind of God*; *America and Political Islam: Clash of Cultures or Clash of Interests?*; *Jihad: The Trail of Political Islam*; and *Religious Fundamentalism: Global, Local and Personal*.[1] Books like these vary in their approaches to the subject. Some regard fundamentalism as a radical response to the forces of globalization, while others see fundamentalism as a globalizing enterprise in itself.

A second focus for work on the subject has been on religion as a discrete aspect of culture affected by forces of globalization. In this corpus we are dealing with work that equates religion with systems of beliefs and values that respond to, or resist, its challenges. Those who write from this perspective have generally been concerned with exploring the impact on—and responses to—globalization surfacing from the local and diasporic experiences of Buddhists, Christians, Muslims, Hindus, etc. These are explorations circumscribed by the systems we sometimes call the "Great Religions" or "new religious movements." Here we find available to us books like *God and Globalization*; *Gods in the Global Village: The World's Religions in Sociological Perspective*; *Religion and Globalization: World Religions in Historical Perspective*; and *The Desecularization of the World: Resurgent Religion and World Politics*.[2]

Finally, some theorists have been concerned with creating ethical standards for guiding transcultural and transnational relationships in our time. In this category we find titles like *Ethics and World Religions: Cross-Cultural Case Studies*; *Conscience across Borders: An Ethics of Global Rights and Religious Pluralism*; *Religion and Ethics in a Globalizing World*; and *Globalization, Spirituality, and Justice: Navigating the Path to Peace*.[3] Many of these books

[handwritten margin notes, right side:]
* religion is a discrete aspect of culture
* particular religions groups – world religions
* what makes something a religion ii. cult vt. spiritual experience

[handwritten note at bottom:]
→ many diff religions, what is shared?
What are shared values & standards?

draw on Western philosophical and theological traditions, seeking to find a universal set of ethical principles. Others seek to reconcile culturally diverse ethical systems with one another to arrive at a shared set of values for conducting transnational and transcultural relationships.

While these are all valid approaches to considering the relationship between religion and globalization, in the collection of readings to follow we will approach the subject from a slightly different vantage point: in essence, we will consider globalization itself as a religious problem.

Globalization

In this sourcebook we will be guided by a basic premise: that the concept of globalization cannot be limited to its conventional definition as a post-WWII economic phenomenon related to Western capitalist expansion and neoliberalism economic policies. There is no doubt that neoliberalism plays a substantive role in our global economy. In fact, it might accurately be said to be the principal economic and political template of late modernity. The crux of neoliberalism, which is generally thought to have emerged under the guiding hands of Ronald Reagan in the United States and Margaret Thatcher in Britain in the 1980s, is the need for a free market where enterprising capitalists and insatiable consumers can play out their relationships with one another. Not surprisingly, the term globalization has also been in the air since the 1980s when it began to appear in the discourses of sociologists and business interests.

The word elicits a variety of responses. Some of us like the idea of globalization and the world it invokes: a place where economic development, and the benefits that will accrue of it, are inevitable and desirable. In this sense globalization is the result of technological ingenuity meeting with transnational trade and the integration of national economies. For those who are in the business of making money globalization understood in this manner is a godsend. Larger markets mean larger volumes of exports, cheaper imports, and greater access to capital flow. More flowing capital means there is simply more money to be made.

Some others among us, however, are troubled by the word globalization. As national economies have supposedly become more integrated, disparities between rich and poor have been amplified. From this perspective, economic expansion and integration has been synonymous with exploitation and deepening social inequalities. Regardless of how we might feel about globalization, however, the word generally invokes two central meanings:

the intensification of worldwide social relations which link distant localities in such a way that local happenings are shaped by events occurring many miles away and vice versa. (Giddens 1990: 64)

[the ascendency of] a capitalist world-economy ... built on having a multiplicity of value systems within it, reflecting the specific functions groups and areas play in the world division of labor. (Wallerstein 2011: 356)

Neoliberalism—and the idea of globalization—however, is also in many ways a recent incarnation of an old set of values and practices whereby a minority of economically and politically powerful entities have pursued unfettered financial gain through their intrusion into as many aspects of people's lives as possible. The roots of our twenty-first-century globalized world run much deeper than the 1980s or even the end of World War II. In fact, as we will see in the entries in our first section of this sourcebook, they can be traced back at least to the beginning of European colonial expansion of the fifteenth century through which the "modern world-system" came into existence.

A quick glance at the list of selections in this sourcebook points to this temporally expansive view of the term globalization, the foundations of which can be argued to trace back to the beginning of the European colonial era and the voyages of Christopher Columbus. Prior to 1492, Europeans moved around a lot. They traded, warred, and exchanged religious and cultural ideas across great geographic distances, sometimes referred to as worlds. But these movements were not thought to be global enterprises. We might think here, for example, of the Silk Road. This was a 4,000-mile trade route that connected China to India, Persia, Arabia, East Africa, Egypt, and ultimately Europe beginning in the first century before the Common Era and continuing until the mid-fifteenth century when the Ottoman Empire broke off relations with Europe. The westward voyages of Christopher Columbus, which were precipitated by this shutdown of eastern trade routes, signaled more than simply a shift in direction. The discovery of a "New World" was essentially the discovery of a global world.

Now, we all know that Columbus did not discover the Americas. Norsemen made the transatlantic trip and founded the village of L' Anse aux Meadows in present-day Newfoundland 500 years before Columbus's excursions. Polynesian sailors landed in South America sometime between three and five centuries before that. And, of course, the ancestors of indigenous peoples found their way to the Americas at least 13,000 years before the Polynesians. While Columbus most certainly did not discover America, he did indeed discover something hitherto unknown: a new global world. With his voyages, the European imagination was opened to the possibility of the globe as a massive contested grid for expanding economic, cultural, and human exchange. Competitive traffic of this magnitude required a conceptual shift from the notion of trade routes linking empires to a planetary network of rival economic interests. It is perhaps a not-so-strange irony that for a great many of us, any mention of the Silk Road now invokes not images of a pre-Columbian network of military, cultural and economic exchange, but an internet prototype for a global black market in illegal drugs (and its spinoffs in various other nefarious trades).

Religion

It is another underlying premise of this sourcebook that we can think differently about globalization if we begin by questioning our common presumption that religion and globalization are distinct entities, autonomous agents as it were that intersect at certain points, but that are also separable in our discourses and our practices. How would our world look to us if we were to regard globalization as a fundamentally religious phenomenon? The readings included in this sourcebook, and the Questions for Discussion that follow them, will seek to raise questions that invite us to consider this possibility.

When we think of religion in conventional terms, the first thing that often comes to mind is the idea of structured institutions or systems of philosophical thought and ethical standards. We tend to equate the term with the so-called "Great Religions" like Buddhism, Christianity, Hinduism, Islam, or Judaism. There is no doubt that religion thus conceived has played a foundational role in the creation of a global world. Contemporary terrorist groups, for example, all too often identify themselves with one or another of these traditions. And long before the rise of this kind of recent violence religious institutions were similarly imbedded in European colonial expansion through which our globalized world came into existence. Christianity was a tool of oppression from earliest colonial contact, travelling hand-in-hand with European economic interests as they crossed oceans and created settler societies around the globe.

But this is not the only way—nor necessarily the most useful way—to understand religion in a global world. In fact, the "Great Religions" model of religion is a Western one, having been variously attached to cultures in which there is no equivalent concept. The Indian term *dharma* or the Native American concept of spirituality, for instance, refer to broad modalities of life that are suffused with sacrality, rather than to distinct entities that can be separated from other arenas of cultural life (economic, political, social, etc.). In these contexts the sacred informs all human interactions, mediates relationships, and binds persons to one another and to other non-human entities." Dis-moi quel est ton Dieu, dis-moi quel es ton monde, et je te dirai qui tu es," wrote the French philosopher Georges Gusdorf: [Tell me who is your God, tell me what is your world, and I will tell you who you are.[4] It is this broader notion of religion that we will take up in this book.

The basic definition of religion that we will employ in this context is that of the historian of religions Charles H. Long. Long proposes that, whatever else may be said about religion, it is always at root a mode of ultimate orientation in the world.[5] Now this definition presupposes a number of factors. First we must remind ourselves that worlds are not necessarily given. We can speak simultaneously of the Old World and New World; World War I and World War II; the First World, Second World and Third World; a global world, a cyber world, the World Bank, and Disney World. Obviously these are not all the same world. Some of us have been, and are, included in them, some of us are not. Thus in thinking about a world, any world, we must immediately take note of the fact that it is not known or experienced the same way by all persons or communities. Furthermore, the rules of engagement in any particular world do not carry over into others. Being accosted by an eight-foot tall mouse, for example, may be perfectly acceptable, even desirable, at Disney World, but few of us would react positively to the same thing occurring, say, in New York City's Central Park.

Worlds, however, also share some basic commonalities. They all, for instance, draw boundaries around what we perceive as meaningful and important at any given time and in any given space. While many of us who are constantly online via our laptops, tablets, and cell phones can speak of a cyber world as a kind of global structure, for example, the fact remains that 2.3 billion people on the planet—about a third of our total population—do not have internet access.[6] Thus we can say that worlds are arbitrary even as they appear real and fixed. They have fluid boundaries that are perceived as at once stable and changeable, and within those boundaries we must of necessity define ourselves. We must establish who and where we are to make any thought or action possible, a process that is never-ending given that worlds are constantly changing, coming into being, and passing away.

This brings us to the second factor to be considered in this definition of religion: that of orientation. This term simply refers to the process of defining ourselves, of establishing the meaning of our individual and social bodies within the framework of any particular world. We find our orientation in relation to the things that impinge on our own sense of who we are in any given temporal and special frame: landscape and climate, for example, and perhaps most importantly other people, both intimates and strangers. The principal way in which we establish our identity is through relationships with these various others, and this is where we begin to speak of that crucial factor in defining religion: ultimacy. Ultimacy refers to that which transcends normal spatial and temporal parameters: gods, spirits, angels, living ancestors, to name just a few forms this transcendent structure can assume for us. Ultimacy is aligned with reciprocity; it is in a sense the surplus value of an exchange that then gives legitimacy to the identities that are being forged.

To get a hold of the religious meaning of what we call globalization it is important that we enter into this religiously charged meaning of exchange. The forces associated with what we now call globalization are experienced as what the French sociologist Marcel Mauss would have described as a total social fact, that is, a phenomenon whose presence is felt at every level of society: in economics, law, politics, and religion. In this sense, globalization is, and has always been, implicated in another "total social fact" that concerned Mauss: the exchange of gifts.

In his classic book *The Gift: The Form and Reason for Exchange in Archaic Societies* Mauss spoke a good deal about the logic of exchange. He argued that gift-giving is not simply about being friendly. Rather, it is the glue that holds persons, cultures and societies together. Gifts, he wrote, exert "a *magical* and *religious* hold" over the recipient.[7] They are dynamic. They compel the recipient to restore to the giver some comparable entity. Refusal to enter into a process of reciprocity with an immediate other is a refusal to negotiate the boundary between persons and communities and, consequently, to acknowledge some manner of shared humanity.

Humans are social beings. For most of our time on this planet, we have exchanged things with one another to maintain our relationships: personal property and wealth, to be sure; but also feasts, acts of kindness, military assistance, dances, and rituals.[8] The things themselves that we have exchanged have been more than simply gross matter. In the act of exchange they assume a significance that is greater than what they seem: they become religiously significant because they introduce a transcendent meaning into relationships, one not limited to the act of passing an object from one person or community to another, nor to the material substance of that which is exchanged. Things that are valued in this way are what give form to relationships. It is no accident that for most of human history exchanges have often been accompanied by frankly religious language, and often too by ritual and the invocation of non-human entities.

Now, the meaning of exchange in our time has been complicated by something peculiar to modernity: the universal use of money as it emerged in mercantile—and later capitalist—economies. The use of money in the first instance seriously subverts barter economies. More broadly, it is a neutral specie that undermines systems of reciprocity. Once a person has paid for an item, or has been paid for their labor, there is no necessity for reciprocating. Working to produce goods or commodities or money does not involve the production of social relationships—the product or money itself becomes the purpose of work. When one works to produce things and money, rather than relationships, alienation results.

Globalization is often referred to as a system of worldwide exchanges. This may not be the most accurate way to speak of it, since it is not clear that the logic of exchange is actually part of our network of global relationships. A lot of money and information and generalized stuff is making its way around the globe at unprecedented speed and in unprecedented volume. But all this trafficking is not generally thought to be enhancing a sense of community among those who are implicated in it. It most assuredly is lacking in a level of religious meaning that binds persons and communities to one another in a mutually enriching way. We might remind ourselves that the word *religion* is derived of the Latin word *religare*—to bind and rebind. For most of human history, exchanges bound us to one another in a way that enhanced our personal and social identities, by legitimizing them in terms of transcendent powers. These are the surpluses generated by the act of exchange to which we have also then been bound. It is no accident therefore that among those who have been most oppressed by the expansion of modern and late modern capitalist enterprise, we often find experiences and invocations of ultimate powers to mediate and ameliorate a dehumanizing situation—calls for reciprocity sanctified by something other than capital accumulation.

Globalization and religion

In a sense "globalization" is a recent term in a string of Western attempts to name and, perhaps more importantly, to map the nature of modernity. A map is a metaphor that seeks to compress a lot of information into a manageable and understandable model. But a map is also about power. Maps in modernity have been inextricably tied to European expansion and territorial claims in the interest of mercantile and capitalist gain. New World lands were initially mapped by European explorers backed by sovereign powers. Soon after, territories that were desired but also inhabited by indigenous societies were designated on maps as *terra nullius*—empty land and thus free for the taking. Later the map of Africa would be redrawn by houseguests of Chancellor Otto Von Bismarck, giving European states control of the continent. And later still, the boundaries of the modern states of India and Pakistan would be drawn in England by Cyril Radcliffe, a chap who knew virtually nothing of the subcontinent.

Maps have thus defined relations of power in modernity. As actual landmasses have been exhaustively depicted on paper, modes of representing economic and political power have become discursive and conceptual. But they have remained exercises in mapping—metaphorical representations of the relationships among human entities in a given landscape. In the post-WWII Cold War era, for example, the capitalist industrialized West began referring to itself as the First World. In this new map of the world the United States and other countries that shared its political ideology and economic interests (i.e. Canada, Western European states, Japan, and Australia) gave themselves pride of place, "first" in an international community composed of three worlds. The term Second World was ascribed to industrialized states aligned with the Soviet Union (i.e. Eastern Europe, some Turkic states, and China). What was left was designated as a Third World (most of Africa, Asia, and Central and South America), places that were very poor, lacking in economic "development" and generally economically dependent on Western industrialized states.

In one manner or another almost every entry in this sourcebook provides us with a map of the world. And we are all insinuated—often by acts of exclusion—in each of them. Each map defines the relationship between the geographic and human elements of these worlds. But each also directs our attention to an ongoing crisis of exchange. And no one can deny that it is indeed a crisis. We are excluding one another from crucial decision-making processes. We are seeking to impose foreign cultural, social, economic, and political values on one another. We are abusing and exploiting one another. We are afraid of one another. Each essay, whether in its foreground or background, highlights this breakdown in reciprocity.

Section I sets the stage, so to speak. Here we will consider three early and later colonial documents, a piece on the global nature of modern militarization, and two now-canonical texts on the emergence of global capitalism. Sections II through IV present us with conventional interpretations of globalization and the ethics of globalization, as well as rejoinders to each. The final section allows us to hear voices that call attention to the struggles of people the world over who have been coerced into a global world at various times over the past 500 years. These are the voices of indigenous historians, political movements, activists, poets, and essayists, all of whom invoke things religious in dealing with their struggles. They are not representatives of religious traditions or factions in conversation or contention with the forces of globalization. They are simply people who are linked to communities in which there is a shared basic experience of being pawns in the deadly serious game of globalization.

The "Questions for Discussion" at the end of each section will provide us with an opportunity to explore this approach to globalization and religion in greater depth. Ultimately these essays each point to the gaps and disruptions in exchange where much of the world's population finds itself calling simply for reciprocity. We cannot disregard the fact that all too often these calls are legitimized by ultimate forces that are resources for affirming and assisting in the struggle to be regarded and treated as meaningful persons. They are not aligned with any specific religious groups. As such, they invite us to understand that globalization, however one feels about it, is an intrinsically religious problem rooted in a lack of meaningful human exchange.

Suggestions for further reading

Globalization

Thomas L. Friedman, *The Lexus and the Olive Tree: Understanding Globalization*, New York: Anchor, 1990.

Anthony Giddens, *Runaway World: How Globalization is Reshaping Our Lives*, New York: Routledge, 2000.

Michael Hardt and Antonio Negri, *Empire*, Cambridge, MA: Harvard University Press, 2001.

David Held, Anthony McGrew, David Goldblatt, and Jonathan Perraton, *Global Transformations: Politics, Economics, and Culture*, Stanford, CA: Stanford University Press, 1999.

Naomi Kline, *No Logo*, London: Falmango, 2000.

Roland Robertson, *Globalization: Social Theory and Global Culture*, London: Sage, 1992.

Robert K. Schaeffer, *Understanding Globalization: The Social Consequences of Political, Economic, and Environmental Change*, second edn, Lanham, MD: Rowman and Littlefield, 2002.

Malcolm Waters, *Globalization*, New York: Routledge, 1995.

Religion and globalization (conventional approaches)

Peter Beyer, *Religion and Globalization*, Thousand Oaks, CA: Sage, 2000.

Harvey Cox, *Fire from Heaven: The Rise of Pentecostal Spirituality and the Reshaping of Religion in the 21st Century*, Cambridge, MA: DaCapo, 1995.

Thomas J. Csordas (ed.), *Transnational Transcendence: Essays on Religion and Globalization*, Berkeley, CA: University of California Press, 2009.

Peter Herriot, *Religious Fundamentalism: Global, Local and Personal*, New York: Routledge, 2008.

Hans Küng, *A Global Ethic for Global Politics and Economics*, John Bowden (trans.), New York: Oxford University Press, 1998.

Section I

Contextualizing globalization

Part 1

We begin this first section of our reader not at the definitive beginning of the global world, but at a (not entirely) arbitrary point that is deeply implicated in the emergence of this world. We will consider here two colonial charters and a British Parliamentary Act—documents that bestowed upon European interests proprietary rights to territories in the New World. The two charters and the Act are maps delineating the boundaries of sovereign claims in the New World. The first two date from the beginning of the colonial era, and the third dates from some 300 years later. Of course, in tracing the roots of our global world we could easily have turned our sights to an even earlier moment, perhaps to 1452 when Pope Nicholas V issued two papal bulls (public legal pronouncements from the Vatican) that established a legal principle by which Europeans could claim enemy territories. In these bulls, Nicholas effectively barred Spain from African exploration, and in response, Spain turned its attention westward with the voyages of Christopher Columbus.

But every story needs to start somewhere and *Inter Caetera*, establishing as it did a fundamental principle of modern international law, seems as good as any. *Inter Caetera* is a pivotal document in the history of Europe's intrusion into the non-European world. It articulates clearly what would later become known as the "Doctrine of Discovery," a Roman Catholic pronouncement on European rights of sovereignty in the New World that would thereafter be a fundamental part of international law. As we have noted, Atlantic exploration became an attractive idea to the Spanish in the wake of Nicholas V's bulls authorizing Portuguese King Alfonso V to conquer North Africa. As a result of the bulls the Spanish Crown, which had its eyes on Africa, began to look westward, and Christopher Columbus was the man of the hour. When he returned from the Caribbean with news of the "discoveries" he had made there, the Spanish monarchs Isabella and Ferdinand immediately requested that Pope Alexander VI validate their claims to lands in the region. Alexander complied and issued three papal bulls that legalized their claims. The most important of these was *Inter Caetera*, a document that spelled out the legal Doctrine of Discovery with specific reference to the Americas.

Inter Caetera split the globe from the North Pole to the South Pole along an imaginary line about 500 miles west of the Azores. Spain was awarded legal title to any land it had discovered, or would later discover, west of the line, in order to carry on the "holy and laudable work" of extending Christendom. A subsequent Bull extended some rights in the region to Portugal. Soon afterward, and until the Protestant Reformation, European sovereigns and their legal and theological advisers began to put a good deal of energy into reinterpreting papal controls over discovery claims. Papal constraints were studied by professionals, especially in England and France, with an eye to justifying their competing claims to territories in the New World. But two things were never questioned during the period: (i) the right of European monarchs to claim sovereignty rights in the New World and (ii) the assumption that indigenous peoples did not have sovereign claims to their own lands under international law. Indeed, these assumptions have continued to hold sway in legal disputes over indigenous land claims the world over. In the United States, Canada, and Australia, for example, Supreme Courts have routinely fallen back on the Doctrine of Discovery in adjudicating such claims, a problem that has compelled some to take their claims to international bodies like the United Nations.

We see this point of international law clearly reflected in the Charter granted to John Cabot and his sons by Henry VII in 1496, a product of the labors of English scholars who quickly became adept at the practice of reinterpreting papal limitations on discovery claims. Henry VII was advised that he would not be in breach of *Inter Caetera* if the English claimed title only to territories that had not yet been "discovered" by Spain or Portugal (or any other Christian nation). Elizabeth I, we might note, would later be assured that claims to territory had to be accompanied by actual settlement—colonial outposts—to be considered legitimate. By the 1496 Charter that Henry VII granted to the Cabots, the King felt quite within his rights to instruct them to assume ownership, for the purpose of sovereign claims and mercantile gain, of any land occupied by "heathens and infidels."

Jumping ahead 300 years, we read next of the British Government's Act relating to the East India Company in 1813. While it renews the Company's rule in India (initiated in 1707 by its predecessor the Honourable East India Company), it also asserts British sovereignty rights over the region and brings an end to the Company's trade monopoly except with regard to trade in tea and with China. According to the Charter all residents of British territories (British or Indian) are subject to Company imposed duties and taxes and to the jurisdiction of provincial courts in matters of "revenue." Furthermore, all such persons working for the Company are subject to the jurisdiction of provincial courts with respect to "all crimes and misdemeanors." It commits the British Parliament and the Company to supporting a civil service college and a military seminary (academy) whose purposes are to train men for the Indian service. Faculty who are clergy are particularly desired in these institutions. The Company is responsible for maintaining a military force comprised of both British and Indian personnel, undertones of what would become known as indirect rule—the exploitation and privileging of traditional ruling classes to maintain colonial order. The Act also establishes a church presence in India, mandating the export of Church of England bishops and archdeacons to serve the spiritual needs of the regions over which Britain claims sovereignty.

1.1 *Inter Caetera*

Pope Alexander VI

Alexander, bishop, servant of the servants of God, to the illustrious sovereigns, our very dear son in Christ, Ferdinand, king, and our very dear daughter in Christ, Isabella, queen of Castile, Leon, Aragon, Sicily, and Granada, health and apostolic benediction. Among other works well pleasing to the Divine Majesty and cherished of our heart, this assuredly ranks highest, that in our times especially the Catholic faith and the Christian religion be exalted and be everywhere increased and spread, that the health of souls be cared for and that barbarous nations be overthrown and brought to the faith itself. Wherefore inasmuch as by the favor of divine clemency, we, though of insufficient merits, have been called to this Holy See of Peter, recognizing that as true Catholic kings and princes, such as we have known you always to be, and as your illustrious deeds already known to almost the whole world declare, you not only eagerly desire but with every effort, zeal, and diligence, without regard to hardships, expenses, dangers, with the shedding even of your blood, are laboring to that end; recognizing also that you have long since dedicated to this purpose your whole soul and all your endeavors—as witnessed in these times with so much glory to the Divine Name in your recovery of the kingdom of Granada from the yoke of the Saracens—we therefore are rightly led, and hold it as our duty, to grant you even of our own accord and in your favor those things whereby with effort each day more hearty you may be enabled for the honor of God himself and the spread of the Christian rule to carry forward your holy and praiseworthy purpose so pleasing to immortal God. We have indeed learned that you, who for a long time had intended to seek out and discover certain islands and mainlands remote and unknown and not hitherto discovered by others, to the end that you might bring to the worship of our Redeemer and the profession of the Catholic faith their residents and inhabitants, having been up to the present time greatly engaged in the siege and recovery of the kingdom itself of Granada were unable to accomplish this holy and praiseworthy purpose; but the said kingdom having at length been regained, as was pleasing to the Lord, you, with the wish to fulfill your desire, chose our beloved son, Christopher Columbus, a man assuredly worthy and of the highest recommendations and fitted for so great an undertaking, whom you furnished with ships and men equipped for like designs, not without the greatest hardships, dangers, and expenses, to make diligent quest for these remote and unknown mainlands and islands through the sea, where hitherto no one had sailed; and they at length, with divine aid and with the utmost diligence sailing in the ocean sea, discovered certain very remote islands and even mainlands that hitherto had not been discovered by others; wherein dwell very many peoples living in peace, and, as reported, going unclothed, and not eating flesh. Moreover, as your aforesaid envoys are of opinion, these very peoples living in the said islands and countries believe in one God, the Creator in heaven, and seem sufficiently disposed to embrace the Catholic faith and be trained in good morals. And it is hoped that, were they instructed, the name of the Savior, our Lord Jesus Christ, would easily be introduced into the said countries and islands. Also, on one of the chief of these aforesaid islands the said Christopher has already caused to be put together and built a fortress fairly equipped, wherein he has stationed as garrison certain Christians, companions of his, who are to make search for other remote and unknown islands and mainlands. In the islands and countries already discovered are found gold, spices, and very many other precious things of divers kinds and qualities. Wherefore, as becomes Catholic kings and princes, after earnest consideration of all matters, especially of the rise and spread of the Catholic faith, as was the fashion of your ancestors, kings of renowned memory, you have purposed with the favor of divine clemency to bring under your sway the said mainlands and islands with their residents and inhabitants and to bring them to the Catholic faith. Hence, heartily commending in the Lord this your holy and praiseworthy purpose, and desirous that it be duly accomplished, and that the name of our Savior be carried into those regions, we exhort you very earnestly in the Lord and by your reception of holy baptism, whereby you are bound to our apostolic commands, and by the bowels of the mercy of our Lord Jesus Christ, enjoy strictly, that inasmuch as with eager zeal for the true faith you design to equip and despatch this expedition, you purpose also, as is your duty, to lead the peoples dwelling in those islands and countries to embrace the Christian religion; nor at any time let dangers or hardships deter you therefrom, with the stout hope and trust in your hearts that Almighty God will further your undertakings. And, in order that you may enter upon so great an undertaking with greater readiness and heartiness endowed with benefit of our apostolic favor, we, of our own accord, not at your instance nor the request of anyone else in your regard, but out of our own sole largess and certain knowledge and out of the fullness of our apostolic power, by the authority of Almighty God conferred upon us in blessed Peter and of the vicarship of Jesus Christ, which we hold on earth, do by tenor of these presents, should any of said islands have been found by your envoys and captains, give, grant, and assign to you and your heirs and successors, kings of Castile and Leon, forever, together with all their dominions, cities, camps, places, and villages, and all rights, jurisdictions, and appurtenances, all islands and mainlands found and to be found, discovered and to be discovered towards the west and south, by drawing and establishing a line from the

Arctic pole, namely the north, to the Antarctic pole, namely the south, no matter whether the said mainlands and islands are found and to be found in the direction of India or towards any other quarter, the said line to be distant one hundred leagues towards the west and south from any of the islands commonly known as the Azores and Cape Verde. With this proviso however that none of the islands and mainlands, found and to be found, discovered and to be discovered, beyond that said line towards the west and south, be in the actual possession of any Christian king or prince up to the birthday of our Lord Jesus Christ just past from which the present year one thousand four hundred ninety-three begins. And we make, appoint, and depute you and your said heirs and successors lords of them with full and free power, authority, and jurisdiction of every kind; with this proviso however, that by this our gift, grant, and assignment no right acquired by any Christian prince, who may be in actual possession of said islands and mainlands prior to the said birthday of our Lord Jesus Christ, is hereby to be understood to be withdrawn or taking away. Moreover we command you in virtue of holy obedience that, employing all due diligence in the premises, as you also promise—nor do we doubt your compliance therein in accordance with your loyalty and royal greatness of spirit—you should appoint to the aforesaid mainlands and islands worthy, God-fearing, learned, skilled, and experienced men, in order to instruct the aforesaid inhabitants and residents in the Catholic faith and train them in good morals. Furthermore, under penalty of excommunication "late sententie" to be incurred "ipso facto," should anyone thus contravene, we strictly forbid all persons of whatsoever rank, even imperial and royal, or of whatsoever estate, degree, order, or condition, to dare without your special permit or that of your aforesaid heirs and successors, to go for the purpose of trade or any other reason to the islands or mainlands, found and to be found, discovered and to be discovered, towards the west and south, by drawing and establishing a line from the Arctic pole to the Antarctic pole, no matter whether the mainlands and islands, found and to be found, lie in the direction of India or toward any other quarter whatsoever, the said line to be distant one hundred leagues towards the west and south, as is aforesaid, from any of the islands commonly known as the Azores and Cape Verde; apostolic constitutions and ordinances and other decrees whatsoever to the contrary notwithstanding. We trust in Him from whom empires and governments and all good things proceed, that, should you, with the Lord's guidance, pursue this holy and praiseworthy undertaking, in a short while your hardships and endeavors will attain the most felicitous result, to the happiness and glory of all Christendom. But inasmuch as it would be difficult to have these present letters sent to all places where desirable, we wish, and with similar accord and knowledge do decree, that to copies of them, signed by the hand of a public notary commissioned therefor, and sealed with the seal of any ecclesiastical officer or ecclesiastical court, the same respect is to be shown in court and outside as well as anywhere else as would be given to these presents should they thus be exhibited or shown. Let no one, therefore, infringe, or with rash boldness contravene, this our recommendation, exhortation, requisition, gift, grant, assignment, constitution, deputation, decree, mandate, prohibition, and will. Should anyone presume to attempt this, be it known to him that he will incur the wrath of Almighty God and of the blessed apostles Peter and Paul. Given at Rome, at Saint Peter's, in the year of the incarnation of our Lord one thousand four hundred and ninety-three, the fourth of May, and the first year of our pontificate.

1.2 First Letters Patent granted by Henry VII to John Cabot (March 5, 1496)

For John Cabot and his Sons

The King, to all to whom, etc. Greeting: Be it known and made manifest that we have given and granted as by these presents we give and grant, for us and our heirs, to our well-beloved John Cabot, citizen of Venice, and to Lewis, Sebastian and Sancio, sons of the said John, and to the heirs and deputies of them, and of any one of them, full and free authority, faculty and power to sail to all parts, regions and coasts of the eastern, western and northern sea, under our banners, flags and ensigns, with five ships or vessels of whatsoever burden and quality they may be, and with so many and with such mariners and men as they may wish to take with them in the said ships, at their own proper costs and charges, to find, discover and investigate whatsoever islands, countries, regions or provinces of heathens and infidels, in whatsoever part of the world placed, which before this time were unknown to all Christians. We have also granted to them and to any one of them, and have given licence to set up our aforesaid banners and ensigns in any town, city, castle, island or mainland whatsoever, newly found by them. And that the before-mentioned John and his sons or their heirs and deputies may conquer, occupy and possess whatsoever such towns, castles, cities and islands by them thus discovered that they may be able to conquer, occupy and possess, as our vassals and governors lieutenants and deputies therein, acquiring for us the dominion, title and jurisdiction of the same towns, castles, cities, islands and mainlands discovered; in such a way nevertheless that of all the fruits, profits, enoluments, commodities, gains and revenues accruing from this voyage, the said John and sons and their heirs and deputies shall be bounden and under obligation for every their voyage, as often as they shall arrive at our port of Bristol, at which they are bound and holden only to arrive, all necessary charges and expenses incurred by them having been deducted, to pay to us, either in goods or money, the fifth part of the whole capital gained, we giving and granting to them and their heirs and deputies, that they shall be free and exempt from all payment of customs on all and singular the goods and merchandise that they may bring back with them from those places newly discovered.

And further we have given and granted to them and to their heirs and deputies, that all mainlands, islands, towns, cities, castles and other places whatsoever discovered by them, however numerous they may happen to be, may not be frequented or visited by any other subjects of ours whatsoever without the licence of the aforesaid John and his sons and of their deputies, on pain of loss as well of the ships or vessels daring to sail to these places discovered, as of all goods whatsoever. Willing and strictly commanding all singular our subjects as well as by land as by sea, that they shall render good assistance to the aforesaid John and his sons and deputies, and that they shall give them all their favour and help as well in fitting out the ships or vessels as in buying stores and provisions with their money and in providing the other things which they must take with them on the said voyage.

In witness whereof, etc.
Witness ourself at Westminster on the fifth day of March.
By the King himself, etc.

1.3 An Act for Continuing in The East India Company, 1813

An Act for Continuing in The East India Company, for a further Term, The Possession of the British Territories in India, together with certain exclusive Privileges for establishing further Regulations for the Government of the said Territories, and the better Administration of Justice within the same; and for regulating the Trade to, and from, the Places within the Limits of the said Company's Charter, July 21, 1813.

Whereas, by an Act of the Parliament of Great Britain, passed in the thirty-third year of His present Majesty's Reign, for continuing in the East India Company for a further term, the possession of the British Territories in India, together with their exclusive trade, under certain limitations, and for other purposes; the possession and government of the British Territories in India, together with an exclusive trade in, to, and from, the East Indies, and other the limits described in an Act made in the ninth year of the reign of King William the Third, or in a certain Charter of the fifth day of September in the tenth year of the same King, were continued in the United Company of Merchants of England trading to the East Indies, for a term thereby limited, under certain regulations and conditions ...

And whereas it is expedient that the territorial acquisitions mentioned in the said Act of Parliament of Great Britain of the thirty-third year of His present Majesty, together with such other territorial acquisitions on the continent of Asia, as are now in the possession and under the government of the said United Company, with the revenues thereof, should, without prejudice to the undoubted sovereignty of the Crown of the United Kingdom of Great Britain and Ireland, in and over the same, or to any claim of the said United Company to any rights of property therein, remain in the possession and under the government of the said United Company, for a further term; subject to such powers and authorities for the superintendence, direction and control over all acts, operations, and concerns, which relate to the civil or military government or revenues of the said territories, and to such further and other powers, authorities, rules, regulations, and restrictions, as have been already made or provided, by any Act or Acts of Parliament in that behalf, or as now are, or hereafter shall be made, and provided by the authority of Parliament ...

May it therefore please Your Majesty,

That it may be enacted; and be it enacted ... That the territorial acqui-sitions mentioned in the said Act of the thirty-third year of His present Majesty, together with such of the territorial acquisitions since obtained upon the continent of Asia, as are now in the possession of, and under the government of the said United Company, with the revenues thereof respectively, shall remain and continue in the possession and under the government of the said United Company, for a further term, to be computed from the said until the same shall be determined, by virtue of the proviso hereinafter contained …

And be it further enacted, That for and during the continuance of the possession and government of the said territorial acquisitions and revenues in the said United Company, the rents, revenues, and profits arising from the said territorial acquisitions, after defraying the charges and expenses of collecting the same, shall be applied and disposed of, to and for the uses and purposes hereinafter expressed, in the following order of preference, and to or for no other use purpose, or in any other manner whatsoever, and Act or Acts of Parliament now in force to the contrary notwithstanding; (that is to say) In the first place, the defraying of all the charges and expences of raising and maintaining the forces, as well European as native, military, artillery, and marine, on the establishments in the East Indies and parts aforesaid, and of maintaining the forts and garrisons there, and providing warlike and naval stores …

Be it therefore enacted and declared, That it was, and is, and shall be lawful, to and for the Governor General in Council of Fort William in Bengal, and to and for the Governor in Council of Fort St. George, and to and for the Governor in Council of Bombay, within the respective Presidencies of Fort William, Fort St. George, and Bombay, to impose all such duties of customs and other taxes, to be levied, raised, and paid within the said towns of Calcutta and Madras, and the said town and island of Bombay, and upon and by all persons whomsoever, resident or being there respectively, and in respect of all goods, wares, merchandises, commodities and property whatsoever also being therein respectively; and upon and by all persons whomsoever, whether British born or foreigners, resident or being in any country or place within the authority of the said governments respectively; and in respect of all goods, wares, merchandises, commodities, and property whatsoever, being in any such country or place, in as full, large, and ample manner, as such Governor General in Council or Governors in Council respectively may now lawfully impose any duties or taxes to be levied, raised, or paid, upon or by any persons whomsoever, or in any place whatsoever, within the authority of the said governments respectively.

And be it further enacted and declared, That is was, and is, and shall and may be lawful to and for the said Governor-general in Council, and the said Governors in Council respectively, within the said presidencies respectively, to erect and establish provincial courts, with jurisdiction in matters of revenue and to give and annex jurisdiction in matters of revenue to any provincial court now in existence, or hereafter to be erected, to be exercised as well within the said towns of Calcutta and Madras, and the said town and island of

Bombay, and over all persons whomsoever, whether British born, foreign, or natives of India, and over all things whatsoever, or to whomsoever belonging, in as full, large, and ample manner as such Governor-general in Council and Governors in Council respectively, within the said presidencies respectively, can now lawfully erect or establish any provincial court, or give or annex any jurisdiction whatsoever to any provincial court whatsoever.

And be it further enacted and declared, That all persons whomsoever, being natives of India, who have been, now are, or hereafter may be employed, by or in the service of His Majesty, the said United Company, or of any of His Majesty's subjects, were, and are, and shall be subject and amenable to all provincial courts of competent jurisdiction for all crimes and misdemenors, and in all actions and suits whatsoever, of which such courts respectively could take cognizance, if the persons having committed such crimes or misdemenors or against whom the causes of such actions or suits shall have arisen, had not been employed by, or had not been in the service of His Majesty, or the said United Company, or any of his Majesty's subjects; and law, usage, or practice to the contrary thereof in any ways not withstanding. Provided always that nothing herein contained shall anywise oust the said supreme courts of judicature of Fort William and Madras, and the said court of the Recorder of Bombay respectively, of any jurisdiction over any natives of India, which such court my now lawfully exercise; but such supreme courts of judicature of Fort William and Madras, and the said court of the Recorder of Bombay respectively, as well as the provincial courts herein referred to, according to their several jurisdictions, shall have a concurrent jurisdiction over Natives of India, employed by or in the service of the said United Company, or any of His Majesty's subjects ...

And whereas the said United Company have lately established, in *England*, a College for the appropriate education of young men designed for their Civil service in India, and also a Military Seminary for the appropriate education of young men designed for their Military service in India: And whereas it is expedient that the said College and Military Seminary should be further continued and maintained, and that proper rules and regulations should be constituted and established, by the authority of law, for the good government of the said College and Military Seminary respectively; Be it therefore enacted, That the said College and Military Seminary shall be continued and maintained by the said United Company during the further term hereby granted to the said Company, and that it shall and may be lawful for the said Court of Directors, and they are hereby required, forthwith, ... to frame such rules and regulations for the good government of the said College and Military Seminary respectively, as in their judgment shall appear best adapted to the purposes aforesaid; and to lay the same before the Board of Commissioners for the Affairs of India, for their revisal and approbation, who shall thereupon proceed to consider the same, and shall and may make such alterations therein and additions thereto as the said Board shall think fit ...

And whereas for the due performance of the public duties of Religion at the said College, as well as for the maintenance of sound learning and religious education, it is expedient that the Principle, and some of the Professors, of the said College, should be Clergymen of the Established Church ...

And whereas no Provision hath hitherto been made for the maintenance and support of such persons as may be appointed by His Majesty to superintend the Christian Church, and to administer holy ceremonies in the British territories of the *East-Indies*, and other parts within the limits of the said Company's Charter; BE it therefore enacted, That in case it shall please His Majesty, by His Royal Letters Patent under the Great Seal of the said United Kingdom, to erect, found and constitute, for the whole of the said British territories in the *East-Indies*, and parts aforesaid, one Bishoprick; for the presidency of Fort William in Bengal, one Archdeaconry; for the presidency of Fort Saint George, on the coast of Coromandel, one Archdeaconry; and for the presidency and island of Bombay, on the coast of Malabar, one Archdeaconry; and from time to time to nominate and appoint a Bishop and Archdeacons to such Bishoprick and Archdeconaries respectively: The Court of Directors of the said Company, during such time as the said territorial acquisitions shall remain in the possession of the said Company, shall and they are hereby required to direct and cause to be paid, certain established salaries to such Bishop[s] and Archdeacon[s] respectively ...

And be it further enacted, That the said person and persons so to be appointed Bishop and Archdeacons, respectively, shall not carry on, nor be concerned in, nor have any dealings or transactions by way of traffic or commerce of any kind whatsoever, either for his or their own use, benefit, profit or advantage, or the use, benefit, profit or advantage of any person whatsoever.

Provided always, and be it further enacted, That such Bishop shall not have or use any jurisdiction, or exercise any episcopal functions whatsoever, either in the East-Indies or elsewhere, but only such jurisdiction and functions as shall or may from time to time be limited to him by His Majesty by Letters Patent under the Great Seal of the United Kingdom ...

Part 2

In this second part of Section I, we explore some of the foundations and results of European economic expansion during the colonial era. Our first two readings remind us that colonial expansion was not only a phenomenon that profoundly altered the worlds of indigenous peoples. Colonial contact and conquest were made possible by economic, technological, and military developments that would come to define the world that we now refer to as globalized. To begin, political theorist Tarak Barkawi focuses in his short essay on the issue of military apparatus as a fundamental part of globalization. While conversations about globalization rarely connect it with militarism, Barkawi points out that soldiers might well be considered to have been among the first modern cosmopolitans. He further argues that European expansion established a pattern of maintaining economic and communication systems through the employment of trained military professionals—something we saw clearly in the East India Company Act of 1813.

We will follow Barkawi with a classic essay by the American sociologist Immanuel Wallerstein. Wallerstein is a key figure in the development of "world-systems analysis," a field of research that combines history and sociology. The modern world-system, he argues, cannot be fully understood without situating it within a long-term economic, political, and social context that has essentially been an exercise in capitalist expansion. The "modern world-system" is an apt map of the "globalized" world that we have inherited in which economic and political power have played out in both centrifugal and centripetal ways, excreting military, economic, and political power in order to reabsorb resources from elsewhere. Wallerstein's map has been 500 years in the making. His map, like all maps, has "boundaries, structures, member groups, rules of legitimation, and coherence." This modern world-system also has some distinct features: a global marketplace for commodities and labor, a class-and-territorially based division of labor, and state-based global relationships. It is a world defined by "the imagination of its profiteers and the counter-assertiveness of the oppressed."

We will close this first section with a reading from the German sociologist Max Weber's classic study of the relationship between the emergence of Protestantism and the development of capitalism. According to Weber, the emergence of our modern capitalist world-system was stimulated and facilitated by a Protestant ethic rooted in the thought of Martin Luther, and developed in later Calvinist ethics. In the medieval period salvation was thought to be determined by a person's partaking in the Catholic sacraments and acquiescing to the authority of the Church in all social and legal matters. Architects of the Protestant Reformation, who regarded salvation as predetermined and merely observable as a completed process, countermanded both of these modes of seeking salvation. Weber suggests that in this context, the accumulation of capital—a product of hard work and austerity—became a mode of demonstrating one's state of salvation in Calvinist and Puritan traditions. This ethic, he adds, became most highly developed in the United States. We might note that other scholars who are not included here have reinforced aspects of Weber's analysis from different vantage points. Benjamin Nelson, for example (see Suggestions for Further Reading, below), wrote extensively on the way in which a shift in Christian notions of usury (charging interest on loans) signaled a breakdown in medieval European notions of Christian cultural and religious fraternity (as over and against Jews) in favor of universal principles of individualism. The lifting of legal injunctions against usury, he argues, was a transition of sorts from medieval to modern economic relations: it was, quite literally, now a case of every man for himself.

1.4 Military globalization is nothing new

Tarak Barkawi

For true believers, globalization is a force for peace. This is globalization as communications technologies. People are brought closer together in a multi-cultural utopia, where tweets and posts bring down authoritarian rulers.

For critics, globalization is the iron cage of neoliberalism. Here, executives in suits jet about in business class, while workers are penned in in *maquiladoras*, denied union representation, and subjected to punishing labor regimes.

Rarely is the military, the supposed bastion of conservative nationalism, associated with globalization. But soldiers have been circulating the globe for centuries, and were visiting exotic places long before cheap air travel.

When the military and globalization are brought together, it is usually in terms of private security companies. An example is R2's new venture in the United Arab Emirates, where a foreign battalion composed largely of Colombians is being trained.

As so often the case with globalization, what seems new actually reflects much older patterns and histories. Bamboozled by patriotic war movies and memorials, and by the efforts of nationalists everywhere to claim the military as their own, we forget that armed forces are often composed of foreigners. Indeed, there are few institutions as cosmopolitan as the military. Where else would you find Arabs, Colombians and US citizens working together?

Naturally, foreign troops are very useful when a government is threatened by its own citizens. Bahrain did not have to hire R2, because its army is already largely composed of Baluchis from Pakistan who were willing to fire when ordered. Along with Saudi assistance, this fact proved decisive in saving the regime in the recent unrest.

But foreign troops are not just praetorian guards for the local potentate. Bahrain, like the UAE, is a crucial node in global networks of military, economic and political power. The UAE has the world's sixth largest reserves of oil, while the US Fifth Fleet is headquartered in Bahrain.

The steel frame of globalization

These global networks, initially erected by European and US imperialism, require pliant, friendly local rulers who respond to international concerns. In turn, those rulers require security forces to maintain them in power. And so every imperial power devotes considerable resources to training, advising and assisting foreign armed forces. Many of Bahrain's officers are trained in the UK and the US, while other Western security specialists are hired privately.

In the era of formal colonies, the Europeans raised large colonial armies officered by whites. The British held India with an Indian army, while France ruled North and West Africa with regiments raised from these very places. But with decolonization, military advice and assistance became more complicated and often covert.

In the 1960s, Britain's client, the Sultan of Oman, was faced with a rebellion in the Dhofar region. The first step, of course, was to redefine this rebellion as "communist." Like "terrorism" today, this was the catch all term for everything that threatened Western interests in the Cold War (R2's UAE battalion is, in part, justified by the threat of "terrorism"). But even so, to openly assist the Sultan would have made him appear a Western client and weakened him further.

What was needed was a force that could appear "Omani." A British officer was seconded to command the Sultan's Armed Forces (SAF), along with British officers and NCOs who volunteered for service. Other British officers were privately hired into the SAF, many having recently been discharged from the Indian army which had continued to employ British officers after 1947. Due to feudal rights, the Sultan could recruit Baluchis, who made up 67 per cent of the SAF in 1961, while Indians and other foreigners were hired into the navy and air force.

The Dhofar rebels pointed all this out in their propaganda. In response the Sultan proclaimed in a speech in 1972 that "everyone knows the air force is an Omani air force, and that the navy is an Omani navy, and that our Omani army is the only force which protects the land of our nation."

Once they broke the back of the rebellion, the Sultan and his British advisors set about creating an "Omanisation" program for the armed forces, recruiting more Omanis. Like Vietnamisation, Iraqi-isation, and Afghanistan-isation, creating indigenous security forces that can hold the country on their own is the key to Western withdrawal and empire on the cheap. When necessary, the local forces are stiffened with foreigners, while their officers are trained abroad.

Needless to say these projects of order making do not always succeed. But in various ways these examples begin to lay bare the steel frame of globalization, the worldwide circulation of military and security professionals who see off local armed challenges to global interests.

Another of the announced purposes of R2's battalion is to put down unrest among the legions of migrant workers in the UAE. From the earliest days of European expansion onwards, globalization has always required back breaking, soul destroying manual labor, on sugar plantations, in mines and elsewhere.

Then, as now, the workers occasionally revolted, while lines of communications with markets and suppliers had to be secured. Then, as now, the cheapest way to do so was to train up indigenous armed forces.

The modern, interconnected world has been made and maintained by getting brown and black men arrayed in warlike order to kill other brown and black people. Whether as economy or as communication, globalization has required a great deal of "security."

1.5 The modern world system: Capitalist agriculture and the origins of the European world-economy in the sixteenth century

Immanuel Wallerstein

In order to describe the origins and initial workings of a world system, I have had to argue a certain conception of a world-system. A world-system is a social system, one that has boundaries, structures, member groups, rules of legitimation, and coherence. Its life is made up of the conflicting forces which hold it together by tension, and tear it apart as each group seeks to remold it to its advantage. It has the characteristics of an organism; in that it has a life-span over which its characteristics change in some respects and remain stable in others. One can define its structures as being at different times strong or weak in terms of the internal logic of its functioning.

What characterizes a social system in my view is the fact that life within it is largely self-contained, and that the dynamics of its development are largely internal. The reader may feel that the use of the term "largely" is a case of academic weaseling. I admit I cannot quantify it. Probably no one ever will be able to do so, as the definition is based on a counterfactual hypothesis: If the system, for any reason, were to be cut off from all external forces, (which virtually never happens), the definition implies that the system would continue to function substantially in the same manner. Again, of course, substantially is difficult to convert into hard operational criteria. Nonetheless the point is an important one, and key to many parts of the empirical analyses of this book. Perhaps we should think of self-containment as a theoretical absolute, a sort of social vacuum, rarely visible and even more implausible to create artificially, but still and all a socially real asymptote, the distance from which is somehow measurable.

Using such a criterion, it is contended here that most entities usually described as social systems—"tribes," communities, nation-states— are not in fact total systems. Indeed, on the contrary, we are arguing that the only real social systems are, on the one hand, those relatively small, highly auton-omous subsistence economies not part of some regular tribute-demanding system and, on the other hand, world-systems. These latter are to be sure distinguished from the former because they are relatively large; that is, they are in common parlance "worlds." More precisely, however, they are defined by the fact that their self-containment as an economic-material entity is based on extensive division of labor and that they contain within them a multiplicity of cultures.

1 political system vs 1 economic system

It is further argued that thus far there have only existed two varieties of such world-systems: world-empires, in which there is a single political system over most of the area, however attenuated the degree of its effective control; and those systems in which a single political system does not exist over all, or virtually all, of the space. For convenience and for want of a better term, we are using the term "world-economy" to describe the latter.

Finally, we have argued that prior to the modern era, world-economies were highly unstable structures which tended either to be converted into empires or to disintegrate. It is the peculiarity of the modern world-system that a world-economy has survived for 500 years and yet has not come to be transformed into a world-empire—a peculiarity that is the secret of its strength.

This peculiarity is the political side of the form of economic organization called capitalism. Capitalism has been able to flourish precisely because the world-economy has had within its bounds not one but a multiplicity of political systems.

I am not here arguing the classic case of capitalist ideology that capitalism is a system based on the noninterference of the state in economic affairs. Quite the contrary! Capitalism is based on the constant absorption of economic loss by political entities, while economic gain is distributed to "private" hands. What I am arguing rather is that capitalism as an economic mode is based on the fact that the economic factors operate either an arena larger than that which any political entity can totally control. This gives capitalists a freedom of maneuver that is structurally based. It has made possible the constant economic expansion of the world-system, albeit a very skewed distribution of its rewards. The only alternative world-system that could maintain a high level of productivity and change the system of distribution would involve the reintegration of the levels of political and economic decision-making. This would constitute a third possible form of world-system, a socialist world government. This is not a form that presently exists, and it was not even remotely conceivable in the sixteenth century.

The historical reasons why the European world-economy came into existence in the sixteenth century and resisted attempts to transform it into an empire have been expounded at length. We shall not review them here. It should however be noted that the size of a world-economy is a function of the state of technology, and in particular of the possibilities of transport and communication within its bounds. Since this is a constantly changing phenomenon, not always for the better, the boundaries of a world-economy are ever fluid.

We have defined a world-system as one in which there is extensive division of labor. This division is not merely functional—that is, occupational— but geographical. That is to say, the range of economic tasks is not evenly distributed throughout the world-system. In part this is the consequence of ecological considerations, to be sure. But for the most part, it is a function of the social organization of work, one which magnifies and legitimizes the ability of some groups within the system to exploit the labor of others, that is, to receive a larger share of the surplus.

While, in a empire, the political structure tends to link culture with occupation, in a world-economy the political structure tends to link culture with spatial location. The reason is that in a world-economy the first point of political pressure available to groups is the local (national) state structure. Cultural homogenization tends to serve the interests of key groups and the pressures build up to create cultural-national identities.

This is particularly the case in the advantaged areas of the world-economy—what we have called the core-states. In such states, the creation of a strong state machinery coupled with a national culture, a phenomenon often referred to as integration, serves both as a mechanism to protect disparities that have arisen within the world-system, and as an ideological mask and justification for the maintenance of these disparities.

World-economies then are divided into core-states and peripheral areas. I do not say peripheral *states* because one characteristic of a peripheral area is that the indigenous state is weak, ranging from its nonexistence (that is, a colonial situation) to one with a low degree of autonomy (that is, a neo-colonial situation).

There are also semiperipheral areas which are in between the core and the periphery on a series of dimensions, such as the complexity of economic activities, strength of the state machinery, cultural integrity, etc. Some of these areas had been core-areas of earlier versions of a given world-economy. Some had been peripheral areas that were later promoted, so to speak, as a result of the changing geopolitics of an expanding world-economy.

The semiperiphery, however, is not an artifice of statistical cutting points, nor is it a residual category. The semiperiphery is a necessary structural element in a world-economy. These areas play a role parallel to that played, *mutatis mutandis*, by middle trading groups in an empire. They are collection points of vital skills that are often politically unpopular. These middle areas (like middle groups in an empire) partially deflect the political pressure which groups primarily located in peripheral areas might otherwise direct against core-states and the groups which operate within and through their state machineries. On the other hand, the interests primarily located in the semiperiphery are located outside the political arena of the core-states, and find it difficult to pursue the ends in political coalitions that might be open to them were they in the same political arena.

The division of a world-economy involves a hierarchy of occupational tasks, in which tasks requiring higher levels of skill and greater capitalization are reserved for higher-ranking areas. Since a capitalist world-economy essentially reward accumulated capital, including human capital, at a higher rate than "raw" labor power, the geographical maldistribution of these occupational skills involves a strong trend toward self-maintenance. The forces of the marketplace reinforce them rather than undermine them. And the absence of a central political mechanism for the world-economy makes it very difficult to intrude counteracting forces to the maldistribution of reward.

Hence, the ongoing process of a world-economy tends to expand the economic and social gaps among its varying areas in the very process of its development. One factor that tends to mask this fact is that the process of development of a world-economy brings about technological advances which make it possible to expand the boundaries of a world-economy. In this case, particular regions of the world may change their structural role in the world-economy, to their advantage, even though the disparity of reward between different sectors of the world-economy as a whole may be simultaneously widening. It is in order to observe this crucial phenomenon clearly that we have insisted on the distinction between a peripheral area of a given world-economy and the external arena of the world-economy. The external arena of one century often becomes the periphery of the next—or its semiperiphery. But then too core-states can become semiperipheral and semiperipheral ones peripheral.

While the advantages of the core-states have not ceased to expand throughout the history of the modern world-system, the ability of a particular state to remain in the core sector is not beyond challenge. The hounds are ever to the hares for the position of top dog. Indeed, it may well be that in this kind of system it is not structurally possible to avoid, over a long period of historical times, a circulation of the elites in the sense that the particular country that is dominant at a given time tends to be replaced in this role sooner or later by another country.

We have insisted that the modern world-economy is, and only can be, a capitalist world-economy. It is for this reason that we have rejected the appellation of "feudalism" for the various forms of capitalist agriculture based on coerced labor which grow up in a world-economy. Furthermore, although this has not been discussed in this volume, it is for this same reason that we will, in future volumes, regard with great circumspection and prudence the claim that there exist in the twentieth century socialist national economies within the framework of the world-economy (as opposed to socialist movements controlling certain state-machineries within the world-economy).

If world-systems are the only real social systems (other than truly isolated subsistence economies), then it must follow that the emergence, consolidation, and political roles of classes and status groups must be appreciated as elements of this *world*-system. And in turn it follows that one of the key elements in analyzing a class or a status-group is not only the state of its self-consciousness but the geographical scope of its self-definition.

Classes always exist potentially (*an sich*). The issue is under what conditions they become class-conscious (*für sich*), that is, operate as a group in the politico-economic arenas and even to some extent as a cultural entity. Such self-consciousness is a function of conflict situations. But for upper strata open conflict, and hence overt consciousness, is always *faute de mieux*. To the extent that class boundaries are not made explicit, to that extent it is more likely that privileges be maintained.

The European world-economy of the sixteenth century tended overall to be a one-class system. It was the dynamic forces profiting from economic expansion and the capitalist system, especially those in the core-areas, who tended to be class-conscious, that is to operate within the political arena as a group defined primarily by their common role in the economy. This common role was in fact defined somewhat broadly from a twentieth-century perspective. It included persons who were farmers, merchants, and industrialists. Individual entrepreneurs often moved back and forth between these activities in any case, or combined them. The crucial distinction was between these men, whatever their occupation, principally oriented to obtaining profit in the world market, and the others not so oriented.

The "others" fought back in terms of their status privileges—those of the traditional aristocracy, those which small farmers had derived from the feudal system, those resulting from guild monopolies that were outmoded. Under the cover of cultural similarities, one can often wield strange alliances. Those strange alliances can take a very activist form and force the political centers to take account of them. We pointed to such instances in our discussion of France. Or they can take a politically passive form that serves well the needs of the dominant forces in the world-system. The triumph of Polish Catholicism as a cultural force was a case in point.

The details of the canvass are filled in with the panoply of multiple forms of status-groups, their particular strengths and accents. But the grand sweep is in terms of the process of class formation. And in this regard, the sixteenth century was indecisive. The capitalist strata formed a class that survived and gained *droit de cite*, but did not yet triumph in the political arena.

The evolution of the state machineries reflected precisely this uncertainty. Strong states serve the interests of some groups and hurt those of others. From however the standpoint of the world-system as a whole, if there is to be a multitude of political entities (that is, is the system is not a world-empire), then it cannot be the case that all these entities be equally strong. For if they were, they would be in the position of blocking the effective operation of transnational economic entities whose locus were in another state. It would then follow that the world division of labor would be impeded, the world-economy decline, and eventually the world-system fall apart.

It also cannot be that *no* state machinery is strong. For in such a case, the capitalist strata would have no mechanisms to protect their interests, guaranteeing their property rights, assuring various monopolies, spreading losses among the larger population, etc.

It follows then that the world-economy develops a pattern where state structures are relatively strong in the core areas and relatively weak in the periphery. Which areas play which roles is in many ways accidental. What is necessary is that in some areas the state machinery be far stronger than in others.

What do we mean by a strong state machinery? We mean strength vis-à-vis other states within the world-economy including other core-states, and strong vis-à-vis local political units within the boundaries of the state. In effect, we mean a sovereignty that is *de facto* as well as *de jure*. We also mean a state that is strong vis-à-vis any particular social group within the state. Obviously such groups vary in the amount of pressure they can bring to bear upon the state. And obviously certain combinations of these groups control the state. It is not that the state is a neutral arbiter. But the state is more than a simple vector of given forces, if only because many of these forces are situated in more than one state or are defined in terms that have little correlation with state boundaries.

A strong state then is a partially autonomous entity in the sense that it has a margin of action available to it wherein it reflects the compromises of multiple interests, even if the bounds of these margins are set by the existence of some groups of primordial strength. To be a partially autonomous entity, there must be a group of people whose direct interests are served by such an entity: state managers and a state bureaucracy.

Such groups emerge within the framework of a capitalist world-economy because a strong state is the best choice between difficult alternatives for the two groups that are strongest in political, economic, and military terms: the emergent capitalist strata, and the old aristocratic hierarchies.

For the former, the strong state in the form of the "absolute monarchies" was a prime customer, a guardian against local and international brigandage, a mode of social legitimation, a preemptive protection against the creation of strong state barriers elsewhere. For the latter, the strong state represented a brake on these same capitalist strata, an upholder of status conventions, a maintainer of order, a promoter of luxury.

No doubt both nobles and bourgeois found the state machineries to be a burdensome drain of funds, and a meddlesome unproductive bureaucracy. But what options did they have? Nonetheless they were always restive and the immediate politics of the world-system was made up of the pushes and pulls resulting from the efforts of both groups to insulate themselves from what seemed to them the negative effects of the state machinery.

A state machinery involves a tipping mechanism. There is a point where strength creates more strength. The tax revenue enables the state to have a larger and more efficient civil bureaucracy and army which in turn leads to greater tax revenue—a process that continues in spiral form. The tipping mechanism works in other direction too—weakness leading to greater weakness. In between these two tipping points lies the politics of state creation. It is in this arena that the skills of particular managerial groups make a difference. And it is because of the two tipping mechanisms that at certain points a small gap in the world-system can very rapidly become a large one.

In those states in which the state machinery is weak, the state managers do not play the role of coordinating a complex industrial-commercial-agricultural mechanism. Rather they simply become one set of landlords amidst others, with little claim to legitimate authority over the whole.

These tend to be called traditional rulers. The political struggle is often phrased in terms of tradition versus change. This is of course a grossly misleading and ideological terminology. It may in fact be taken as a general sociological principle that, at any given point in time, what is thought to be traditional is of more recent origin than people generally imagine it to be, and represents primarily the conservative instincts of some group threatened with declining social status. Indeed, there seems to be nothing which emerges and evolves as quickly as a "tradition" when the need presents itself.

In a one-class system, the "traditional" is that in the name of which the "others" fight the class-conscious group. If they can encrust their values by legitimating them widely, even better by enacting them into legislative barriers, they thereby change the system I a way favorable to them.

The traditionalists may win in some states, but if a world-economy is to survive, they must lose more or less in the others. Furthermore, the gain in one region is the counterpart of the loss in another.

This is not quite a zero-sum game, but it is also inconceivable that all elements in a capitalist world-economy shift their values in a given direction simultaneously. The social system is built on having a multiplicity of value systems within it, reflecting the specific functions groups and areas play in the world division of labor.

We have not exhausted here the theoretical problems relevant to the functioning of a world-economy. We have tried only to speak to those illustrated by the early period of the world-economy in creation, to wit, sixteenth-century Europe. Many other problems emerged at later stages and will be treated, both empirically and theoretically, in later volumes.

In the sixteenth century, Europe was like a bucking bronco. The attempt of some groups to establish a world-economy based on a particular division of labor, to create national states in the core areas as politico-economic guarantors of this system, and to get the workers to pay not only the profits but the costs of maintaining the system was not easy. It was to Europe's credit that it was done, since without the thrust of the sixteenth century the modern world would not have been born and, for all its cruelties, it is better that it was born than had it not been.

It is also to Europe's credit that it was not easy, and particularly that it was not easy because the people who paid the short-term costs screamed lustily at the unfairness of it all. The peasants and workers in Poland and England and Brazil and Mexico were all rambunctious in their various ways. As R.H. Tawney says of the agrarian disturbances of sixteenth-century England: "Such movements are a proof of blood and sinew and of a high and gallant spirit … Happy the nation whose people has not forgotten how to rebel."

The mark of the modern world is the imagination of its profiteers and the counter-assertiveness of the oppressed. Exploitation and the refusal to accept exploitation as either inevitable or just constitute the continuing antinomy of the modern era, joined together in a dialectic which has far from reached its climax in the twentieth century.

↳ ways to make money & the impact that it has on those oppressed

1.6 The Protestant ethic and the spirit of capitalism

Max Weber

This worldly Protestant asceticism, as we may recapitulate up to this point, acted powerfully against the spontaneous enjoyment of possessions; it restricted consumption, especially of luxuries. On the other hand, it had the psychological effect of freeing the acquisition of goods from the inhibitions of traditionalistic ethics. It broke the bonds of the impulse of acquisition in that it not only legalized it, but (in the sense discussed) looked upon it as directly willed by God. The campaign against the temptations of the flesh, and the dependence on external things, was, as besides the Puritans the great Quaker apologist Barclay expressly says, not a struggle against the rational acquisition, but against the irrational use of wealth.

But this irrational use was exemplified in the outward forms of luxury which their code condemned as idolatry of the flesh, however natural they had appeared to the feudal mind. On the other hand, they approved the rational and utilitarian uses of wealth which were willed by God for the needs of the individual and the community. They did not wish to impose mortification on the man of wealth, but the use of his means for necessary and practical things. The idea of comfort characteristically limits the extent of ethically permissible expenditures. It is naturally no accident that the development of a manner of living consistent with that idea may be observed earliest and most clearly among the most consistent representatives of this whole attitude toward life. Over against the glitter and ostentation of feudal magnificence which, resting on an unsound economic basis, prefers a sordid elegance to a sober simplicity, they set the clean and solid comfort of the middle-class home as an ideal.

On the side of the production of private wealth, asceticism condemned both dishonesty and impulsive avarice. What was condemned as covetousness, Mammonism, etc., was the pursuit of riches for their own sake. For wealth in itself was a temptation. But here asceticism was the power "which ever seeks the good but ever creates evil" what was evil in its sense was possession and its temptations. For, in conformity with the Old Testament and in analogy to the ethical valuation of good works, asceticism looked upon the pursuit of wealth as an end in itself as highly reprehensible; but the attainment of it as a fruit of labor in a calling was a sign of God's blessing. And even more important: the religious valuation of restless, continuous, systematic work in a worldly calling, a the highest means to asceticism, and at the same time the surest and most evident proof of rebirth and genuine faith, must have been the most powerful conceivable lever for the expansion of that attitude toward life which we have here called the spirit of capitalism.

When the limitation of consumption is combined with this release of acquisitive activity, the inevitable practical result is obvious: accumulation of capital through ascetic compulsion to save. The restraints which were imposed upon the consumption of wealth naturally served to increase it by making possible the productive investment of capital. How strong this influence was is not, unfortunately, susceptible to exact statistical demonstration. In New England the connection is so evident that it did not escape the eye of so discerning a historian as Doyle. But also in Holland, which was really only dominated by strict Calvinism for seven years, the greater simplicity of life in the more seriously religious circles, in combination with great wealth, led to an excessive propensity to accumulation.

That, furthermore, the tendency which has existed everywhere and at all times, being quite strong in Germany today, for middle-class fortunes to be absorbed into the nobility, was necessarily checked by the Puritan antipathy to the feudal way of life, is evident. English Mercantilist writers of the seventeenth century attributed the superiority of Dutch capital to English to the circumstance that newly acquired wealth there did not regularly seek investment in land. Also, since it is not simply a question of the purchase of land, it did not there seek to transfer itself to feudal habits of life, and thereby to remove itself from the possibility of capitalistic investment. The high esteem for agriculture as a peculiarly important branch of activity, also especially consistent with piety, which the Puritans shared, applied (for instance in Baxter) not to the landlord, but to the yeoman and farmer, in the eighteenth century not to the squire, but the rational cultivator. Through the whole of English society in the time since the seventeenth century goes the conflict between the squirearchy, the representatives of "merrie old England," and the Puritan circles of widely varying social influence. Both elements, that of an unspoiled naive joy of life, and of a strictly regulated, reserved self-control, and conventional ethical conduct are even today combined to form the English national character. Similarly, the early history of the North American Colonies is dominated by the sharp contrast of the adventurers, who wanted to set up plantations with the labor of indentured servants, and live as feudal lords, and the specifically middle-class outlook of the Puritans.

As far as the influence of the Puritan outlook extended, under all circumstances—and this is, of course, much more important than the mere encouragement of capital accumulation—it favoured the development of a rational bourgeois economic life; it was the most important, and above all the only consistent influence in the development of that life. It stood at the cradle of the modern economic man.

To be sure, these Puritanical ideals tended to give way under excessive pressure from the temptations of wealth, as the Puritans themselves knew very well. With great regularity we find the most genuine adherents of Puritanism among the classes which were rising from a lowly status, the small bourgeois and farmers, while the *beati possidentes*, even among Quakers, are often found tending to repudiate the old ideals. It was the same fate which again and again befell the predecessor of this worldly asceticism, the monastic asceticism of the Middle Ages. In the latter case, when rational economic activity had worked out its full effects by strict regulation of conduct and limitation of consumption, the wealth accumulated either succumbed directly to the nobility, as in the time before the Reformation, or monastic discipline threatened to break down, and one of the numerous reformations became necessary.

In fact the whole history of monasticism is in a certain sense the history of a continual struggle with the problem of the secularizing influence of wealth. The same is true on a grand scale of the worldly asceticism of Puritanism. The great revival of Methodism, which preceded the expansion of English industry toward the end of the eighteenth century, may well be compared with such a monastic reform. We may hence quote here a passage from John Wesley himself which might well serve as a motto for everything which has been said above. For it shows that the leaders of these ascetic movements understood the seemingly paradoxical relationships which we have here analysed perfectly well, and in the same sense that we have given them. He wrote:

I fear, wherever riches have increased, the essence of religion has decreased in the same proportion. Therefore I do not see how it is possible, in the nature of things, for any revival of true religion to continue long. For religion must necessarily produce both industry and frugality, and these cannot but produce riches. But as riches increase, so will pride, anger, and love of the world in all its branches. How then is it possible that Methodism, that is, a religion of the heart, though it flourishes now as a green bay tree, should continue in this state? For the Methodists in every place grow diligent and frugal; consequently they increase in goods. Hence they proportionately increase in pride, in anger, in the desire of the flesh, the desire of the eyes, and the pride of life. So, although the form of religion remains, the spirit is swiftly vanishing away. Is there no way to prevent this—this continual decay of pure religion? We ought not to prevent people from being diligent and frugal; we must exhort all Christians to gain all they can, and to save all they can; that is, in effect, to grow rich.

There follows the advice that those who gain all they can and save all they can should also give all they can, so that they will grow in grace and lay up a treasure in heaven. It is clear that Wesley here expresses, even in detail, just what we have been trying to point out. As Wesley here says, the full economic effect of those great religious movements, whose significance for economic development lay above all in their ascetic educative influence, generally came only after the peak of the purely religious enthusiasm was past. Then the intensity of the search for the Kingdom of God commenced gradually to pass over into sober economic virtue; the religious roots died out slowly, giving way to utilitarian worldliness. Then, as Dowden puts it, as in Robinson Crusoe, the isolated economic man who carries on missionary activities on the side takes the place of the lonely spiritual search for the Kingdom of Heaven of Bunyan's pilgrim, hurrying through the market-place of Vanity. When later the principle "to make the most of both worlds" became dominant in the end, as Dowden has remarked, a good conscience simply became one of the means of enjoying a comfortable bourgeois life, as is well expressed in the German proverb about the soft pillow. What the great religious epoch of the seven-teenth century bequeathed to its utilitarian successor was, however, above all an amazingly good, we may even say a pharisaically good, conscience in the acquisition of money, so long as it took place legally. Every trace of the *deplacere vix potest* has disappeared.

A specifically bourgeois economic ethic had grown up. With the consciousness of standing in the fullness of God's grace and being visibly blessed by Him, the bourgeois business man, as long as he remained within the bounds of formal correctness, as long as his moral conduct was spotless and the use to which he put his wealth was not objectionable, could follow his pecuniary interests as he would and feel that he was fulfilling a duty in doing so. The power of religious asceticism provided him in addition with sober, conscientious, and unusually industrious workmen, who clung to their work as to a life purpose willed by God.

Finally, it gave him the comforting assurance that the unequal distribution of the goods of this world was a special dispensation of Divine Providence, which in these differences, as in particular grace, pursued secret ends unknown to men. Calvin himself had made the much-quoted statement that only when the people, i.e. the mass of laborers and craftsmen, were poor did they remain obedient to God. In the Netherlands (Pieter de la Court and others), that had been secularized to the effect that the mass of men only labor when necessity forces them to do so. This formulation of a leading idea of capitalistic economy later entered into the current theories of the productivity of low wages. Here also, with the dying out of the religious root, the utilitarian interpretation crept in unnoticed, in the line of development which we have again and again observed. Mediaeval ethics not only tolerated begging but actually glorified it in the mendicant orders. Even secular beggars, since they gave the person of means opportunity for good works through giving alms, were sometimes considered an estate and treated as such. Even the Anglican social ethic of the Stuarts was very close to this attitude. It remained for Puritan Asceticism to take part in the severe English Poor Relief Legislation which fundamentally changed the situation. And it could do that because the Protestant sects and the strict Puritan communities actually did not know any begging in their own midst.

On the other hand, seen from the side of the workers, the Zinzendorf branch of Pietism, for instance, glorified the loyal worker who did not seek acquisition, but lived according to the apostolic model, and was thus endowed with the charisma of the disciples. Similar ideas had originally been prevalent among the Baptists.

Now naturally the whole ascetic literature of almost all denominations is saturated with the idea that faithful labor, even at low wages, on the part of those whom, life offers no other opportunities, is highly pleasing to God. In this respect Protestant Asceticism added in itself nothing new. But it not only deepened this idea most powerfully, it also created the force which was alone decisive for its effectiveness: the psychological sanction of it through the conception of this labor as a calling, as the best, often in the last analysis the only means of attaining certainty of grace. And on the other hand it legalized the exploitation of this specific willingness to work, in that it also interpreted the employer's business activity as a calling. It is obvious how powerfully the exclusive search for the Kingdom of God only through the fulfilment of duty in the calling, and the strict asceticism which Church discipline naturally imposed, especially on the propertyless classes, was bound to affect the productivity of labor in the capitalistic sense of the word. The treatment of labor as a calling became as characteristic of the modern worker as the corresponding attitude toward acquisition of the business man. It was a perception of this situation, new at his time, which caused so able an observer as Sir William Petty to attribute the economic power of Holland in the seventeenth century to the fact that the very numerous dissenters in that country (Calvinists and Baptists) "are for the most part thinking, sober men, and such as believe that Labor and Industry is their duty towards God."

Calvinism opposed organic social organization in the fiscal-monopolistic form which it assumed in Anglicanism under the Stuarts, especially in the conceptions of Laud, this alliance of Church and State with the monopolists on the basis of a Christian, social ethical foundation. Its leaders were universally among the most passionate opponents of this type of politically privileged commercial, putting-out, and colonial capitalism. Over against it they placed the individualistic motives of rational legal acquisition by virtue of one's own ability and initiative. And, while the politically privileged monopoly industries in England all disappeared in short order, this attitude played a large and decisive part in the development of the industries which grew up in spite of and against the authority of the State. The Puritans (Prynne, Parker) repudiated all connection with the large-scale capitalistic courtiers and projectors as an ethically suspicious class. On the other hand, they took pride in their own superior middle-class business morality, which formed the true reason for the persecutions to which they were subjected on the part of those circles. Defoe proposed to win the battle against dissent by boycotting bank credit and withdrawing deposits. The difference of the two types of capitalistic attitude went to a very large extent hand in hand with religious differences. The opponents of the Nonconformists, even in the eighteenth century, again and again ridiculed them for personifying the spirit of shopkeepers, and for having, ruined the ideals of old England. Here also lay the difference of the Puritan economic ethic from the Jewish; and contemporaries (Prynne) knew well that the former and not the latter was the bourgeois capitalistic ethic.

One of the fundamental elements of the spirit of modern capitalism, and not only of that but of all modern culture: rational conduct on the basis of the idea of the calling, was born—that is what this discussion has sought to demonstrate—from the spirit of Christian asceticism. One has only to reread the passage from Franklin, quoted at the beginning of this essay, in order to see that the essential elements of the attitude which was there called the spirit of capitalism are the same as what we have just shown to be the content of the Puritan worldly asceticism, only without the religious basis, which by Franklin's time had died away. The idea that modern labor has an ascetic character is of course not new. Limitation to specialized work, with a renunciation of the Faustian universality of man which it involves, is a condition of any valuable work in the modern world; hence deeds and renunciation inevitably condition each other today. This fundamentally ascetic trait of middle-class life, if it attempts to be a way of life at all, and not simply the absence of any, was what Goethe wanted to teach, at the height of his wisdom, in the *Wanderjahren*, and in the end which he gave to the life of his Faust. For him the realization meant a renunciation, a departure from an age of full and beautiful humanity, which can no more be repeated in the course of our cultural development than can the flower of the Athenian culture of antiquity.

The Puritan wanted to work in a calling; we are forced to do so. For when asceticism was carried out of monastic cells into everyday life, and began to dominate worldly morality, it did its part in building the tremendous cosmos of the modern economic order. This order is now bound to the technical and economic conditions of machine production which today determine the lives of all the individuals who are born into this mechanism, not only those directly concerned with economic acquisition, with irresistible force. Perhaps it will so determine them until the last ton of fossilized coal is burnt. In Baxter's view tile care for external goods should only lie on the shoulders of the "saint like a light cloak, which can be thrown aside at any moment." But fate decreed that the cloak should become an iron cage.

Since asceticism undertook to remodel the world and to work out its ideals in the world, material goods have gained an increasing and finally an inexorable power over the lives of men as at no previous period in history. Today the spirit of religious asceticism—whether finally, who knows?—has escaped from the cage. But victorious capitalism, since it rests on mechanical foundations, needs its support no longer. The rosy blush of its laughing heir, the Enlightenment, seems also to be irretrievably fading, and the idea of duty in one's calling prowls about in our lives like the ghost of dead religious beliefs. Where the fulfilment of the calling cannot directly be related to the highest spiritual and cultural values, or when, on the other hand, it need not be felt simply as economic compulsion, the individual generally abandons the attempt to justify it at all. In the field of its highest development, in the United States, the pursuit of wealth, stripped of its religious and ethical meaning, tends to become associated with purely mundane passions, which often actually give it the character of sport.

No one knows who will live in this cage in the future, or whether at the end of this tremendous development, entirely new prophets will arise, or there will be a great rebirth of old ideas and ideals, or, if neither, mechanized petrification, embellished with a sort of convulsive self-importance. For of the fast stage of this cultural development, it might well be truly said: "Specialists without spirit, sensualists without heart; this nullity imagines that it has attained a level of civilization never before achieved."

But this brings us to the world of judgments of value and of faith, with which this purely historical discussion need not be burdened. The next task would be rather to show the significance of ascetic rationalism which has only been touched in the foregoing sketch for the content of practical social ethics, thus for the types of organization and the functions of social groups from the conventicle to the State. Then its relations to humanistic rationalism, its ideals of life and cultural influence; further to the development of philosophical and scientific empiricism, to technical development and to spiritual ideals would have to be analysed. Then its historical development from the mediaeval beginnings of worldly asceticism to its dissolution into pure utilitarianism would have to be traced out through all the areas of ascetic religion. Only then could the quantitative cultural significance of ascetic Protestantism in its relation to the other plastic elements of modern culture be estimated.

Here we have only attempted to trace the fact and the direction of its influence to their motives in one, though a very important point. But it would also further be necessary to investigate how Protestant Asceticism was in turn influenced in its development and its character by the totality of social conditions, especially economic. The modern man is in general, even with the best will, unable to give religious ideas a significance for culture and national character which they deserve. But it is, of course, not my aim to substitute for a one-sided materialistic an equally one-sided spiritualistic causal interpretation of culture and of history. Each is equally possible, but each, if it does not serve as the preparation, but as the conclusion of an investigation, accomplish equally little in the interest of historical truth.

Questions for discussion

1   How do the early colonial Charters establish a "legal" foundation for undermining the possibility of reciprocal relationships between Europeans and non-Europeans in the modern world? By extension, how transnational is international law?

2   How is the system of governance set out in the *East India Company Act* implicated in the creation of deep rifts in Asian societies that have persisted to this day?

3   Tarak Barkawi suggests that mercantile and later capitalist interests have always required military enforcement. Thomas Friedman similarly wrote in the *New York Times* in 1999: "The hidden hand of the market will never work without a hidden fist—McDonald's cannot flourish without McDonnell-Douglas, the builder of the F-15."[1] In what ways are contemporary economic interests implicated in transnational military action (and inaction)?

4   Immanuel Wallerstein writes of the modern world-system as, while "not quite a zero-sum game," one in which the global capitalist economy rests on a balancing of gain and loss. That is, gains achieved by regional value systems are met with concomitant losses by others. As economic power increasingly shifts from the Western to the Eastern hemisphere, what will be the impact on long-standing social and cultural patterns within the Western hemisphere?

5   Critics of Max Weber have pointed to the fact that nascent capitalist forces were present before the Protestant Reformation, in Venice and Florence, and in parts of Germany,

for example. Some have further argued that European "discoveries" in the New World and the capitalist impulses they unleashed shaped Protestantism rather than the inverse. Weber, in fact, was open to these criticisms, as we see in the final paragraphs of the reading. What then are the more salient implications of his argument when considering the ascendency of—and prospects for—global capitalism?

Suggestions for further reading

Tarak Barkawi, *Globalization and War*, Lanham, MD: Rowman and Littlefield, 2005.

Tonya Gonnella Frichner, "Impact on indigenous peoples of the international legal construct known as the doctrine of discovery, which has served as the foundation of the violation of their human rights," section 7, New York, United Nations Economic and Social Council: 2010. http://www.google.com/url?sa=t&rct=j&q=&esrc=s&source=web&cd=1&ved=0CCgQFjAA&url=http%3A%2F%2Fwww.un.org%2Fesa%2Fsocdev%2Funpfii%2Fdocuments%2FE%2520C.19%25202010%252013.DOC&ei=Sg2GU6TlLcHisATdulKoDQ&usg=AFQjCNHILAJtAiDelRhbwGlHFDLEjSoNTg&bvm=bv.67720277,d.cWc

Benjamin Nelson, *The Idea of Usury: From Tribal Brotherhood to Universal Otherhood*, Chicago, IL: University of Chicago Press, 1969.

Paul Tillich, *The Protestant Era*, Charleston, SC: Nabu Press, 2011.

Section II

Religion and globalization: A dialogue with prevailing wisdom

Part 1

The first three readings in Section II provide rather dichotomous maps of the late modern world. Each deals in one fashion or another with a polarized cultural view of the globe. The first essay is written by the eminent American political scientist Samuel Huntington, whose work on "civilizations" in late modernity has received a great deal of scholarly and popular attention. The second by Benjamin Barber has catapulted the phrase "Jihad vs. McWorld" into the public sphere.

While Huntington is unmistakably the person most associated with the phrase "the clash of civilizations" he did not actually coin the phrase. If anything, Huntington was placing himself in a lineage of scholars who have been consistently concerned with the divide between the West and the Islamic world. Basil Matthews invoked the term in his 1926 *Young Islam on Trek: A Study in the Clash of Civilizations*, where he concluded that Islam was a "fixed system of theocracy" entirely incompatible with modern democratic government. In 1990 Bernard Lewis again used the term in an essay published in the *Atlantic Monthly*. While the essay explored the relationship between contemporary resentment in some Muslim states and the history of Western imperialism and meddling in the affairs of these states (as well as those of their geographical neighbors), there was much of Basil Matthews here. The discourses of hardline Muslim regimes (i.e. Libya and Iran), Lewis wrote, are undoubtedly jarring to the "modern outsider," while their violent actions are a "war against modernity."

Huntington's now famous thesis is set firmly in this tradition. With the end of the Cold War, argues Huntington, global conflicts will henceforth turn non-ideological, erupting along the "fault lines" running between civilizations and especially between the West and Islam. The formal collapse of the Soviet Union in 1991 provides the back-drop for Huntington's argument, an event that opened new spaces for global capitalism to flourish, and spurred some to celebrate the apparent ascendency of Western political ideology. In 1992, for example, the American political economist Francis Fukuyama now famously announced: "What we may be witnessing is not just the end of the Cold War, but the end of history as such: that is, the endpoint of mankind's ideological evolution and the universalization of Western liberal democracy as the final form of human government."[1] Where Fukuyama saw in the dissolution of the Soviet Union a future to be celebrated, Huntington anticipated a less positive turn in global power structures. From his perspective civilizations are now the preeminent form of cultural organization. With an increasingly globalized world, local cultural factions are identifying themselves with larger civilizations, developing "kin-country syndrome" which will inevitably lead to increased confrontations between the West and the rest of the world.

American political theorist Benjamin Barber proposes a different kind of polarized global environment, organized loosely around two different approaches to modernity. Barber explores a pair of antithetical contemporary phenomena that he regards as threatening to democracy: tribalism (cultural and religious fundamentalism) and globalism (a commercial culture of uniformity). Tribalism provides persons with a sense of distinct local identity, kinship and community in a world dominated by the homogenizing machinations of consumer culture. Globalism offers an ephemeral promise of peace and prosperity, a counter to the threats posed by a world of politically volatile tribalism. Thus they are, Barber tells us, antithetical ways of dealing with globalization that are at the same time unmistakably implicated in one another.

The third reading in this section deals with a polarized late modernity from a different perspective, asserting the necessity for the extension of Western economic norms into a global context where they are not being practiced. Bill George, a businessman and a professor of management practice at Harvard Business School, introduces the notion of business ethics, a subject that will come up in different ways in subsequent entries. The view he espouses is important to note. It is the idea that global business cannot be conducted without an ethical framework that reflects Western European and American values and promotes Western European and American interests. This assumption lies in the background of another conventional view of globalization—that transnational capitalist interests must avoid as much as possible non-Western ethical voices in shaping business interests and practices.

2.1 The clash of civilizations?

Samuel P. Huntington

World politics is entering a new phase, and intellectuals have not hesitated to proliferate visions of what it will be—the end of history, the return of traditional rivalries between nation states, and the decline of the nation state from the conflicting pulls of tribalism and globalism, among others. Each of these visions catches aspects of the emerging reality. Yet they all miss a crucial, indeed a central, aspect of what global politics is likely to be in the coming years.

It is my hypothesis that the fundamental source of conflict in this new world will not be primarily ideological or primarily economic. The great divisions among humankind and the dominating source of conflict will be cultural. Nation states will remain the most powerful actors in world affairs, but the principal conflicts of global politics will occur between nations and groups of different civilizations. The clash of civilizations will dominate global politics. The fault lines between civilizations will be the battle lines of the future …

The nature of civilizations

During the Cold War the world was divided into the First, Second and Third Worlds. Those divisions are no longer relevant. It is far more meaningful now to group countries not in terms of their political or economic systems or in terms of their level of economic development but rather in terms of their culture and civilization.

What do we mean when we talk of a civilization? A civilization is … the highest cultural grouping of people and the broadest level of cultural identity people have short of that which distinguishes humans from other species. It is defined both by common objective elements, such as language, history, religion, customs, institutions, and by the subjective self-identification of people …

Westerners tend to think of nation states as the principal actors in global affairs. They have been that, however, for only a few centuries. The broader reaches of human history have been the history of civilizations. In *A Study of History*, Arnold Toynbee identified 21 major civilizations; only six of them exist in the contemporary world.

Why civilizations will clash

Civilization identity will be increasingly important in the future, and the world will be shaped in large measure by the interactions among seven or eight major civilizations. These include Western, Confucian, Japanese, Islamic, Hindu, Slavic-Orthodox, Latin American and possibly African civilization. The most important conflicts of the future will occur along the cultural fault lines separating these civilizations from one another.

Why will this be the case?

First, differences among civilizations are not only real; they are basic. Civilizations are differentiated from each other by history, language, culture, tradition and, most important, religion ... Differences do not necessarily mean conflict, and conflict does not necessarily mean violence. Over the centuries, however, differences among civilizations have generated the most prolonged and the most violent conflicts.

Second, the world is becoming a smaller place The interactions between peoples of different civilizations are increasing; these increasing interactions intensify civilization consciousness and awareness of differences between civilizations and commonalities within civilizations ... The interactions among peoples of different civilizations enhance the civilization-consciousness of people that, in turn, invigorates differences and animosities stretching or thought to stretch back deep into history.

Third, the processes of economic modernization and social change throughout the world are separating people from long-standing local identities. They also weaken the nation state as a source of identity. In much of the world religion has moved in to fill this gap, often in the form of movements that are labeled "fundamentalist." ...

Fourth, the growth of civilization-consciousness is enhanced by the dual role of the West. On the one hand, the West is at a peak of power. At the same time, however, and perhaps as a result, a return to the roots phenomenon is occurring among non-Western civilizations ...

A de-Westernization and indigenization of elites is occurring in many non-Western countries at the same time that Western, usually American, cultures, styles and habits become more popular among the mass of the people.

Fifth, cultural characteristics and differences are less mutable and hence less easily compromised and resolved than political and economic ones. In the former Soviet Union, communists can become democrats, the rich can become poor and the poor rich, but Russians cannot become Estonians and Azeris cannot become Armenians ...

Finally, economic regionalism is increasing ... The importance of regional economic blocs is likely to continue to increase in the future. On the one hand, successful economic regionalism will reinforce civilization-consciousness, On the other hand, economic regionalism may succeed only when it is rooted in a common civilization. The European Community rests on the shared foundation of European culture and Western Christianity. The success of the North American Free Trade Area depends on the convergence now underway of Mexican, Canadian and American cultures. Japan, in contrast, faces difficulties in creating a comparable economic entity in East Asia because Japan is a society and civilization unique to itself ...

As people define their identity in ethnic and religious terms, they are likely to see an "us" versus "them" relation existing between themselves and people of different ethnicity or religion. The end of ideologically defined states in Eastern Europe and the former Soviet Union permits traditional ethnic identities and animosities to come to the fore. Differences in culture and religion create differences over policy issues, ranging from human rights to immigration to trade and commerce to the environment. Geographical propinquity gives rise to conflicting territorial claims from Bosnia to Mindanao. Most important, the efforts of the West to promote its values of democracy and liberalism as universal values, to maintain its military predominance and to advance its economic interests engender countering responses from other civilizations ...

The clash of civilizations thus occurs at two levels. At the micro-level, adjacent groups along the fault lines between civilizations struggle, often violently, over the control of territory and each other. At the macro-level, states from different civilizations compete for relative military and economic power, struggle over the control of international institutions and third parties, and competitively promote their particular political and religious values.

The fault lines between civilizations

The fault lines between civilizations are replacing the political and ideological boundaries of the Cold War as the flash points for crisis and bloodshed ... As the ideological division of Europe has disappeared, the cultural division of Europe between Western Christianity, on the one hand, and Orthodox Christianity and Islam, on the other, has reemerged. The most significant dividing line in Europe, as William Wallace has suggested, may well be the eastern boundary of Western Christianity in the year 1500 ...

Conflict along the fault line between Western and Islamic civilizations has been going on for 1,300 years ... In the nineteenth and early twentieth centuries as Ottoman power declined Britain, France, and Italy established Western control over most of North Africa and the Middle East.

After World War II, the West, in turn, began to retreat; the colonial empires disappeared; first Arab nationalism and then Islamic fundamentalism manifested themselves; the West became heavily dependent on the Persian Gulf countries for its energy; the oil-rich Muslim countries became money-rich and, when they wished to, weapons-rich ... [W]arfare between Arabs and the West culminated in 1990, when the United States sent a massive army to the Persian Gulf to defend some Arab countries against aggression by another. In its aftermath NATO planning is increasingly directed to potential threats and instability along its "southern tier." ...

On both sides the interaction between Islam and the West is seen as a clash of civilization ...

Historically, the other great antagonistic interaction of Arab Islamic civilization has been with the pagan, animist, and now increasingly Christian black peoples to the south ... It has been reflected in the on-going civil war in the Sudan between Arabs and blacks, the fighting in Chad between Libyan-supported insurgents and the government, the tensions between Orthodox Christians and Muslims in the Horn of Africa, and the political conflicts, recurring riots and communal violence between Muslims and Christians in Nigeria ...

On the northern border of Islam, conflict has increasingly erupted between Orthodox and Muslim peoples, including the carnage of Bosnia and Sarajevo, the simmering violence between Serb and Albanian ... the tense relations between Russians and Muslims in Central Asia, and the deployment of Russian troops to protect Russian interests in the Caucasus and Central Asia. Religion reinforces the revival of ethnic identities and restimulates Russian fears about the security of their southern borders ...

The conflict of civilizations is deeply rooted elsewhere in Asia. The historic clash between Muslim and Hindu in the subcontinent manifests itself now not only in the rivalry between Pakistan and India but also in intensifying religious strife within India between increasingly militant Hindu groups and India's substantial Muslim minority ...

Civilization rallying: The kin-country syndrome

Groups or states belonging to one civilization that become involved in war with people from a different civilization naturally try to rally support from other members of their own civilization. As the post-Cold War world evolves, civilization commonality, what H.D.S. Greenway has termed the "kin-country" syndrome, is replacing political ideology and traditional balance of power considerations as the principal basis for cooperation and coalitions ...

First, in the Gulf War one Arab state invaded another and then fought a coalition of Arab, Western and other states. While only a few Muslim governments overtly supported Saddam Hussein, many Arab elites privately cheered him on, and he was highly popular among large sections of the Arab publics. Islamic fundamentalist movements universally supported Iraq rather than the Western-backed governments of Kuwait and Saudi Arabia ...

Second, the kin-country syndrome also appeared in conflicts in the former Soviet Union. Armenian military successes in 1992 and 1983 stimulated Turkey to become increasingly supportive of its religious, ethnic and linguistic brethren in Azerbaijan ...

Third, with respect to the fighting in the former Yugoslavia, Western publics manifested sympathy and support for the Bosnian Muslims and the horrors they suffered at the hands of the Serbs. Relatively little concern was expressed, however, over Croatian attacks on Muslims and participation in the dismemberment of Bosnia-Herzegovina. In the early stages of the Yugoslav breakup, Germany, in an unusual display of diplomatic initiative and muscle, induced the other 11 members of the European Community to follow its lead in recognizing Slovenia and Croatia. As a result of the pope's determination to provide strong backing to the two Catholic countries, the Vatican extended recognition even before the Community did. The United States followed the European lead. Thus the leading actors in Western civilization rallied behind their coreligionists. Subsequently Croatia was reported to be receiving substantial quantities of arms from Central European and other Western countries ...

Conflicts and violence will also occur between states and groups within the same civilization. Such conflicts, however, are likely to be less intense and less likely to expand than conflicts between civilizations. Common membership in a civilization reduces the probability of violence in situations where it might otherwise occur ...

Civilization rallying to date has been limited, but it has been growing, and it clearly has the potential to spread much further ... In the coming years, local conflicts most likely to escalate into major wars will be those, as in Bosnia and the Caucasus, along the fault lines between civilizations. The next world war, if there is one, will be a war between civilizations.

The West versus the rest

The West is now at an extraordinary peak of power in relation to other civilizations ... The very phrase "the world community" has become the euphemistic collective noun (replacing "the Free World") to give global legitimacy to actions reflecting the interests of the United States and other

Western powers. Through the IMF and other international economic institutions, the West promotes its economic interests and imposes on other nations the economic policies it thinks appropriate. In any poll of non-Western peoples, the IMF undoubtedly would win the support of finance ministers and a few others, but get an overwhelmingly unfavorable rating from just about everyone else …

Western domination of the U.N. Security Council and its decisions, tempered only by occasional abstention by China, produced U.N. legitimation of the West's use of force to drive Iraq out of Kuwait and its elimination of Iraq's sophisticated weapons and capacity to produce such weapons. It also produced the quite unprecedented action by the United States, Britain and France in getting the Security Council to demand that Libya hand over the Pan Am 103 bombing suspects and then to impose sanctions when Libya refused. After defeating the largest Arab army, the West did not hesitate to throw its weight around in the Arab world. The West in effect is using international institutions, military power and economic resources to run the world in ways that will maintain Western predominance, protect Western interests and promote Western political and economic values.

That at least is the way in which non-Westerners see the new world, and there is a significant element of truth in their view. Differences in power and struggles for military, economic and institutional power are thus one source of conflict between the West and other civilizations. Differences in culture, that is basic values and beliefs, are a second source of conflict. V.S. Naipaul has argued that Western civilization is the "universal civilization" that "fits all men." At a superficial level much of Western culture has indeed permeated the rest of the world. At a more basic level, however, Western concepts differ fundamentally from those prevalent in other civilizations. Western ideas of individualism, liberalism, constitutionalism, human rights, equality, liberty, the rule of law, democracy, free markets, the separation of church and state, often have little resonance in Islamic, Confucian, Japanese, Hindu, Buddhist or Orthodox cultures. Western efforts to propagate such ideas produce instead a reaction against "human rights imperialism" and a reaffirmation of indigenous values, as can be seen in the support for religious fundamentalism by the younger generation in non-Western cultures. The very notion that there could be a "universal civilization" is a Western idea, directly at odds with the particularism of most Asian societies and their emphasis on what distinguishes one people from another …

The central axis of world politics in the future is likely to be, in Kishore Mahbubani's phrase, the conflict between "the West and the Rest" and the responses of non-Western civilizations to Western power and values …

The torn countries

In the future, as people differentiate themselves by civilization, countries with large numbers of peoples of different civilizations, such as the Soviet Union and Yugoslavia, are candidates for dismemberment. Some other countries have a fair degree of cultural homogeneity but are divided over whether their society belongs to one civilization or another. These are torn countries. Their leaders typically wish to pursue a bandwagoning strategy and to make their countries members of the West, but the history, culture and traditions of their countries are non-Western. The most obvious and prototypical torn country is Turkey. The late twentieth-century leaders of Turkey have followed in the Attaturk tradition and defined Turkey as a modern, secular, Western nation state. They allied Turkey with the West in NATO and in the Gulf War; they applied for membership in the European Community. At the same time, however, elements in Turkish society have supported an Islamic revival and have argued that Turkey is basically a Middle Eastern Muslim society …

During the past decade Mexico has assumed a position somewhat similar to that of Turkey. Just as Turkey abandoned its historic opposition to Europe and attempted to join Europe, Mexico has stopped defining itself by its opposition to the United States and is instead attempting to imitate the United States and to join it in the North American Free Trade Area …

… Globally the most important torn country is Russia. The question of whether Russia is part of the West or the leader of a distinct Slavic-Orthodox civilization has been a recurring one in Russian history. That issue was obscured by the communist victory in Russia, which imported a Western ideology, adapted it to Russian conditions and then challenged the West in the name of that ideology. The dominance of communism shut off the historic debate over Westernization versus Russification. With communism discredited Russians once again face that question …

To redefine its civilization identity, a torn country must meet three requirements. First, its political and economic elite has to be generally supportive of and enthusiastic about this move. Second, its public has to be willing to acquiesce in the redefinition. Third, the dominant groups in the recipient civilization have to be willing to embrace the convert …

The Confucian–Islamic connection

The obstacles to non-Western countries joining the West vary considerably. They are easy for Latin American and East European countries. They are greater for the Orthodox countries of the former Soviet Union. They are still greater for Muslim, Confucian, Hindu and Buddhist societies. Japan has established a unique position for itself as an associate member of the West: it is in the West in some respects but clearly not of the West in important dimensions. Those countries that for reason of culture and power do not wish to, or cannot, join the West compete with the West by developing their own economic, military and political power. They do this by promoting their internal development and by cooperating with other non-Western countries. The most prominent form of this cooperation is the Confucian-Islamic connection that has emerged to challenge Western interests, values and power.

Almost without exception, Western countries are reducing their military power; under Yeltsin's leadership so also is Russia. China, North Korea and several Middle Eastern states, however, are significantly expanding their military capabilities. They are doing this by the import of arms from Western and non-Western sources and by the development of indigenous arms industries. One result is the emergence of what Charles Krauthammer has called "Weapon States," and the Weapon States are not Western states. Another result is the redefinition of arms control, which is a Western concept and a Western goal ...

The conflict between the West and the Confucian-Islamic states focuses largely, although not exclusively, on nuclear, chemical and biological weapons, ballistic missiles and other sophisticated means for delivering them, and the guidance, intelligence and other electronic capabilities for achieving that goal. The West promotes nonproliferation as a universal norm and nonproliferation treaties and inspections as means of realizing that norm. It also threatens a variety of sanctions against those who promote the spread of sophisticated weapons and proposes some benefits for those who do not. The attention of the West focuses, naturally, on nations that are actually or potentially hostile to the West.

The non-Western nations, on the other hand, assert their right to acquire and to deploy whatever weapons they think necessary for their security ...

Centrally important to the development of counter-West military capabilities is the sustained expansion of China's military power and its means to create military power. Buoyed by spectacular economic development, China is rapidly increasing its military spending and vigorously moving forward with the modernization of its armed forces ... China is also a major exporter of arms and weapons technology ... North Korea has had a nuclear weapons program under way for some while and has sold advanced missiles and missile technology to Syria and Iran. The flow of weapons and weapons technology is generally from East Asia to the Middle East. There is, however, some movement in the reverse direction; China has received Stinger missiles from Pakistan.

A Confucian-Islamic military connection has thus come into being, designed to promote acquisition by its members of the weapons and weapons technologies needed to counter the military power of the West. It may or may not last. At present, however, it is, as Dave McCurdy has said, "a renegades' mutual support pact, run by the proliferators and their backers." ...

Implications for the West

... [D]ifferences between civilizations are real and important; civilization-consciousness is increasing; conflict between civilizations will supplant ideological and other forms of conflict as the dominant global form of conflict; international relations, historically a game played out within Western civilization, will increasingly be de-Westernized and become a game in which non-Western civilizations are actors and not simply objects; successful political, security and economic international institutions are more likely to develop within civilizations than across civilizations; conflicts between groups in different civilizations will be more frequent, more sustained and more violent than conflicts between groups in the same civilization; violent conflicts between groups in different civilizations are the most likely and most dangerous source of escalation that could lead to global wars; the paramount axis of world politics will be the relations between "the West and the Rest"; the elites in some torn non-Western countries will try to make their countries part of the West, but in most cases face major obstacles to accomplishing this; a central focus of conflict for the immediate future will be between the West and several Islamic-Confucian states.

... These implications should be divided between short-term advantage and long-term accommodation. In the short term it is clearly in the interest of the West to promote greater cooperation and unity within its own civilization, particularly between its European and North American components; to incorporate into the West societies in Eastern Europe and Latin America whose cultures are close to those of the West; to promote and maintain cooperative relations with Russia and Japan; to prevent escalation of local inter-civilization conflicts into major inter-civilization wars; to limit the expansion of the military strength of Confucian and Islamic states; to moderate the reduction of Western military capabilities and maintain military superiority in East and Southwest Asia; to exploit differences and conflicts among Confucian and Islamic states; to support in other civilizations groups sympathetic to Western values and interests; to strengthen international institutions that reflect and legitimate Western interests and values and to promote the involvement of non-Western states in those institutions.

In the longer term other measures would be called for. Western civilization is both Western and modern. Non-Western civilizations have attempted to become modern without becoming Western. To date only Japan has fully succeeded in this quest. Non-Western civilizations will continue to attempt to acquire the wealth, technology, skills, machines and weapons that are part of being modern. They will also attempt to reconcile this modernity with their traditional culture and values. Their economic and military strength relative to the West will increase. Hence the West will increasingly have to accommodate these non-Western modern civilizations whose power approaches that of the West but whose values and interests differ significantly from those of the West. This will require the West to maintain the economic and military power necessary to protect its interests in relation to these civilizations. It will also, however, require the West to develop a more profound understanding of the basic religious and philosophical assumptions underlying other civilizations and the ways in which people in those civilizations see their interests. It will require an effort to identify elements of commonality between Western and other civilizations. For the relevant future, there will be no universal civilization, but instead a world of different civilizations, each of which will have to learn to coexist with the others.

2.2 Jihad vs. McWorld

Benjamin R. Barber

Just beyond the horizon of current events lie two possible political futures—both bleak, neither democratic. The first is a retribalization of large swaths of humankind by war and bloodshed: a threatened Lebanonization of national states in which culture is pitted against culture, people against people, tribe against tribe—a Jihad in the name of a hundred narrowly conceived faiths against every kind of interdependence, every kind of artificial social cooperation and civic mutuality. The second is being borne in on us by the onrush of economic and ecological forces that demand integration and uniformity and that mesmerize the world with fast music, fast computers, and fast food—with MTV, Macintosh, and McDonald's, pressing nations into one commercially homogenous global network: one McWorld tied together by technology, ecology, communications, and commerce. The planet is falling precipitantly apart *AND* coming reluctantly together at the very same moment …

The tendencies of what I am here calling the forces of Jihad and the forces of McWorld operate with equal strength in opposite directions, the one driven by parochial hatreds, the other by universalizing markets, the one re-creating ancient subnational and ethnic borders from within, the other making national borders porous from without. They have one thing in common: neither offers much hope to citizens looking for practical ways to govern themselves democratically …

McWorld, or the globalization of politics

Four imperatives make up the dynamic of McWorld: a market imperative, a resource imperative, an information-technology imperative, and an ecological imperative. By shrinking the world and diminishing the salience of national borders, these imperatives have in combination achieved a considerable victory over factiousness and particularism, and not least of all over their most virulent traditional form—nationalism …

THE MARKET IMPERATIVE. Marxist and Leninist theories of imperialism assumed that the quest for ever-expanding markets would in time compel nation-based capitalist economies to push against national boundaries in search of an international economic imperium. Whatever else has happened to the scientistic predictions of Marxism, in this domain they have proved farsighted. All national economies are now vulnerable to the inroads of larger, transnational markets within which trade is free, currencies are convertible,

[margin note: can you have some globalization, or does it have to be all or nothing?]

access to banking is open, and contracts are enforceable under law. In Europe, Asia, Africa, the South Pacific, and the Americas such markets are eroding national sovereignty and giving rise to entities—international banks, trade associations, transnational lobbies like OPEC and Greenpeace, world news services like CNN and the BBC, and multinational corporations that increasingly lack a meaningful national identity—that neither reflect nor respect nationhood as an organizing or regulative principle.

The market imperative has also reinforced the quest for international peace and stability, requisites of an efficient international economy. Markets are enemies of parochialism, isolation, fractiousness, war. Market psychology attenuates the psychology of ideological and religious cleavages and assumes a concord among producers and consumers—categories that ill fit narrowly conceived national or religious cultures … In the context of common markets, international law ceases to be a vision of justice and becomes a workaday framework for getting things done—enforcing contracts, ensuring that governments abide by deals, regulating trade and currency relations, and so forth.

Common markets demand a common language, as well as a common currency, and they produce common behaviors of the kind bred by cosmopolitan city life everywhere. Commercial pilots, computer programmers, international bankers, media specialists, oil riggers, entertainment celebrities, ecology experts, demographers, accountants, professors, athletes—these compose a new breed of men and women for whom religion, culture, and nationality can seem only marginal elements in a working identity …

THE RESOURCE IMPERATIVE. Democrats once dreamed of societies whose political autonomy rested firmly on economic independence …

… [I]t has been harder for Americans than for most to accept the inevitability of interdependence. But the rapid depletion of resources even in a country like ours, where they once seemed inexhaustible, and the maldistribution of arable soil and mineral resources on the planet, leave even the wealthiest societies ever more resource-dependent and many other nations in permanently desperate straits.

Every nation, it turns out, needs something another nation has; some nations have almost nothing they need.

THE INFORMATION-TECHNOLOGY IMPERATIVE. Enlightenment science and the technologies derived from it are inherently universalizing. They entail a quest for descriptive principles of general application, a search for universal solutions to particular problems, and an unswerving embrace of objectivity and impartiality.

Scientific progress embodies and depends on open communication, a common discourse rooted in rationality, collaboration, and an easy and regular flow and exchange of information …

Business, banking, and commerce all depend on information flow and are facilitated by new communication technologies. The hardware of these technologies tends to be systemic and integrated—computer, television, cable, satellite, laser, fiber-optic, and microchip technologies combining to create a vast interactive communications and information network that can potentially give every person on earth access to every other person, and make every datum, every byte, available to every set of eyes ... Individual cultures speak particular languages; commerce and science increasingly speak English; the whole world speaks logarithms and binary mathematics ...

The new technology's software is perhaps even more globalizing than its hardware. The information arm of international commerce's sprawling body reaches out and touches distinct nations and parochial cultures, and gives them a common face chiseled in Hollywood, on Madison Avenue, and in Silicon Valley ... This kind of software supremacy may in the long term be far more important than hardware superiority, because culture has become more potent than armaments. What is the power of the Pentagon compared with Disneyland? Can the Sixth Fleet keep up with CNN? McDonald's in Moscow and Coke in China will do more to create a global culture than military colonization ever could. It is less the goods than the brand names that do the work, for they convey life-style images that alter perception and challenge behavior. They make up the seductive software of McWorld's common (at times much too common) soul.

Yet in all this high-tech commercial world there is nothing that looks particularly democratic. It lends itself to surveillance as well as liberty, to new forms of manipulation and covert control as well as new kinds of participation, to skewed, unjust market outcomes as well as greater productivity. The consumer society and the open society are not quite synonymous. Capitalism and democracy have a relationship, but it is something less than a marriage. An efficient free market after all requires that consumers be free to vote their dollars on competing goods, not that citizens be free to vote their values and beliefs on competing political candidates and programs ...

THE ECOLOGICAL IMPERATIVE. The impact of globalization on ecology is a cliche even to world leaders who ignore it ... Yet this ecological consciousness has meant not only greater awareness but also greater inequality, as modernized nations try to slam the door behind them, saying to developing nations, "The world cannot afford your modernization; ours has wrung it dry!"

Each of the four imperatives just cited is transnational, transideological, and transcultural. Each applies impartially to Catholics, Jews, Muslims, Hindus, and Buddhists; to democrats and totalitarians; to capitalists and socialists. The Enlightenment dream of a universal rational society has to a remarkable degree been realized—but in a form that is commercialized, homogenized, depoliticized, bureaucratized, and, of course, radically incomplete, for the movement toward McWorld is in competition with forces of global breakdown, national dissolution, and centrifugal corruption. These forces, working in the opposite direction, are the essence of what I call Jihad.

Jihad, or the Lebanonization of the world

… Nationalism was once a force of integration and unification, a movement aimed at bringing together disparate clans, tribes, and cultural fragments under new, assimilationist flags. But as Ortega y Gasset noted more than sixty years ago, having won its victories, nationalism changed its strategy. In the 1920s, and again today, it is more often a reactionary and divisive force, pulverizing the very nations it once helped cement together …

There were more than thirty wars in progress last year, most of them ethnic, racial, tribal, or religious in character, and the list of unsafe regions doesn't seem to be getting any shorter. Some new world order!

The aim of many of these small-scale wars is to redraw boundaries, to implode states and resecure parochial identities: to escape McWorld's dully insistent imperatives. The mood is that of Jihad: war not as an instrument of policy but as an emblem of identity, an expression of community, an end in itself. Even where there is no shooting war, there is fractiousness, secession, and the quest for ever smaller communities …

Among the tribes, religion is also a battlefield. ("Jihad" is a rich word whose generic meaning is "struggle"—usually the struggle of the soul to avert evil. Strictly applied to religious war, it is used only in reference to battles where the faith is under assault, or battles against a government that denies the practice of Islam. My use here is rhetorical, but does follow both journalistic practice and history.) … [L]ike the new forms of hypernationalism, the new expressions of religious fundamentalism are fractious and pulverizing, never integrating …

The atmospherics of Jihad have resulted in a breakdown of civility in the name of identity, of comity in the name of community. International relations have sometimes taken on the aspect of gang war—cultural turf battles featuring tribal factions that were supposed to be sublimated as integral parts of large national, economic, postcolonial, and constitutional entities.

The darkening future of democracy

These rather melodramatic tableaux vivants do not tell the whole story, however. For all their defects, Jihad and McWorld have their attractions. Yet, to repeat and insist, the attractions are unrelated to democracy …

McWorld does manage to look pretty seductive in a world obsessed with Jihad. It delivers peace, prosperity, and relative unity—if at the cost of independence, community, and identity (which is generally based on difference). The primary political values required by the global market are order and tranquillity, and freedom—as in the phrases "free trade," "free press," and "free love." Human rights are needed to a degree, but not citizenship or participation—and no more social justice and equality than are necessary to promote efficient economic production and consumption. Multinational corporations sometimes seem to prefer doing business with local oligarchs, inasmuch as they can take confidence from dealing with the boss on all crucial matters. Despots who slaughter their own populations are no problem, so long as they leave markets in place and refrain from making war on their neighbors (Saddam Hussein's fatal mistake). In trading partners, predictability is of more value than justice.

The Eastern European revolutions that seemed to arise out of concern for global democratic values quickly deteriorated into a stampede in the general direction of free markets and their ubiquitous, television-promoted shopping malls ...

Jihad delivers a different set of virtues: a vibrant local identity, a sense of community, solidarity among kinsmen, neighbors, and countrymen, narrowly conceived. But it also guarantees parochialism and is grounded in exclusion. Solidarity is secured through war against outsiders. And solidarity often means obedience to a hierarchy in governance, fanaticism in beliefs, and the obliteration of individual selves in the name of the group. Deference to leaders and intolerance toward outsiders (and toward "enemies within") are hallmarks of tribalism—hardly the attitudes required for the cultivation of new democratic women and men capable of governing themselves ...

To the extent that either McWorld or Jihad has a *NATURAL* politics, it has turned out to be more of an antipolitics. For McWorld, it is the antipolitics of globalism: bureaucratic, technocratic, and meritocratic, focused (as Marx predicted it would be) on the administration of things—with people, however, among the chief things to be administered. In its politico-economic imperatives McWorld has been guided by laissez-faire market principles that privilege efficiency, productivity, and beneficence at the expense of civic liberty and self-government.

For Jihad, the antipolitics of tribalization has been explicitly antidemocratic: one-party dictatorship, government by military junta, theocratic fundamentalism—often associated with a version of the *Führerprinzip* that empowers an individual to rule on behalf of a people ...

The confederal option

How can democracy be secured and spread in a world whose primary tendencies are at best indifferent to it (McWorld) and at worst deeply antithetical to it (Jihad)? My guess is that globalization will eventually vanquish retribalization. The ethos of material "civilization" has not yet encountered an obstacle it has been unable to thrust aside …

Jihad may be a last deep sigh before the eternal yawn of McWorld … [T]here is nonetheless a form of democratic government that can accommodate parochialism and communitarianism, one that can even save them from their defects and make them more tolerant and participatory: decentralized participatory democracy. And if McWorld is indifferent to democracy, there is nonetheless a form of democratic government that suits global markets passably well—representative government in its federal or, better still, confederal variation.

With its concern for accountability, the protection of minorities, and the universal rule of law, a confederalized representative system would serve the political needs of McWorld as well as oligarchic bureaucratism or meritocratic elitism is currently doing. As we are already beginning to see, many nations may survive in the long term only as confederations that afford local regions smaller than "nations" extensive jurisdiction. Recommended reading for democrats of the twenty-first century is not the U.S. Constitution or the French Declaration of Rights of Man and Citizen but the Articles of Confederation, that suddenly pertinent document that stitched together the thirteen American colonies into what then seemed a too loose confederation of independent states but now appears a new form of political realism, as veterans of Yeltsin's new Russia and the new Europe created at Maastricht will attest.

By the same token, the participatory and direct form of democracy that engages citizens in civic activity and civic judgment and goes well beyond just voting and accountability—the system I have called "strong democracy"— suits the political needs of decentralized communities as well as theocratic and nationalist party dictatorships have done. Local neighborhoods need not be democratic, but they can be. Real democracy has flourished in diminutive settings: the spirit of liberty, Tocqueville said, is local. Participatory democracy, if not naturally apposite to tribalism, has an undeniable attractiveness under conditions of parochialism.

Democracy in any of these variations will, however, continue to be obstructed by the undemocratic and antidemocratic trends toward uniformitarian globalism and intolerant retribalization which I have portrayed here. For democracy to persist in our brave new McWorld, we will have to commit acts of conscious political will—a possibility, but hardly a probability, under these conditions. Political will requires much more than the quick fix of the transfer of institutions. Like technology transfer, institution transfer rests on foolish assumptions about a uniform world of the kind that once fired the imagination of colonial administrators. Spread English justice to the colonies by exporting wigs. Let an East Indian trading company act as the vanguard to Britain's free parliamentary institutions. Today's well-intentioned quick-fixers in the National Endowment for Democracy and the Kennedy School of Government, in the unions and foundations and universities zealously nurturing contacts in Eastern Europe and the Third World, are hoping to democratize by long distance. Post Bulgaria a parliament by first-class mail. Fed Ex the Bill of Rights to Sri Lanka. Cable Cambodia some common law.

Yet Eastern Europe has already demonstrated that importing free political parties, parliaments, and presses cannot establish a democratic civil society; imposing a free market may even have the opposite effect. Democracy grows from the bottom up and cannot be imposed from the top down. Civil society has to be built from the inside out. The institutional superstructure comes last ...

Democrats need to seek out indigenous democratic impulses. There is always a desire for self-government, always some expression of participation, accountability, consent, and representation, even in traditional hierarchical societies. These need to be identified, tapped, modified, and incorporated into new democratic practices with an indigenous flavor ...

It certainly seems possible that the most attractive democratic ideal in the face of the brutal realities of Jihad and the dull realities of McWorld will be a confederal union of semi-autonomous communities smaller than nation-states, tied together into regional economic associations and markets larger than nation-states—participatory and self-determining in local matters at the bottom, representative and accountable at the top. The nation-state would play a diminished role, and sovereignty would lose some of its political potency. The Green movement adage "Think globally, act locally" would actually come to describe the conduct of politics.

This vision reflects only an ideal, however—one that is not terribly likely to be realized. Freedom, Jean-Jacques Rousseau once wrote, is a food easy to eat but hard to digest. Still, democracy has always played itself out against the odds. And democracy remains both a form of coherence as binding as McWorld and a secular faith potentially as inspiring as Jihad.

2.3 Ethics must be global, not local

Bill George

To build a truly great, global business, business leaders need to adopt a global standard of ethical practices.

In business school, we used to debate whether your business ethics should adapt to the local environment or be the same around the world. Many of my classmates argued, "When in Rome, do as the Romans do." In other words, follow local practices. Those were the days when leading ethicists like Joseph Fletcher and James Adams at Harvard were promoting "situation ethics," based on flexible, pragmatic approaches to complex dilemmas.

I listened to their arguments but never could figure out how leaders of business organizations could operate with one set of principles in their homeland and another overseas.

In the 1970s, the Foreign Corrupt Practices Act (FCPA) sent a chill throughout the business community by criminalizing the act of making payments outside the U.S. in pursuit of contracts. Yet the practice persisted. Many U.S. executives lobbied to relax the FCPA's provisions, arguing that they were at a competitive disadvantage in bidding against non-U.S. companies.

Risking the company's reputation

These days the business world has gone global, which has intensified the ethics debate. Making payments to obtain business is common practice in many developing markets in Asia, Africa, the Middle East, and Eastern Europe, and some companies feel obliged to play the game to compete. Witness Germany's Siemens (SI), which has admitted to nearly $2 billion in bribes, leading to the resignations of both its board chairman and its CEO in 2007. Then there's Britain's BAE Systems, which has been accused of making a $2 billion payment to a Saudi prince to secure $80 billion in government contracts. (The company denied the allegation, which is being investigated by the U.S. Justice Dept.)

What's significant about these ethical scandals is the damage they do to great institutions. If you were leading such an organization, would you risk permanently damaging your company in order to win a few overseas contracts? Regrettably, for some executives the answer is yes.

Forty years of experience has strengthened my belief that the only way to build a great global company is with a single global standard of business practices, vigorously communicated and rigorously enforced. Applying "situation ethics" in developing countries is the fastest way to destroy a global organization. To sustain their success, companies must follow the same standards of business conduct in Shanghai, Mumbai, Kiev, and Riyadh as in Chicago.

Engage the CEO in the process

How else will employees in far-flung locations know what to do when pressured by customers or competitors to deviate from company standards? If overseas managers miss their financial targets because they adhere to strict ethical standards, can they be confident management will back them up?

Operating ethically requires much more than a code of conduct. The CEO and top management must engage with employees around the world to insist on transparency and compliance. Otherwise, they will never know what's going on. The company must have a closed-loop system of monitoring and auditing local marketing practices. The "don't look, don't tell" approach is bound to destroy your company's reputation. High standards must be enforced with a zero tolerance policy.

This well-established approach is employed by the companies on whose boards I serve—ExxonMobil (XOM), Goldman Sachs (GS), and Novartis (NOVN). Their employees throughout the world know precisely what is expected of them. Nothing is more important to these companies than their reputations, and they know that nothing destroys reputations faster than ethical violations.

Ethics create shareholder value

General Electric's (GE) former general counsel, Ben Heineman, writes in "Avoiding Integrity Land Mines" in the Harvard Business Review about high performance with high integrity, proposing that performance and ethics go hand in hand. Heineman argues persuasively that CEOs can't just publish their policies and enforce them. Rather, they must get personally involved in ensuring ethical behavior and engaging employees in vigorous discussions of real-world issues. Otherwise, marginal practices like using agents to make payments will abound.

Despite the best efforts, there will be deviations. That's when leaders are watched most closely by their subordinates. Will management make an exception for a top performer?

Early in my time as CEO of Medtronic (MDT) I had to deal with numerous such deviations that led to the termination of such high-performing executives as the president of our European operations and country managers of

Japan, Argentina, and Italy. These actions sent a powerful message that we were serious about company standards, and no one was exempt.

The bottom line is that good ethics is good business. There is a direct correlation between behaving ethically and creating long-term shareholder value. Furthermore, high integrity in external business dealings goes hand in hand with creating greater transparency and increased integrity in internal relationships. This necessitates choosing leaders who are not only ethical themselves but also committed to ensuring their organizations operate ethically at all times.

Bill's True North Principle: Great global organizations can be built only from a solid ethical foundation.

Part 2

The views of globalization represented in our previous readings have not been without their critiques. Before moving to these, however, we should note the work of Peter Berger. Berger, an Australian-born American sociologist, has been a notable voice in public discourses concerning religion and globalization. In many respects Berger's work provides us with a transition from the more conventional approaches we have seen in Huntington and Barber to those we will explore in the remainder of this, and in subsequent, sections. We were unable to obtain permission to reproduce material that is relevant to our discussion here, but we will briefly consider his contribution to the conversation in relation to his essay "Wisdom from the East," published in the online journal *The American Interest*.[2]

In this essay Berger finds much of value in Barber's notion of a "McWorld" in which Westernizing—and more particularly Americanizing—cultural and economic forces are infiltrating every corner of the globe.

The prevailing view of the cultural aspect of globalization is that of a massive process of Westernization. It is producing a synthetic international culture. On the popular level it is sometimes called "McWorld" (a term felicitously coined by Benjamin Barber), sometimes "airport culture." Here the world dances to American music, eats American fast food, affirms (in rhetoric if not always in practice) American notions about love and sexuality. In this world people communicate in a kind of pidgin English, which also adorns T-shirts in luxurious forms of misspelling. On the elite level there has been an equally catchy term (this one invented by Samuel Huntington): the "Davos culture," named after the Swiss mountain village in which every January world leaders from business, government, and (to a lesser extent) academia trudge through the snowdrifts to assure each other of their importance. The English here is of better quality, but it too has an American intonation. Perhaps the denizens of this culture can be succinctly described as people, wherever they originally come from, who find Woody Allen funny.

Yet while Berger finds this vision of late modernity apt, he also suggests that it is insufficient: "Yes, the mighty train of Westernizing culture has left the station. But other trains are coming in from the opposite direction." Here Berger is reflecting the arguments of David Chidester (below) and Srinivas Aravamudan (Section 3) concerning the dialectical nature of the global movement of cultural capital. He notes that North America and Europe, too, are experiencing undeniable cultural infiltration originating principally in

Asia. This "Easternization," he argues, is having a pronounced impact on many facets of traditional Western culture, and it is particularly noticeable in relation to religious beliefs and practices.

> Practices deriving from Asian religion have proliferated—yoga, meditation, alternative therapeutic techniques (such as acupuncture and Ayurvedic medicine). To be sure, sometimes these practices have been detached from their original religious meanings. One may do yoga to lose weight (to misquote Freud—"sometimes a cigar is just a cigar"). Much of the time, though, the religious/"spiritual" intention is deliberate and overt. That is even clearer with expressed beliefs. Large numbers of Westerners believe in reincarnation, and some think that they can, with the right exercises, remember previous lives. A survey in Europe reported that a surprising number of Catholics think that reincarnation is a doctrine of their church. Probably more importantly, many people believe that Western civilization has disrupted the harmony between human beings and nature, and that this is a pathology that should be remedied. There is a strong anti-individualistic theme in the latter belief, often linked to leftist ideology (capitalism as the source of "excessive individualism"), environmentalism (reconciling with a supposedly benign Mother Nature, or with Gaia, the earth as a living being), and radical feminism (the healing power of female spirituality).

With Berger's considerations in the background, we move now to four essays all of which seek to map our global environment. In these essays, however, the maps lack the distinct fault lines that we saw in the earlier part of this Section. Here we read of transcultural contact zones, overlapping spheres of local influence shaped by global forces, and multinational businesses as at once trans-civilizational, exploitative, and susceptible to mutation by local forces.

Our first reading, "The Clash of Ignorance" was written by the literary theorist Edward Said. Said (who was born a Palestinian Arab but also held American citizenship through his father) wrote the essay in direct response to Huntington's "The Clash of Civilizations." His critique is scathing, accusing Huntington of abstracting contemporary cultures to the point of making them into static and immutable entities, and thus portraying them in a "cartoonlike fashion." He goes on to write that the notion of civilizations in conflict not only glosses over the reality of transcultural contacts and reciprocal relationships, but it poses a distinct threat to global security by nudging Western public discourses in a post-9/11 world into a potentially dangerous "us vs. them" mentality. The viable alternative, argues Said, is to approach our current global situation with an eye to divisions of power and "universal principles of justice and injustice."

In the second essay, cultural anthropologist Arjun Appadurai (who was born and educated in Mumbai before moving the United States) also objects strongly to the kind of bifurcated world that we find in the work of Huntington and others. Appadurai argues that the colonial period ushered in an era of unprecedented cultural interactions that have given rise to novel constructed and imagined identities. Furthermore, changes in transportation and information technologies over the past century have set our period apart from the previous 400 years in terms of the sheer volume of transcultural migrations, exchanges, and imaginative possibilities. This has created a unique problem of globalization in our time: a pronounced friction between cultural homogenization and cultural heterogenization, a tension between imported cultural forms (i.e. Americanization), and the indigenization of these forms in local contexts. The result of this is that our current global cultural economy is complex, with a pronounced fragmentation of cultures, politics and economics.

To think about these, Appadurai suggests we employ the idea of global "scapes," protean spaces in which identities, ideologies, technologies, money, and information are negotiated at local (often diasporic) levels. These are the spaces in which new worlds and identities are being imagined into being. But since these scapes are increasingly disconnected from one another, the imagined worlds (especially among immigrants) are fraught with tension.

Like Said, the Bengali economist and Nobel laureate Amartya Sen sees Huntington-styled categorizations as not only ill-conceived but as potentially inflammatory in their reduction of multi-faceted communities to broad ideologically based cultural monoliths. The stereotypes, he writes, merely serve to impoverish the "power and reach of our social and political reasoning." Like Appadurai, he directs our attention to the variety of cultural spheres—class, gender, work, politics—that are the tangled context within which identities are forged and choices made about how we wish to be in the world. Unlike Appadurai, however, he regards these spheres as inescapably overlapping.

An essay by historian of religions David Chidester (an American who has spent most of his career in South Africa) closes this section. Chidester's interest is in how cross-cultural business is remapping the world, and the possibility that business itself is assuming a religious character. Highlighting the ways in which multinational corporations employ frankly religious language in speaking about themselves (i.e. Ray Kroc, for example, speaking of the creation of a McDonald's French fry as "a ritual to be followed religiously") and how corporate photographers pair their products with acknowledged religious symbols (i.e. photos of Saudi Arabian Muslims bowing in prayer with a Coke machine nearby), and drawing parallels between the machinations of global commerce and colonial missionary enterprises that sought to transcend national borders, Chidester raises the implicit question of whether global business is now in the business of religion too, blurring the dichotomies relied upon by writers like Huntington, Barber, and Berger, seeking to forge transnational identities that are legitimized under the "sacred" signs of commodities.

2.4 The clash of ignorance

Edward W. Said

Samuel Huntington's article "The Clash of Civilizations?" appeared in the Summer 1993 issue of *Foreign Affairs*, where it immediately attracted a surprising amount of attention and reaction. Because the article was intended to supply Americans with an original thesis about "a new phase" in world politics after the end of the cold war, Huntington's terms of argument seemed compellingly large, bold, even visionary. He very clearly had his eye on rivals in the policy-making ranks, theorists such as Francis Fukuyama and his "end of history" ideas, as well as the legions who had celebrated the onset of globalism, tribalism and the dissipation of the state. But they, he allowed, had understood only some aspects of this new period. He was about to announce the "crucial, indeed a central, aspect" of what "global politics is likely to be in the coming years." …

Most of the argument in the pages that followed relied on a vague notion of something Huntington called "civilization identity" and "the interactions among seven or eight [*sic*] major civilizations," of which the conflict between two of them, Islam and the West, gets the lion's share of his attention. In this belligerent kind of thought, he relies heavily on a 1990 article by the veteran Orientalist Bernard Lewis, whose ideological colors are manifest in its title, "The Roots of Muslim Rage." In both articles, the personification of enormous entities called "the West" and "Islam" is recklessly affirmed, as if hugely complicated matters like identity and culture existed in a cartoonlike world where Popeye and Bluto bash each other mercilessly, with one always more virtuous pugilist getting the upper hand over his adversary. Certainly neither Huntington nor Lewis has much time to spare for the internal dynamics and plurality of every civilization, or for the fact that the major contest in most modern cultures concerns the definition or interpretation of each culture, or for the unattractive possibility that a great deal of demagogy and downright ignorance is involved in presuming to speak for a whole religion or civilization. No, the West is the West, and Islam Islam.

The challenge for Western policy-makers, says Huntington, is to make sure that the West gets stronger and fends off all the others, Islam in particular. More troubling is Huntington's assumption that his perspective, which is to survey the entire world from a perch outside all ordinary attachments and hidden loyalties, is the correct one, as if everyone else were scurrying around looking for the answers that he has already found. In fact, Huntington is an ideologist, someone who wants to make "civilizations" and "identities" into what they are not: shut-down, sealed-off entities that have been purged of the myriad currents and countercurrents that animate human history, and that over centuries have made it possible for that history not only to contain wars of religion and imperial conquest but also to be one of exchange, cross-fertilization and sharing. This far less visible history is ignored in the rush to highlight the ludicrously compressed and constricted warfare that "the clash of civilizations" argues is the reality ...

The basic paradigm of West versus the rest (the cold war opposition refor-mulated) ... has persisted, often insidiously and implicitly, in discussion since the terrible events of September 11. The carefully planned and horrendous, pathologically motivated suicide attack and mass slaughter by a small group of deranged militants has been turned into proof of Huntington's thesis. Instead of seeing it for what it is—the capture of big ideas (I use the word loosely) by a tiny band of crazed fanatics for criminal purposes—international luminaries from former Pakistani Prime Minister Benazir Bhutto to Italian Prime Minister Silvio Berlusconi have pontificated about Islam's troubles, and in the latter's case have used Huntington's ideas to rant on about the West's superiority, how "we" have Mozart and Michelangelo and they don't ...

But why not instead see parallels, admittedly less spectacular in their destructiveness, for Osama bin Laden and his followers in cults like the Branch Davidians or the disciples of the Rev. Jim Jones at Guyana or the Japanese Aum Shinrikyo? Even the normally sober British weekly *The Economist*, in its issue of September 22–28, can't resist reaching for the vast generalization, praising Huntington extravagantly for his "cruel and sweeping, but nonetheless acute" observations about Islam. "Today," the journal says with unseemly solemnity, Huntington writes that "the world's billion or so Muslims are 'convinced of the superiority of their culture, and obsessed with the inferiority of their power.'" Did he canvas 100 Indonesians, 200 Moroccans, 500 Egyptians and fifty Bosnians? Even if he did, what sort of sample is that?

Uncountable are the editorials in every American and European newspaper and magazine of note adding to this vocabulary of gigantism and apocalypse, each use of which is plainly designed not to edify but to inflame the reader's indignant passion as a member of the "West," and what we need to do. Churchillian rhetoric is used inappropriately by self-appointed combatants in the West's, and especially America's, war against its haters, despoilers, destroyers, with scant attention to complex histories that defy such reduc-tiveness and have seeped from one territory into another, in the process overriding the boundaries that are supposed to separate us all into divided armed camps.

This is the problem with unedifying labels like Islam and the West: They mislead and confuse the mind, which is trying to make sense of a disorderly reality that won't be pigeonholed or strapped down as easily as all that. I remember interrupting a man who, after a lecture I had given at a West Bank university in 1994, rose from the audience and started to attack my ideas as "Western," as opposed to the strict Islamic ones he espoused. "Why are you wearing a suit and tie?" was the first retort that came to mind. "They're Western too." He sat down with an embarrassed smile on his face, but I recalled the incident when information on the September 11 terrorists started to come in: how they had mastered all the technical details required to inflict their homicidal evil on the World Trade Center, the Pentagon and the aircraft they had commandeered. Where does one draw the line between "Western" technology and, as Berlusconi declared, "Islam's" inability to be a part of "modernity"? ...

In a remarkable series of three articles published between January and March 1999 in *Dawn*, Pakistan's most respected weekly, the late Eqbal Ahmad, writing for a Muslim audience, analyzed what he called the roots of the religious right, coming down very harshly on the mutilations of Islam by absolutists and fanatical tyrants whose obsession with regulating personal behavior promotes "an Islamic order reduced to a penal code, stripped of its humanism, aesthetics, intellectual quests, and spiritual devotion." ... As a timely instance of this debasement, Ahmad proceeds first to present the rich, complex, pluralist meaning of the word *jihad* and then goes on to show that in the word's current confinement to indiscriminate war against presumed enemies, it is impossible "to recognize the Islamic—religion, society, culture, history or politics—as lived and experienced by Muslims through the ages." The modern Islamists, Ahmad concludes, are "concerned with power, not with the soul; with the mobilization of people for political purposes rather than with sharing and alleviating their sufferings and aspirations. Theirs is a very limited and time-bound political agenda." What has made matters worse is that similar distortions and zealotry occur in the "Jewish" and "Christian" universes of discourse.

It was Conrad ... who understood that the distinctions between civilized London and "the heart of darkness" quickly collapsed in extreme situations, and that the heights of European civilization could instantaneously fall into the most barbarous practices without preparation or transition. And it was Conrad also, in *The Secret Agent* (1907), who described terrorism's affinity for abstractions like "pure science" (and by extension for "Islam" or "the West"), as well as the terrorist's ultimate moral degradation.

For there are closer ties between apparently warring civilizations than most of us would like to believe; both Freud and Nietzsche showed how the traffic across carefully maintained, even policed boundaries moves with often terrifying ease. But then such fluid ideas, full of ambiguity and skepticism about notions that we hold on to, scarcely furnish us with suitable, practical guidelines for situations such as the one we face now. Hence the altogether more reassuring battle orders (a crusade, good versus evil, freedom against fear, etc.) drawn out of Huntington's alleged opposition between Islam and the West, from which official discourse drew its vocabulary in the first days after the September 11 attacks. There's since been a noticeable de-escalation in that discourse, but to judge from the steady amount of hate speech and actions, plus reports of law enforcement efforts directed against Arabs, Muslims and Indians all over the country, the paradigm stays on.

One further reason for its persistence is the increased presence of Muslims all over Europe and the United States … But what is so threatening about that presence? Buried in the collective culture are memories of the first great Arab-Islamic conquests, which began in the seventh century and which … shattered once and for all the ancient unity of the Mediterranean, destroyed the Christian-Roman synthesis and gave rise to a new civilization dominated by northern powers (Germany and Carolingian France) whose mission … is to resume defense of the "West" against its historical-cultural enemies … [I] n the creation of this new line of defense the West drew on the humanism, science, philosophy, sociology and historiography of Islam, which had already interposed itself between Charlemagne's world and classical antiquity. Islam is inside from the start, as even Dante, great enemy of Mohammed, had to concede when he placed the Prophet at the very heart of his *Inferno*.

Then there is the persisting legacy of monotheism itself, the Abrahamic religions … Beginning with Judaism and Christianity, each is a successor haunted by what came before; for Muslims, Islam fulfills and ends the line of prophecy. There is still no decent history or demystification of the many-sided contest among these three followers—not one of them by any means a monolithic, unified camp—of the most jealous of all gods, even though the bloody modern convergence on Palestine furnishes a rich secular instance of what has been so tragically irreconcilable about them. Not surprisingly, then, Muslims and Christians speak readily of crusades and *jihads*, both of them eliding the Judaic presence with often sublime insouciance. Such an agenda, says Eqbal Ahmad, is "very reassuring to the men and women who are stranded in the middle of the ford, between the deep waters of tradition and modernity."

But we are all swimming in those waters, Westerners and Muslims and others alike. And since the waters are part of the ocean of history, trying to plow or divide them with barriers is futile. These are tense times, but it is better to think in terms of powerful and powerless communities, the secular politics of reason and ignorance, and universal principles of justice and injustice, than to wander off in search of vast abstractions that may give momentary satisfaction but little self-knowledge or informed analysis. "The Clash of Civilizations" thesis is a gimmick like "The War of the Worlds," better for reinforcing defensive self-pride than for critical understanding of the bewildering interdependence of our time.

2.5 Disjuncture and difference in a global cultural economy

Arjun Appadurai

The central problem of today's global interactions is the tension between cultural homogenization and cultural heterogenization. A vast array of empirical facts could be brought to bear on the side of the homogenization argument, and much of it has come from the left end of the spectrum of media studies. Most often, the homogenization argument subspeciates into either an argument about Americanization or an argument about commoditization, and very often the two arguments are closely linked. What these arguments fail to consider is that as rapidly as forces from various metropolises are brought into new societies they tend to become indigenized in one or another way: this is true of music and housing styles as much as it is true of science and terrorism, spectacles and constitutions. The dynamics of such indigenization have just begun to be explored systematically, and much more needs to be done. But it is worth noticing that for the people of Irian Jaya, Indonesianization may be more worrisome than Americanization, as Japanization may be for Koreans, Indianization for Sri Lankans, Vietnamization for the Cambodians, and Russianization for the people of Soviet Armenia and the Baltic republics. Such a list of alternative fears to Americanization could be greatly expanded, but it is not a shapeless inventory: for polities of smaller scale, there is always a fear of cultural absorption by polities of larger scale, especially those that are nearby. One man's imagined community is another man's political prison.

...

The new global cultural economy has to be seen as a complex, overlapping, disjunctive order that cannot any longer be understood in terms of existing center-periphery models (even those that might account for multiple centers and peripheries). Nor is it susceptible to simply models of push and pull (in terms of migration theory), or of surpluses and deficits (as in traditional models of balance of trade), or of consumers and producers (as in most neo-Marxist theories of development) ...

...

I propose that an elementary framework for exploring such disjunctures is to look at the relationship among five dimensions of global cultural flows that can be termed (a) *ethnoscapes*, (b) *mediascapes*, (c) *technoscapes*, (d) *financescapes*, and (e) *ideoscapes*. The suffix-*scape* allows us to point to the fluid, irregular shapes of these landscapes, shapes that characterize international capital as deeply as they do international clothing styles. These terms with the common suffix-*scape* also indicate that these are not objectively given relations that look the same from every angle of vision but, rather, that they are deeply perspectival constructs, inflected by the historical, linguistic, and political situatedness of different sorts of actors: nation-states, multinationals, diasporic communities, as well as subnational groupings and movements (whether religious, political, or economic), and even intimate face-to-face groups, such as villages, neighborhoods, and families. Indeed, the individual actor is the last locus of this perspectival set of landscapes, for these landscapes are eventually navigated by agents who both experience and constitute larger formations, in part from their own sense of what these landscapes offer.

These landscapes thus are the building blocks of what (extending Benedict Anderson) I would like to call *imagined worlds*, that is, the multiple worlds that are constituted by the historically situated imaginations of persons and groups spread around the globe. An important fact of the world we live in today is that many persons on the globe live in such imagined worlds (and not just in imagined communities) and thus are able to contest and even sometimes subvert the imagined worlds of the official mind and of the entrepreneurial mentality that surround them.

By *ethnoscape*, I mean the landscape of persons who constitute the shifting world in which we live: tourists, immigrants, refugees, exiles, guest workers, and other moving groups and individuals constitute an essential feature of the world and appear to effect the politics of (and between) nations to a hitherto unprecedented degree. This is not to say that there are no relatively stable communities and networks of kinship, friendship, work and leisure, as well as of birth residence, and other filial forms. But it is to say that the warp of these stabilities is everywhere shot through with the woof of human motion, as more persons and groups deal with the realities of having to move or the fantasies of wanting to move …

…

By *technoscape*, I mean the global configuration, also ever fluid, of technology and the fact that technology, both high and low, both mechanical and informational, now moves at high speeds across various kinds of previously impervious boundaries. Many countries now are the roots of multinational enterprise: a huge steel complex in Libya may involve interests from India, China, Russia, and Japan, providing different components of new technological configurations. The odd distribution of technologies, and thus the peculiarities of these technoscapes, are increasingly driven not by any obvious economies of scale, of political control, or of market rationality but by increasingly complex relationships among money flows, political possibilities, and the availability of both un- and highly skilled labor …

…

Thus it is useful to speak as well of *financescapes*, as the disposition of global capital is now a more mysterious, rapid, and difficult landscape to follow than ever before, as currency markets, national stock exchanges, and commodity speculations move megamonies through national turnstiles at blinding speed, with vast, absolute implications for small differences in percentage points and time units. But the critical point is that the global relationship among ethnoscapes, technoscapes, and financescapes is deeply disjunctive and profoundly unpredictable because each of these landscapes is subject to its own constraints and incentives (some political, some informational, and some technoenvironmental), at the same time as each acts as a constraint and a parameter for movements in the others. Thus, even an elementary model of global political economy must take into account the deeply disjunctive relationships among human movement, technological flow, and financial transfers.

Further refracting these disjunctures (which hardly form a simple, mechanical global infrastructure in any case) are what I call *mediascapes* and *ideoscapes*, which are closely related landscapes of images. *Mediascapes* refer both to the distribution of the electronic capabilities to produce and disseminate information (newspapers, magazines, television stations, and film-production studios), which are now available to a growing number of private and public interests throughout the world, and to the images of the world created by these media … What this means is that many audiences around the world experience the media themselves as a complicated and interconnected repertoire of print, celluloid, electronic screens, and billboards. The lines between the realistic and the fictional landscapes they see are blurred, so that the farther away these audiences are from the direct experiences of metropolitan life, the more likely they are to construct imagined worlds that are chimerical, aesthetic, even fantastic objects, particularly if assessed by the criteria of some other perspective, some other imagined world.

…

Ideoscapes are also concatenations of images, but they are often directly political and frequently have to do with the ideologies of states and the counterideologies of movements explicitly oriented to capturing state power or a piece of it. These ideoscapes are composed of elements of the

Enlightenment worldview, which consists of a chain of ideas, terms and images, including *freedom*, *welfare*, *rights*, *sovereignty*, *representation*, and the master term *democracy*. The master narrative of the Enlightenment (and its many variants in Britain, France, and the United States) was constructed with a certain internal logic and presupposed a certain relationship between reading, representation, and the public sphere. But the diaspora of these terms and images across the world, especially since the nineteenth century, has loosened the internal coherence that held them together in a Euro-American master narrative and provided instead a loosely structured synopticon of politics, in which different nation-states, as part of their evolution, have organized their political cultures around different key words.

...

... Thus *democracy* has clearly become a master term, with profound echoes from Haiti and Poland to the former Soviet Union and China, but it sits at the center of a variety of ideoscapes, composed of distinctive pragmatic configu-rations of rough translations of other central terms form the vocabulary of the Enlightenment. This creates ever new terminological kaleidoscopes, as states (and the groups that seek to capture them) seek to pacify populations whose own ethnoscapes are in motion and whose mediascapes may create severe problems for the ideoscapes with which they are presented. The fluidity of ideoscapes is complicated in particular by the growing diasporas (both voluntary and involuntary) by intellectuals who continuously inject new meaning-streams into the discourse of democracy in different parts of the world.

This extended terminological discussion of the five terms I have coined sets the basis for a tentative formulation about the conditions under which current global flows occur: they occur in the through the growing disjunctures among ethnoscapes, technoscapes, financescapes, mediascapes, and ideoscapes. This formulation, the core of my model of global cultural flow, needs some explanation. First, people, machinery, money, images, and ideas now follow increasingly nonisomorphic paths; of course, at all periods of human history, there have been some disjunctures in the flows of these things, but the sheer speed, scale, and volume of each of these flows are now so great that the disjunctures have become central to the politics of global culture. The Japanese are notoriously hospitable to ideas and are stereotyped as inclined to export (all) and import (some) goods, but they are also notoriously closed to immigration, like the Swiss, the Swedes, and the Saudis. Yet the Swiss and the Saudis accept populations of guest workers, thus creating labor diasporas of Turks, Italians, and other circum-Mediterranean groups. Some such guest-worker groups maintain continuous contact with their home nations, like the

Turks, but others, like high-level South Asian migrants, tend to desire lives in their new homes, raising anew the problem of reproduction in a deterritorialized context.

Deterritorialization, in general, is one of the central forces of the modern world because it brings laboring populations into the lower-class sectors and spaces of relatively wealthy societies, while sometimes creating exaggerated and intensified senses of criticism or attachment to politics in the home state. Deterritorialization, whether of Hindus, Sikhs, Palestinians, or Ukrainians, is now at the core of a variety of global fundamentalisms, including Islamic and Hindu fundamentalism. In the Hindu case, for example, it is clear that the overseas movement of Indians has been exploited by a variety of interests both within and outside India to create a complicated network of finances and religious identifications, by which the problem of cultural reproduction for Hindus abroad has become tied to the politics of Hindu fundamentalism at home.

At the same time, deterritorialization creates new markets for film companies, art impresarios, and travel agencies, which thrive on the need of the deterritorialized population for contact with its homeland. Naturally, these invented homelands, which constitute the mediascapes of deterritorialized groups, can often become sufficiently fantastic and one-sided that they provide the material for new ideoscapes in which ethnic conflicts can begin to erupt ...

It is in the fertile ground of deterritorialization, in which money, commodities, and persons are involved in ceaselessly chasing each other around the world, that the mediascapes and ideoscapes of the modern world find their fractured and fragmented counterpart. For the ideas and images produced by mass media often are only partial guides to the goods and experiences that deterritorialized populations transfer to one another ...

While far more could be said about the cultural politics of deterritorialization and the larger sociology of displacement that it expresses, it is appropriate at this juncture to bring in the role of the nation-state in the disjunctive global economy of culture today. The relationship between states and nations is everywhere an embattled one. It is possible to say that in many societies the nation and the state have become one another's projects. That is, while nations (or more properly groups with ideas about nationhood) seek to capture or co-opt states and state power, states simultaneously seek to capture and monopolize ideas about nationhood ...

... This disjunctive relationship between nation and state has two levels: at the level of any given nation-state, it means that there is a battle of the imagination, with state and nation seeking to cannibalize one another. Here is the seedbed of brutal separatisms—majoritarianisms that seem to have appeared from nowhere and microidentities that have become political projects within the nation-state. At another level, this disjunctive relationship is deeply entangled with the global disjunctures discussed throughout this chapter: ideas of nationhood appear to be steadily increasing in scale and regularly crossing existing state boundaries, sometimes, as with the Kurds, because previous identities stretched across vast national spaces or, as with the Tamils in Sri Lanka, the dominant threads of a transnational diaspora have been activated to ignite the micro-politics of a nation-state.

In discussing the cultural politics that have subverted the hyphen that links the nation to the state, it is especially important not to forget the mooring of such politics in the irregularities that now characterize disorganized capital. Because labor, finance, and technology are now so widely separated, the volatilities that underlie movements for nationhood (as large as transnational Islam on the one hand, or as small as the movement of the Gurkhas for a separate state in Northeast India) grind against the vulnerabilities that characterize the relationships between states. States find themselves pressed to stay open by the forces of media, technology, and travel that have fueled consumerism throughout the world and have increased the craving, even in the non-Western world, for new commodities and spectacles. On the other hand, these very cravings can become caught up in in new ethnoscapes, mediascapes, and, eventually, ideoscapes, such as democracy in China, that the state cannot tolerate as threats to its own control over ideas of nationhood and peoplehood ...

The transnational movement of the martial arts, particularly through Asia, as mediated by the Hollywood and Hong Kong film industries is a rich illustration of the ways in which long-standing martial arts traditions, reformulated to meet the fantasies of contemporary (sometimes lumpen) youth populations, create new cultures of masculinity and violence, which are in turn the fuel for increased violence in national and international politics. Such violence is in turn the spur to an increasingly rapid and amoral arms trade that penetrates the entire world. The world-wide spread of the AK-47 and the Uzi, in films, in corporate and state security, in terror, and in police and military activity, is a reminder that apparently simple technological uniformities often conceal an increasingly complex set of loops, linking images of violence to aspirations for community in some imagined world.

...

The globalization of culture is not the same as its homogenization, but globalization involves the use of a variety of instruments of homogenization (armaments, advertising techniques, language hegemonies, and clothing styles) that are absorbed into local political and cultural economies, only to be repatriated as heterogeneous dialogues of national sovereignty, free enterprise, and fundamentalism in which the state plays an increasingly delicate role: too much openness to global flows, and the nation-state is threatened by revolt, as in the China syndrome, too little, and the state exits the international stage, as Burma, Albania, and North Korea in various ways have done. In general, the state has become the arbitrageur of this *repatriation of difference* (in the form of goods, signs, slogans, and styles). But this repatriation or export of the designs and commodities of difference continuously exacerbates the internal politics of majoritarianism and homogenization, which is most frequently played out in debates over heritage.

Thus the central feature of global culture today is the politics of the mutual effort of sameness and difference to cannibalize one another and thereby proclaim their successful hijacking of the twin Enlightenment ideas of the triumphantly universal and the resiliently particular. This mutual cannibalization shows it ugly face in riots, refugee flows, state-sponsored torture, and ethnocide (with or without state support). Its brighter side is in the expansion of many individual horizons of hope and fantasy, in the global spread of oral rehydration therapy and other low-tech instruments of well-being, in the susceptibility even of South Africa to the force of global opinion, in the inability of the Polish state to repress its own working classes, and in the growth of a wide range of progressive, transnational alliances. Examples of both sorts can be multiplied. The critical point is that both sides of the coin of global cultural process today are products of the infinitely varied mutual contest of sameness and difference on a stage characterized by radical disjunctures between different sorts of global flows and the uncertain landscapes created in and through these disjunctures.

2.6 What clash of civilization?

Amartya Sen

That some barbed cartoons of the Prophet Mohammed could generate turmoil in so many countries tells us some rather important things about the contemporary world. Among other issues, it points up the intense sensitivity of many Muslims about representation and derision of the prophet in the Western press (and the ridiculing of Muslim religious beliefs that is taken to go with it) and the evident power of determined agitators to generate the kind of anger that leads immediately to violence. But stereotyped representations of this kind do another sort of damage as well, by making huge groups of people in the world to look peculiarly narrow and unreal.

The portrayal of the prophet with a bomb in the form of a hat is obviously a figment of imagination and cannot be judged literally, and the relevance of that representation cannot be dissociated from the way the followers of the prophet may be seen. What we ought to take very seriously is the way Islamic identity, in this sort of depiction, is assumed to drown, if only implicitly, all other affiliations, priorities, and pursuits that a Muslim person may have. A person belongs to many different groups, of which a religious affiliation is only one. To see, for example, a mathematician who happens to be a Muslim by religion mainly in terms of Islamic identity would be to hide more than it reveals. Even today, when a modern mathematician at, say, MIT or Princeton invokes an "algorithm" to solve a difficult computational problem, he or she helps to commemorate the contributions of the ninth-century Muslim mathematician Al-Khwarizmi, from whose name the term algorithm is derived (the term "algebra" comes from the title of his Arabic mathematical treatise "Al Jabr wa-al-Muqabilah"). To concentrate only on Al-Khwarizmi's Islamic identity over his identity as a mathematician would be extremely misleading, and yet he clearly was also a Muslim. Similarly, to give an automatic priority to the Islamic identity of a Muslim person in order to understand his or her role in the civil society, or in the literary world, or in creative work in arts and science, can result in profound misunderstanding.

The increasing tendency to overlook the many identities that any human being has and to try to classify individuals according to a single allegedly pre-eminent religious identity is an intellectual confusion that can animate dangerous divisiveness. An Islamist instigator of violence against infidels may want Muslims to forget that they have any identity other than being Islamic. What is surprising is that those who would like to quell that violence promote, in effect, the same intellectual disorientation by seeing Muslims primarily as members of an Islamic world. The world is made much more incendiary by the advocacy and popularity of single-dimensional categorization of human beings, which combines haziness of vision with increased scope for the exploitation of that haze by the champions of violence.

A remarkable use of imagined singularity can be found in Samuel Huntington's influential 1998 book *The Clash of Civilizations and the Remaking of the World Order*. The difficulty with Huntington's approach begins with his system of unique categorization, well before the issue of a clash—or not—is even raised. Indeed, the thesis of a civilizational clash is conceptually parasitic on the commanding power of a unique categorization along so-called civilizational lines, which closely follow religious divisions to which singular attention is paid. Huntington contrasts Western civilization with "Islamic civilization," "Hindu civilization," "Buddhist civilization," and so on. The alleged confrontations of religious differences are incorporated into a sharply carpentered vision of hardened divisiveness.

In fact, of course, the people of the world can be classified according to many other partitions, each of which has some—often far-reaching— relevance in our lives: nationalities, locations, classes, occupations, social status, languages, politics, and many others. While religious categories have received much airing in recent years, they cannot be presumed to obliterate other distinctions, and even less can they be seen as the only relevant system of classifying people across the globe. In partitioning the population of the world into those belonging to "the Islamic world," "the Western world," "the Hindu world," "the Buddhist world," the divisive power of classificatory priority is implicitly used to place people firmly inside a unique set of rigid boxes. Other divisions (say, between the rich and the poor, between members of different classes and occupations, between people of different politics, between distinct nationalities and residential locations, between language groups, etc.) are all submerged by this allegedly primal way of seeing the differences between people.

The difficulty with the clash of civilizations thesis begins with the presumption of the unique relevance of a singular classification. Indeed, the question "Do civilizations clash?" is founded on the presumption that humanity can be pre-eminently classified into distinct and discrete civilizations, and that the relations between different human beings can somehow be seen, without serious loss of understanding, in terms of relations between different civilizations.

This reductionist view is typically combined, I am afraid, with a rather foggy perception of world history that overlooks, first, the extent of internal diversities within these civilizational categories, and second, the reach and influence of interactions—intellectual as well as material—that go right across the regional borders of so-called civilizations. And its power to befuddle can trap not only those who would like to support the thesis of a clash (varying from Western chauvinists to Islamic fundamentalists), but also those who would like to dispute it and yet try to respond within the straitjacket of its prespecified terms of reference.

The limitations of such civilization-based thinking can prove just as treacherous for programs of "dialogue among civilizations" (much in vogue these days) as they are for theories of a clash of civilizations. The noble and elevating search for amity among people seen as amity between civilizations speedily reduces many-sided human beings to one dimension each and muzzles the variety of involvements that have provided rich and diverse grounds for cross-border interactions over many centuries, including the arts, literature, science, mathematics, games, trade, politics, and other arenas of shared human interest. Well-meaning attempts at pursuing global peace can have very counterproductive consequences when these attempts are founded on a fundamentally illusory understanding of the world of human beings.

Increasing reliance on religion-based classification of the people of the world also tends to make the Western response to global terrorism and conflict peculiarly ham-handed. Respect for "other people" is shown by praising their religious books, rather than by taking note of the many-sided involvements and achievements, in nonreligious as well as religious fields, of different people in a globally interactive world. In confronting what is called "Islamic terrorism" in the muddled vocabulary of contemporary global politics, the intellectual force of Western policy is aimed quite substantially at trying to define—or redefine—Islam.

To focus just on the grand religious classification is not only to miss other significant concerns and ideas that move people. It also has the effect of generally magnifying the voice of religious authority. The Muslim clerics, for example, are then treated as the ex officio spokesmen for the so-called Islamic world, even though a great many people who happen to be Muslim by religion have profound differences with what is proposed by one mullah or another. Despite our diverse diversities, the world is suddenly seen not as a collection of people, but as a federation of religions and civilizations. In Britain, a confounded view of what a multiethnic society must do has led to encouraging the development of state-financed Muslim schools, Hindu schools, Sikh schools, etc., to supplement pre-existing state-supported Christian schools. Under this system, young children are placed in the domain of singular affiliations well before they have the ability to reason about different systems of identification that may compete for their attention. Earlier on, state-run denominational schools in Northern Ireland had fed the political distancing of Catholics and Protestants along one line of divisive categorization assigned at infancy. Now the same predetermination of "discovered" identities is now being allowed and, in effect encouraged, to sow even more alienation among a different part of the British population.

Religious or civilizational classification can be a source of belligerent distortion as well. It can, for example, take the form of crude beliefs well exemplified by U.S. Lt. Gen. William Boykin's blaring—and by now well-known—remark describing his battle against Muslims with disarming coarseness: "I knew that my God was bigger than his," and that the Christian God "was a real God, and [the Muslim's] was an idol." The idiocy of such bigotry is easy to diagnose, so there is comparatively limited danger in the uncouth hurling of such unguided missiles. There is, in contrast, a much more serious problem in the use in Western public policy of intellectual "guided missiles" that present a superficially nobler vision to woo Muslim activists away from opposition through the apparently benign strategy of defining Islam appropriately. They try to wrench Islamic terrorists from violence by insisting that Islam is a religion of peace, and that a "true Muslim" must be a tolerant individual ("so come off it and be peaceful"). The rejection of a confrontational view of Islam is certainly appropriate and extremely important at this time, but we must ask whether it is necessary or useful, or even possible, to try to define in largely political terms what a "true Muslim" must be like.

…

A person's religion need not be his or her all-encompassing and exclusive identity. Islam, as a religion, does not obliterate responsible choice for Muslims in many spheres of life. Indeed, it is possible for one Muslim to take a confrontational view and another to be thoroughly tolerant of heterodoxy without either of them ceasing to be a Muslim for that reason alone.

The response to Islamic fundamentalism and to the terrorism linked with it also becomes particularly confused when there is a general failure to distinguish between Islamic history and the history of Muslim people. Muslims, like all other people in the world, have many different pursuits, and not all their priorities and values need be placed within their singular identity of being Islamic. It is, of course, not surprising at all that the champions of Islamic fundamentalism would like to suppress all other identities of Muslims in favor of being only Islamic. But it is extremely odd that those who want to overcome the tensions and conflicts linked with Islamic fundamentalism also seem unable to see Muslim people in any form other than their being just Islamic.

People see themselves—and have reason to see themselves—in many different ways. For example, a Bangladeshi Muslim is not only a Muslim but also a Bengali and a Bangladeshi, typically quite proud of the Bengali language, literature, and music, not to mention the other identities he or she may have connected with class, gender, occupation, politics, aesthetic taste, and so on. Bangladesh's separation from Pakistan was not based on religion at all, since a Muslim identity was shared by the bulk of the population in the two wings of undivided Pakistan. The separatist issues related to language, literature, and politics.

Similarly, there is no empirical reason at all why champions of the Muslim past, or for that matter of the Arab heritage, have to concentrate specifically on religious beliefs only and not also on science and mathematics, to which Arab and Muslim societies have contributed so much, and which can also be part of a Muslim or an Arab identity. Despite the importance of this heritage, crude classifications have tended to put science and mathematics in the basket of "Western science," leaving other people to mine their pride in religious depths. If the disaffected Arab activist today can take pride only in the purity of Islam, rather than in the many-sided richness of Arab history, the unique prioritization of religion, shared by warriors on both sides, plays a major part in incarcerating people within the enclosure of a singular identity.

Even the frantic Western search for "the moderate Muslim" confounds moderation in political beliefs with moderateness of religious faith. A person can have strong religious faith—Islamic or any other—along with tolerant politics. Emperor Saladin, who fought valiantly for Islam in the Crusades in the 12th century, could offer, without any contradiction, an honored place in his Egyptian royal court to Maimonides as that distinguished Jewish philosopher fled an intolerant Europe. When, at the turn of the 16th century, the heretic Giordano Bruno was burned at the stake in Campo dei Fiori in Rome, the Great Mughal emperor Akbar (who was born a Muslim and died a Muslim) had just finished, in Agra, his large project of legally codifying minority rights, including religious freedom for all.

The point that needs particular attention is that while Akbar was free to pursue his liberal politics without ceasing to be a Muslim, that liberality was in no way ordained—nor of course prohibited—by Islam. Another Mughal emperor, Aurangzeb, could deny minority rights and persecute non-Muslims without, for that reason, failing to be a Muslim, in exactly the same way that Akbar did not terminate being a Muslim because of his tolerantly pluralist politics.

The insistence, if only implicitly, on a choiceless singularity of human identity not only diminishes us all, it also makes the world much more flammable. The alternative to the divisiveness of one pre-eminent categorization is not any unreal claim that we are all much the same. Rather, the main hope of harmony in our troubled world lies in the plurality of our identities, which cut across each other and work against sharp divisions around one single hardened line of vehement division that allegedly cannot be resisted. Our shared humanity gets savagely challenged when our differences are narrowed into one devised system of uniquely powerful categorization.

Perhaps the worst impairment comes from the neglect—and denial—of the roles of reasoning and choice, which follow from the recognition of our plural identities. The illusion of unique identity is much more divisive than the universe of plural and diverse classifications that characterize the world in which we actually live. The descriptive weakness of choiceless singularity has the effect of momentously impoverishing the power and reach of our social and political reasoning. The illusion of destiny exacts a remarkably heavy price.

2.7 Doing cross-cultural religious business: Globalization, Americanization, Cocacolonization, McDonaldization, Disneyization, Tupperization, and other local dilemmas of global signification in the study of religion

David Chidester

Cocacolonization

As the supreme icon of American cultural imperialism, Coca-Cola has often been rendered in religious terms. Recalling the words of the company's advertising director, Delony Sledge, in the early 1950s, the Coca-Cola Company has operated as if its "work is a religion rather than a business." What kind of religion is this? As I have argued, the religion of Coca-Cola revolves around a sacred object, the fetish of Coca-Cola, that is both desired object and the objectification of desire. "Coca-Cola is the holy grail," as one company executive observed. "Wherever I go, when people find out I work for Coke, it's like being a representative from the Vatican, like you've touched God. I'm always amazed. There's such reverence toward the product." In these potent images of an original holy blood and an enduring sacred tradition, this Coca-Cola executive invoked a religious aspiration for touching what cannot be touched because it is a materiality that is also an icon of holy desire.

The Coca-Cola Company has produced a massive network of global exchanges and local effects that must be regarded as significant forces in any notion of globalization. As company president Roberto Goizueta put it, "Our success will largely depend on the degree to which we make it impossible for the consumer around the globe to escape Coca-Cola." While the vast exchanges that have established and empowered the Coca-Cola empire are obvious, some of the local effects can be surprising. Coca-Cola is not only transnational; it is also translational. Coca-Cola trades on the translation of information, imagery, and desire among vastly different cultural contexts all over the world. In fashioning this worldwide enterprise, foreign governments, trade restrictions, access to supplies, and local competition have often presented problems; but so has cultural translation. Not only signifying "the global high-sign," Coca-Cola has sometimes generated a chaos of signification in its attempts at global translation. For example, the Chinese characters that most closely reproduced the sound of "Coca-Cola" apparently trans-lated as "bite the wax tadpole." In Dutch, "Refresh Yourself with Coca-Cola" meant "Wash Your Hands with Coca-Cola." French speakers misheard the French version of the song, "Have a Coke and a Smile," as "Have a Coke and a Mouse," while Spanish speakers in Cuba reportedly misread the sky writing for "Tome Coca-Cola" (Drink Coca-Cola) as "Teme Coca-Cola" (Fear Coca-Cola) ...

John Tomlinson, author of *Cultural Imperialism*, has suggested that if goods are actually desired by people rather than imposed upon them by force, then their entry into global markets should not be regarded as cultural imperialism but as "the spread of modernity." Certainly, this benign reading of the role of a desired commodity, especially the supreme commodity that nobody needs but everyone desires, the sacred beverage, bottle, and icon of Coca-Cola, misrepresents the power relations in which the translation of desire is precisely what is at stake. Like the Bible, the Cross, or European styles of housing, clothing, and weapons in other colonial situations of Christian missionary intervention, Coca-Cola marks fundamental oppositions, signifying the slash between primitive and civilized, traditional and modern, or communist and capitalist. In a range of popular imagery, the sacred object of Coca-Cola stands at the frontier of competing religions in a global contact zone. For example, a widely reproduced photographic image from Saudi Arabia shows Muslims bowing in prayer, facing Mecca, but inadvertently also bowing before a bright red soft-drink vending machine, assuming what appears from the photograph to be a posture of religious submission before the sacred logo of Coca-Cola. Visiting the World of Coca-Cola Museum in Atlanta, a group of Tibetan Buddhist monks, wearing robes, were photographed one by one sticking their heads through a cardboard cutout of a waiter pouring a glass of Coca-Cola. They enjoyed making such "modern discoveries," a translator explained. In different ways, these images reinforced stereotypes—Arabian Muslims bowing in blind devotion that made them oblivious to a modernity that was overwhelming them, Tibetan Buddhists encountering that same bewildering modernity with wide-eyed surprise—that elevated Coca-Cola as the crucial sacred object in a frontier zone of interreligious relations ...

McDonaldization

In his popular analysis of modernization, sociologist George Ritzer coined the term *McDonaldization* to represent "the process by which the principles of the fast-food restaurant are coming to dominate more and more sectors of American society as well as of the rest of the world." Updating the classic work of Max Weber, who argued that the principles of bureaucratic rationalization, organization, management, and control were the hallmarks of modernization, Ritzer proposed that the fast-food restaurant has extended the scope of those same principles throughout every aspect of personal and social life. Concentrating on McDonald's as the principal model, the ideal type, or the paradigm for this process, Ritzer identified four principles of rationalization—efficiency, calculability, predictability, and control over labor by replacing human with nonhuman technology. Not merely selling burgers, fries, and milkshakes, therefore, McDonald's is actively advancing these principles of rationalization in America and the larger world.

As Ritzer recognized, a social force with such awesome and pervasive power seems to function like a global religion. Certainly, Ray Kroc employed religious language. "The french fry would become almost sacrosanct for me," Kroc reported, "its preparation, a ritual to be followed religiously." But McDonald's was more than a sacrosanct object. "To many people throughout the world," as George Ritzer has observed, "McDonald's has become a sacred institution." As evidence, Ritzer cited a newspaper account of the opening of McDonald's in Moscow "as if it were the Cathedral in Chartres." Reportedly, a Moscow worker described McDonald's as a place to experience "celestial joy." What kind of religion is this? Anchored in a sacred institution, a "cathedral of consumption," McDonaldization might be regarded as a powerful sect within a broader "consumer religion." In that consumer religion, with its sacred places of pilgrimage, sacred times of ritualized gift giving, and sacred objects of holy desire, McDonald's fast-food restaurant could be regarded as a sect competing for religious market share in the same political economy of the sacred with other sacred institutions, such as the shopping mall, that celebrate the spiritual ecstasy of consumerism. According to Ritzer, however, the "sacred institution" of McDonald's has established a religion that is based not on spiritual ecstasy, despite the Russian worker's claims about experiencing "celestial joy," but on spiritual discipline, a kind of inner-worldly asceticism that regulates desire according to the require-ments of bureaucratic rationalization. Unlike the religion of Cocacolonization, with its cross-cultural translation of desire for the sacred object, the religion of McDonaldization represents a cross-cultural rationalization of desire and desire for rationalization. Embedded in the "sacred institution" of McDonald's, but extending through all social institutions, McDonaldization is the religious rationality of modern institutionalized life …

Although McDonaldization represents a universalizing rationality of efficiency, calculability, predictability, and control, McDonald's restaurants have had to adapt to local situations and circumstances. Adapting to local tastes, rather than simply imposing a global, homogenized "convergence of taste," McDonald's has produced such culturally specific variations as McSpaghetti in the Philippines, McLaks (grilled salmon sandwich) in Norway,

McHuevo (poached egg hamburger) in Uruguay, and MacChao (Chinese fried rice) in Japan. Like Coca-Cola, however, McDonald's has also been actively engaged in interreligious relations, especially when the menu set by its headquarters in the heartland of America, at Hamburger University, Oak Brook, Illinois, conflicts with religious customs, ethics, or laws governing diet. More intimately than Coca-Cola, McDonald's enters into and occasionally comes into conflict with the foodways of the world. Since those foodways are intimately related to religion, the conflicts over food are intensely negotiated. Consistently, although not without conflict, McDonald's has shown a willingness to adapt to local religious requirements. After considerable controversy, McDonald's in Israel agreed to provide hamburgers without cheese, at several outlets, to avoid violating Jewish dietary law. In Malaysia, Singapore, and other countries with a large Muslim presence, McDonald's submitted to inspection by Muslim clerics to ensure the ritual cleanliness, and absence of pork, in the preparation and presentation of meat. In opening new franchises in India, again after considerable controversy, McDonald's introduced a range of new products—mutton-based Maharaja Macs for Hindus who do not eat beef, Vegetable McNuggets and the potato-based McAloo Tikki burger for Hindus who do not eat meat at all—to accommodate religious interests in food, even though Hindu fundamentalists of the Bharatiya Janata Party (BJP) campaigned against McDonald's on religious grounds. In all of these corporate negotiations over the religious significance of food, McDonald's demonstrated an impressive responsiveness to local traditions ...

As defined by George Ritzer, McDonaldization represents a globalizing steamroller in which the American mastery of the rational arts of efficiency, calculability, predictability, and control is subjecting people in America and the rest of the world to a regime of rationalization that is basically dehumanizing. Certainly, the critical perspective advanced by Ritzer echoed the dehumanizing conditions of colonial situations, except that the imperial, colonizing power, in this case, is ideologically legitimated not by God, country, or manifest destiny but by a Big Mac, fries, and a Coke. As in the case of Coca-Cola, however, McDonald's meaning and power has also been appropriated by consumers all over the world as a local production, as if it were a local, indigenous institution. Reversing the thrust in the classic colonial narratives of "first contact" between Europeans and startled natives, many versions have been told of the story about a child coming from some other part of the world to the United States and expressing astonishment to find a McDonald's restaurant. "Look!" exclaimed the son of a Japanese executive visiting America, "They even have McDonald's in the United States!"

Disneyization

While *McDonaldization* has emerged as a technical term for bureaucratic rationalization, a contrasting, but complementary, term, *Disneyization*, has been advanced to capture the importance of managing, engineering, and molding the human imagination. As defined by sociologist Alan Bryman, Disneyization refers to "the process by which *the principles* of the Disney theme parks are coming to dominate more and more sectors of American society as well as the rest of the world." Those principles—theming, dedifferentiation of consumption, multisector merchandising, and emotional labor—undergird the imagineering of cross-cultural business most clearly exemplified by the Walt Disney Company but increasingly informing the way business is conducted. Taking Disneyland as paradigm, businesses apply the principle of theming to create imaginary worlds that evoke a thematic coherence through architecture, landscaping, costuming, and other theatrical effects to establish a focused, coherent experience. In the process, the activity of consumption is dedifferentiated from entertainment, dissolving the distinction between shopping and playing, so that, as Umberto Eco observed, "you buy obsessively, believing that you are still playing." ...

In the end, Disneyization is a system of emotional labor that is empowered, not only through the emotional investments made by consumers, but also in the management of emotions by workers at the point of production. As workers, or "cast members" in Disney-speak, perform their scripted interactions with the public—the "friendly smile," the "friendly phrases"—they master a kind of emotional labor that conveys the impression that work is not work but play ... The Walt Disney Company, however, has set the global standards for imagining happiness, especially through its "classic" animated films and its theme parks, each proclaimed as the "happiest place on earth," where employees and consumers, cast members and guests, both engage in the emotional labor necessary for the success of Disneyization ...

In assessing the religious work of Disney, the theme parks provide a more obvious point of reference. As many cultural analysts have observed, these alternative worlds—Disneyland in Anaheim, Disney World in Orlando, EuroDisney outside of Paris, and Disneyland in Tokyo—have become sacred places of pilgrimage in American and global popular culture. While operating as sacred sites within global tourism, the Disney parks also represent a sacred time, a transcendence of the everyday, ordinary time of the present. Passing through the gates, visitors are informed, "Here you leave today, and enter the world of yesterday, tomorrow, and fantasy." ...

In analyzing the cross-cultural religious business of the Walt Disney Company, the success of Tokyo Disneyland provides an important test case for theories of globalization and cultural imperialism. Clearly, Tokyo

Disneyland is American. "We really tried to avoid creating a Japanese version of Disneyland," spokesperson Toshiharu Akiba recalled. "We wanted the Japanese visitors to feel they were taking a foreign vacation." Nevertheless, Tokyo Disneyland is a particular kind of "America"—a foreign America—that is owned and operated by the Japanese. The success of Tokyo Disneyland has depended entirely upon detailed local negotiations over the processes that we have been considering in reviewing the global dynamics of cross-cultural business—translation, rationalization, and imagination. These dynamics can only briefly be suggested here.

First, the challenge of translation involved not only the task of rendering the English scripts for popular rides into Japanese but also the challenge of mediating the intercultural dynamics of body language. Although the "friendly smile" might fail to translate easily into Japanese, the high-pitched voice of Mickey Mouse curiously resonated with the conventional "service voice" expected from women waiting on customers in department stores.

Second, the principles of bureaucratic rationalization—efficiency, calcu-lability, predictability, and control—exemplified by American management were quickly taken out of the hands of Disney managers from America and mobilized by Japanese managers of Tokyo Disneyland. As sociologist and former Disney cast member John van Maanen observed, "the Japanese have intensified the orderly nature of Disneyland. If Disneyland is clean, Tokyo Disneyland is impeccably clean; if Disneyland is efficient, Tokyo Disneyland puts the original to shame by being absurdly efficient."

Finally, with respect to imagination, especially the temporal imagineering of the past, future, and fantasy, Tokyo Disneyland incorporated important features of the Disney orientation in time, the future of Tomorrowland and the fantasy of Fantasyland, but it fundamentally recast the past. Although its landscape included modified versions of Adventureland and Frontierland (Westernland), Tokyo Disneyland replaced Main Street, USA, with the World Bazaar, which was still an avenue of shops leading from the park's entrance, but it suggested a different past, not a small-town American past, that might lead to a different future. One attraction that was unique to Tokyo Disneyland, "Meet the World," presented the most thorough reworking of the past as an act of Disney imagineering that was presented as thoroughly Japanese. Featuring the traditional White Crane as a guide to the past, initiating two cartoon children into their legacy, "Meet the World" developed a Disneyized version of Japanese history that showed the Japanese people arising from the primordial waters, forming an island nation, and meeting the other people of the world, from the Chinese, but not the Koreans, to the Americans, with all the gains and losses entailed in those encounters, in ways that prepared everyone to sing, "We Meet the World with Love." ...

In the shifting terrain that we call globalization, cross-cultural business has generated multinational corporations that operate like religions in providing material organization for the organization of matter, especially for the translation, rationalization, and imagination of matter, in a new political economy of the sacred. Through vast global exchanges, these material signs of the sacred—the sacred object of Cocacolonized desire, the sacred institution of McDonaldized rationality, the sacred, wonderful world of Disneyized imagineering—have produced profound local effects. But they have also marked out new sites of struggle, contact zones, or contested frontiers for renegotiating what it means to be a human person in a human place. As I have tried to suggest, these intercultural negotiations over the sacred are not always controlled by corporate headquarters. Indigenous versions of global signification are constantly being developed through local appropriations of Coca-Cola, McDonald's, Disney, and other transnational forces. As we have seen, many analysts have used the term *religion* for these global exchanges and local appropriations. If religion is about human identity and orientation, then cross-cultural business has been doing a kind of religious work through the material mediations of plastic signs of the sacred.

Questions for discussion

1   Is Samuel P. Huntington's categorization of the world in monolithic blocks an adequate blueprint for the world as we know it? He divides the world into a handful of civilizations: Western, Latin America, Slavic-Orthodox, Confucian, Japanese, Hindu, Islamic and "possibly African." Additionally he identifies some countries like Ethiopia as unaffiliated with civilizations, and others like India as torn between civilizations. The lines are relatively neat (if we forget about the states that are deemed peripheral or confused), but we must ask whether they reflect reality.

   Is it possible to say that the countries of Latin America are not part of the modern West? They are, after all, products of the same colonial posturing that created the United States and Canada and share with these latter countries fundamental postcolonial attributes (multicultural societies comprised of the descendants of indigenous, African, and European peoples in addition to more recent immigrant populations, disequilibriums of power among these groups, sovereign nation state status). For that matter, can we say that any postcolonial state is not in some manner part of the late modern West, shaped by the historical imperial West and in turn reshaping the meaning of the West (as Srinivas Aravamudan will argue in our excerpt from his *Guru English* in Section III)?

2   Benjamin Barber sees both globalism and tribalism (what he calls "jihad") as threats to democracy. The securing and expansion of democracy is of primary concern to him, and this under girds the importance he places on the universal rule of law and the need for civil society. Yet there are unmistakable resonances between his argument for tapping, modifying and incorporating indigenous democratic impulses with the colonial tradition of indirect rule (exemplified by the British Raj in India). Could a democracy based on this kind of intervention succeed in the long-term?

3   In a 1998 essay "Between Worlds" Said writes:

> With an unexceptionally Arab family name like "Said," connected to an improbably British first name (my mother much admired Prince of Wales [Edward VIII] in 1935, the year of my birth), I was an uncomfortably anomalous student all through my early years: a Palestinian going to school in Egypt, with an English first name, an American passport, and no certain identity, at all. To make matters worse, Arabic, my native language, and English, my school language, were inextricably mixed: I have never known which was my first language, and have felt fully at home in neither, although I dream in both. Every time I speak an English sentence, I find myself echoing it in Arabic, and vice versa.[1]

In what way might Said's own experience of being "between worlds" have influenced his ideas about what it means to be a modern person? His critique of Huntington's fixed cultural identities is powerful, but does he leave us with anything concrete to say about cultural identities in the contemporary world?

4   Does Arjun Appadurai's notion of "scapes" fragment our discussion of global experience even as it seeks to order it? What is the relationship between particular scapes and what kinds of worlds might be operative at their intersections?

5   Appadurai says our global world cannot be understood in terms of older models of center/periphery, push/pull or surplus/deficit. Consider the fact that 80 percent of the world's population lives on the equivalent of less that $2.50 per day, and half the world's population exists on less than $1.00. Almost 20 percent of the world's population does not have access to safe water. Half the world's children live in poverty and 30,000 children die every day as a result of that poverty. In fact, every 3.6 seconds one person, generally a child, dies of starvation. These statistics are drawn largely from the southern hemisphere. Is it appropriate to entirely jettison the older models as Appadurai suggests?

6   While Amartua Sen's criticism is, as is Said's, important in terms of diffusing the powder keg that Huntington has placed in our discourses about late modernity, does it run the risk of being too speculative? While divisive and rigid collective ideologies may well be an inappropriate vantage point from which to view the entire global community, the fact remains that these ideologies fuel thought and action beyond the writing of Huntington. Can we simply "reason" our way through them to something that more accurately represents contemporary identities?

7   David Chidester notes that the products of multinational corporations seeking to link disparate communities for the sake of profit are shaped by the very communities they seek to penetrate. In this sense he is exploring the process of cultural heterogenization that Appadurai sets out as a defining property of late modernity. Bowing to customary practices, for example, mutton Maharaja Macs and vegetarian McAloo Tikki burgers are available in McDonalds restaurants in India for patrons who do not eat beef or who are vegetarian. Chidester invites us to consider not only the question of whether multinationals are doing religious business, but whether they are being forced to acquiesce to a kind of religious meaning of exchange. Is this a case of corporations exploitatively swindling consumers into padding the corporate bottom line, or is it possible that sacred frameworks are reshaping the meaning of the exchange of commodities at a local level?

Suggestions for further reading

Benjamin Barber, *Jihad vs. McWorld: Terrorism's Challenge to Democracy*, New York: Ballantine Books, 2001.

Manuel Castells, *The Power of Identity, Vol. 2: "The Information Age: Economy, Society and Culture,"* Malden, MA: Blackwell, 2004.

David Chidester, *Authentic Fakes: Religion and American Popular Culture*, Berkeley, CA: University of California Press, 2005.

Noam Chomsky, *Profit over People: Neoliberalism and Global Order*, New York: Seven Stories Press, 2011.

Samuel P. Huntington, *The Clash of Civilizations and the Remaking of World Order*, New York: Touchstone, 1996.

George Ritzer, *The McDonaldization of Society*, Thousand Oaks, CA: Pine Forge Press, Sage Publications, 2011.

Amartya Sen, *Identity and Violence: The Illusion of Destiny*, New York: W. W. Norton & Company, 2007.

Michel-Rolph Troulliot, *Global Transformations: Anthropology and the Modern World*, New York: Palgrave Macmillan, 2003.

Section III

Cosmopolitanism

citizen of the world

Part 1

What is to be done in a globalized world characterized by inequities and tensions, but where nonetheless the big fault lines suggested by scholars like Huntington and others are not necessarily accurate or helpful? A solution posed by many is that of "cosmopolitanism." The word cosmopolitanism is somewhat mercurial. For a long time it was a rather negative term, referring to persons who rejected the notion of a national identity. By the 1960s and 1970s, it had shifted to evoke an image of a suave and sophisticated, well-traveled person, someone at home in any urban setting. By the close of the twentieth century, however, the word had assumed an older Western philosophical meaning in some circles, invoked by intellectuals in the service of ethics: specifically, it had become a mode of expressing a universal vision of an ethical system of global democratic regulation intended to curb the pernicious effects of free-market capitalism.

From this perspective cosmopolitanism is essentially a philosophical position that maintains that a shared universal sense of moral responsibility among all people (one that would end global sectarianism and violence) is possible. The first five readings in this section are representative of this trend, reflecting the writers' recognition that a disruption in reciprocal relations has occurred in the late modern period. Each proposes an ethical framework that she or he believes can put things right. These writers, from a variety of vantage points, are generally concerned with moral universalism—the conviction that all people, regardless of geographical or cultural situation, are subject to the same moral imperatives. Their ethical formulations come out of an authentic concern with the adverse effects of globalization—inequality, poverty, ecological destruction—and they seek a way out of this pattern of global devastation. Yet their ethics are also distinctly related to the end of the Cold War and a subsequent desire by Western-trained scholars to find a way to mediate global relationships based on the primacy of the rule of law and democratic governance.

This understanding of cosmopolitanism, regardless of its specific configuration, is generally thought to trace back to Diogenes (412 BCE) and forward in our own day to philosophers like Jürgen Habermas and Jacques Derrida. The way that it has come to be understood in recent years, however, owes a huge debt to the Enlightenment philosopher Immanuel Kant who was undoubtedly the most influential thinker of the Enlightenment period. His essay "Perpetual Peace" laid a foundation for Western thought concerning a need for a cosmopolitan system of law applicable to a "universal community."

Kant's commitment to reason and its relationship with natural law indelibly shaped his approach to politics, and led him to posit a universal ethical basis for governance that trumps local allegiances and simple patriotism. His notions of perpetual peace and cosmopolitanism are fully grounded in his commitment to discovering universal laws of both nature and history. His argument is thus the first Western philosophical claim that universal peace is part of natural law. In his view universal peace is the terminus of our ethical progression as a species, and it will ultimately be realized in a league of nations committed to upholding (although not coercively) cosmopolitan values. Thus, while individual persons are incurably bound to their own good and bad impulses, the species is unmistakably progressing to this state through the evolution of our systems of statutory law. Perpetual peace will finally be achieved with the alliance of republican states committed to upholding this (natural) "law of nations."[1]

Social theorist David Harvey has noted that elsewhere Kant presents a much less benign view of the world (alluded to in our reading through a reference to "American savages" who eat their enemies). In "Perpetual Peace" Kant writes specifically about cosmopolitan right (*ius cosmopoliticum*), which is composed of two distinct rights: civil right (*ius civitis*) and international right (*ius genitum*). The first concerns rights of persons in any specific state and the second concerns rights among states. Together these rights constitute a universal law that eclipses that of the state. The result of exercising these universal laws is that persons become "citizens of the world" who enjoy "universal hospitality"—freedom to move unobstructed among states and to engage in commercial activity across state boundaries. The vision is rather lovely (especially for emerging capitalist interests) when all is said and done.

Yet it would be a mistake to isolate the vision from the corpus of Kant's work, and important in this respect is his geography. Kant was passionate about geography. Throughout his teaching career he taught courses in geography as often as he taught logic and metaphysics; and his *Geography*, a compilation of course notes, reveals a very different view of the world than his cosmopolitanism. Here we find Kant claiming that temperate climates allow humans to develop to their full potential. "Yellow Indians," living in a warmer climate are less developed, "negroes" are "much inferior," and some indigenous Americans rate below them. Heat breeds laziness, he claims. According to Kant, these developmentally challenged peoples dress indecently, seek pregnancies with European men, are unsanitary and smell foul, steal, cheat and are generally servile. He adds that people who live in far northern climates also suffer the same developmental limitations.

Kant's cosmopolitanism and his geography cannot be considered discreetly. They are part of the totality of his thought. After all, he maintained that geography provided the foundation for all practical knowledge. Considering them in tandem leaves us at an ambivalent place, but it is one that we cannot avoid if we take Kant seriously. As Harvey notes:

> What happens when normative ideals get inserted as a principle of political action into a world in which some people are considered inferior and others are thought indolent, smelly, or just plain ugly? Some of Kant's more temporizing remarks on the principle of "perpetual peace" are precisely when such actual geographical cases present themselves. But it boils down to this: either the smelly Hottentots and the lazy Samoyards have to reform themselves to qualify for consideration under the universal ethical code (thereby flattening out all geographical differences), or the universal principles operate as an intensely discriminatory code masquerading as the universal good.[2]

3.1 Perpetual peace: A philosophical essay

Immanuel Kant

Second definitive article for a perpetual peace

"The law of nations shall be founded on a federation of free states"

Nations, as states, may be judged like individuals who, living in the natural state of society—that is to say—uncontrolled by external law injure one another through their very proximity. Every state, for the sake of its own security, may—and ought to—demand that its neighbour should submit itself to conditions, similar to those of the civil society where the right of every individual is guaranteed.

This would give rise to a federation of nations which, however, would not have to be a State of nations. That would involve a contradiction. For the term "state" implies the relation of one who rules to those who obey—that is to say, of lawgiver to the subject people: and many nations in one state would constitute only one nation, which contradicts our hypothesis, since here we have to consider the right of one nation against another, in so far as they are so many separate states and are not to be fused into one.

The attachment of savages to their lawless liberty, the fact that they would rather be at hopeless variance with one another than submit themselves to a legal authority constituted by themselves, that they therefore prefer their senseless freedom to a reason-governed liberty, is regarded by us with profound contempt as barbarism and uncivilisation and the brutal degradation of humanity. So one would think that civilised races, each formed into a state by itself, must come out of such an abandoned condition as soon as they possibly can. On the contrary, however, every state thinks rather that its majesty (the "majesty" of a people is an absurd expression) lies just in the very fact that it is subject to no external legal authority; and the glory of the ruler consists in this, that, without his requiring to expose himself to danger, thousands stand at his command ready to let themselves be sacrificed for a matter of no concern to them. The difference between the savages of Europe and those of America lies chiefly in this, that, while many tribes of the latter have been entirely devoured by their enemies, Europeans know a better way of using the vanquished than by eating them; and they prefer to increase through them the number of their subjects, and so the number of instruments at their command for still more widely spread war.

The depravity of human nature shows itself without disguise in the unrestrained relations of nations to each other, while in the law-governed civil state much of this is hidden by the check of government. This being so, it is astonishing that the word "right" has not yet been entirely banished from the politics of war as pedantic, and that no state has yet ventured to publicly advocate this point of view. For Hugo Grotius, Puffendorf, Vattel and others—Job's comforters, all of them—are always quoted in good faith to justify an attack, although their codes, whether couched in philosophical or diplomatic terms, have not—nor can have—the slightest legal force, because states, as such, are under no common external authority; and there is no instance of a state having ever been moved by argument to desist from its purpose, even when this was backed up by the testimony of such great men. This homage which every state renders—in words at least—to the idea of right, proves that, although it may be slumbering, there is, notwithstanding, to be found in man a still higher natural moral capacity by the aid of which he will in time gain the mastery over the evil principle in his nature, the existence of which he is unable to deny. And he hopes the same of others; for otherwise the word "right" would never be uttered by states who wish to wage war, unless to deride it like the Gallic Prince who declared:—"The privilege which nature gives the strong is that the weak must obey them."

The method by which states prosecute their rights can never be by process of law—as it is where there is an external tribunal—but only by war. Through this means, however, and its favourable issue, victory, the question of right is never decided. A treaty of peace makes, it may be, an end to the war of the moment, but not to the conditions of war which at any time may afford a new pretext for opening hostilities; and this we cannot exactly condemn as unjust, because under these conditions everyone is his own judge. Notwithstanding, not quite the same rule applies to states according to the law of nations as holds good of individuals in a lawless condition according to the law of nature, namely, "that they ought to advance out of this condition." This is so, because, as states, they have already within themselves a legal constitution, and have therefore advanced beyond the stage at which others, in accordance with their ideas of right, can force them to come under a wider legal constitution. Meanwhile, however, reason, from her throne of the supreme law-giving moral power, absolutely condemns war as a morally lawful proceeding, and makes a state of peace, on the other hand, an immediate duty. Without a compact between the nations, however, this state of peace cannot be established or assured. Hence there must be an alliance of a particular kind which we may call a covenant of peace (*foedus pacificum*) which would differ from a treaty of peace (*pactum pacis*) in this respect, that the latter merely puts an end to one war, while the former would seek to put an end to war for ever. This alliance does not aim at the gain of any power whatsoever of the state, but merely at the preservation and security of the freedom of the state for itself and of other allied states at the same time. The latter do not, however, require, for this reason, to submit themselves like individuals in the state of nature to public laws and coercion. The practicability or objective reality of this idea of federation which is to extend gradually over all states and so lead to perpetual peace can be shewn. For, if Fortune ordains that a powerful and enlightened people should form a republic,—which by its very nature is inclined to perpetual peace—this would serve as a centre of federal union for other states wishing to join, and thus secure conditions of freedom among the states in accordance with the idea of the law of nations. Gradually, through different unions of this kind, the federation would extend further and further.

It is quite comprehensible that a people should say:—"There shall be no war among us, for we shall form ourselves into a state, that is to say, constitute for ourselves a supreme legislative, administrative and judicial power which will settle our disputes peaceably." But if this state says:— "There shall be no war between me and other states, although I recognise no supreme law-giving power which will secure me my rights and whose rights I will guarantee;" then it is not at all clear upon what grounds I could base my confidence in my right, unless it were the substitute for that compact on which civil society is based—namely, free federation which reason must necessarily connect with the idea of the law of nations, if indeed any meaning is to be left in that concept at all.

There is no intelligible meaning in the idea of the law of nations as giving a right to make war; for that must be a right to decide what is just, not in accordance with universal, external laws limiting the freedom of each individual, but by means of one-sided maxims applied by force. We must then understand by this that men of such ways of thinking are quite justly served, when they destroy one another, and thus find perpetual peace in the wide grave which covers all the abominations of acts of violence as well as the authors of such deeds. For states, in their relation to one another, there can be, according to reason, no other way of advancing from that lawless condition which unceasing war implies, than by giving up their savage lawless freedom, just as individual men have done, and yielding to the coercion of public laws. Thus they can form a State of nations (*civitas gentium*), one, too, which will be ever increasing and would finally embrace all the peoples of the earth. States, however, in accordance with their understanding of the law of nations, by no means desire this, and therefore reject *in hypothesi* what is correct *in thesi*. Hence, instead of the positive idea of a world-republic, if all is not to be lost, only the negative substitute for it, a federation averting war, maintaining its ground and ever extending over the world may stop the current of this tendency to war and shrinking from the control of law. But even then there will be a constant danger that this propensity may break out. "*furor impius intus—fremit horridus ore cruento.*" (Virgil.)

Third definitive article for a perpetual peace

"The rights of men, as citizens of the world, shall be limited to the conditions of universal hospitality"

We are speaking here, as in the previous articles, not of philanthropy, but of right; and in this sphere hospitality signifies the claim of a stranger entering foreign territory to be treated by its owner without hostility. The latter may send him away again, if this can be done without causing his death; but, so long as he conducts himself peaceably, he must not be treated as an enemy. It is not a right to be treated as a guest to which the stranger can lay claim—a special friendly compact on his behalf would be required to make him for a given time an actual inmate, but he has a right of visitation. This right to present themselves to society belongs to all mankind in virtue of our common right of possession on the surface of the earth on which, as it is a globe, we cannot be infinitely scattered, and must in the end reconcile ourselves to existence side by side: at the same time, originally no one individual had more right than another to live in any one particular spot. Uninhabitable portions of the surface, ocean and desert, split up the human community, but in such a way that ships and camels—"the ship of the desert"—make it possible for men to come into touch with one another across these unappropriated regions and to take advantage of our common claim to the face of the earth with a view to a possible intercommunication. The inhospitality of the inhabitants of certain sea coasts—as, for example, the coast of Barbary—in plundering ships in neighbouring seas, or making slaves of shipwrecked mariners; or the behaviour of the Arab Bedouins in the deserts, who think that proximity to nomadic tribes constitutes a right to rob, is thus contrary to the law of nature. This right to hospitality, however—that is to say, the privilege of strangers arriving on foreign soil—does not amount to more than what is implied in a permission to make an attempt at intercourse with the original inhabitants. In this way far distant territories may enter into peaceful relations with one another. These relations may at last come under the public control of law, and thus the human race may be brought nearer the realization of a cosmopolitan constitution.

Let us look now, for the sake of comparison, at the inhospitable behaviour of the civilised nations, especially the commercial states of our continent.

The injustice which they exhibit on visiting foreign lands and races—this being equivalent in their eyes to conquest—is such as to fill us with horror. America, the negro countries, the Spice Islands, the Cape etc. were, on being discovered, looked upon as countries which belonged to nobody; for the native inhabitants were reckoned as nothing. In Hindustan, under the pretext of intending to establish merely commercial depots, the Europeans introduced foreign troops; and, as a result, the different states of Hindustan were stirred up to far-spreading wars. Oppression of the natives followed, famine, insurrection, perfidy and all the rest of the litany of evil which can afflict mankind.

China and Japan (Nipon) which had made an attempt at receiving guests of this kind, have now taken a prudent step. Only to a single European people, the Dutch, has China given the right of access to her shores (but not of entrance into the country), while Japan has granted both these concessions; but at the same time they exclude the Dutch who enter, as if they were prisoners, from social intercourse with the inhabitants. The worst, or from the standpoint of ethical judgment the best, of all this is that no satisfaction is derived from all this violence, that all these trading companies stand on the verge of ruin, that the Sugar Islands, that seat of the most horrible and deliberate slavery, yield no real profit, but only have their use indirectly and for no very praiseworthy object—namely, that of furnishing men to be trained as sailors for the men-of-war and thereby contributing to the carrying on of war in Europe. And this has been done by nations who make a great ado about their piety, and who, while they are quite ready to commit injustice, would like, in their orthodoxy, to be considered among the elect.

The intercourse, more or less close, which has been everywhere steadily increasing between the nations of the earth, has now extended so enormously that a violation of right in one part of the world is felt all over it. Hence the idea of a cosmopolitan right is no fantastical, high-flown notion of right, but a complement of the unwritten code of law—constitutional as well as inter-national law—necessary for the public rights of mankind in general and thus for the realisation of perpetual peace. For only by endeavouring to fulfil the conditions laid down by this cosmopolitan law can we flatter ourselves that we are gradually approaching that ideal.

Part 2

The four essays that follow are written by scholars who have all been deeply influenced by Kant's cosmopolitanism in different ways. Jürgen Habermas, a German sociologist and philosopher, takes as his point of departure Kant's notion of the "cosmopolitan condition." This, he argues, is a state of affairs that provides only two possibilities for global governance: (i) an international commonwealth (an alliance with a relatively loose legal structure) and (ii) a "world republic" (a system with a strong international government that Habermas believes is unsatisfactorily represented in a contemporary "Pax Americana"). Habermas proposes something in between these two extremes: a transnational constitutional system of governance that nonetheless preserves the political integrity of individual states. This would be a legal system in which international, national, and intranational bodies would be able to work in concert with one another. In this regard he believes the European Union may provide a model.

Unlike Habermas, the American philosopher Martha Nussbaum generally questions the efficacy of local, regional, and national identities, calling for a system of education focused on the values of global citizenship, a point of view that has had wide influence.[3] Following in the tradition of Kant, Nussbaum suggests that we need to provide our children with a global education that requires them to know about geographies and cultures that are distant from their own.

Her essay here is considered to have been a catalyst for renewed interest in cosmopolitanism among philosophers, social scientists, and educators at the end of the twentieth century. It was, and continues to be, a seminal piece of work in which Nussbaum defines a cosmopolitan as "the person whose primary allegiance is to the community of human beings in the entire world," and cosmopolitanism as the "possibility of a more international basis for political emotion and concern." From this perspective, nationalism and patriotism are not viable forms of contemporary allegiances. We should, rather, be educating our children to be world citizens. It is only through such a shift in perspective that we will be better able to understand ourselves in our global environment, to more effectively deal with issues that require transnational initiatives, and to appreciate our global "moral obligations." Drawing on the tradition established by Kant in the second chapter of "Perpetual Peace" Nussbaum's cosmopolitanism is based on what she regards as the universality of reason and universal principles of moral obligation.

The British political theorist David Held provides our next essay in this section. While remaining in the tradition of Kant, Held also believes that

Kant's cosmopolitanism was insufficient. He argues, for instance, that universal hospitality cannot be exercised in situations where persons are subject to economic and social forces over which they have little control. In essence, it is untenable in a neoliberal economic environment. Consequently he advocates the establishment of international representative bodies with the power to regulate issues relating to human rights (political, economic, and social). He has no problem with maintaining the rights of sovereign states. In fact, he sees contemporary states as inextricably enmeshed in a global complex of social and economic relations. They are, however, not fully capable of dealing with new global pressures. His cosmopolitan democracy thus calls for the creation of new kinds of global institutions (patterned on the policy statements of the United Nations) that balance global, national, regional, and local interests.

The final essay in the section is written by the philosopher and cultural theorist Kwame Anthony Appiah. Appiah, though born in England, had an Asante father and was raised in Ghana. In his work Appiah seeks to counter the divisive frameworks of writers like Huntington. He believes the most effective means of doing this is by developing a global ethic that, he argues, can be divined out of the Western philosophical tradition. Thus he proposes a form of cosmopolitanism with its roots in ancient Greek philosophy and running through the European Enlightenment, Revolutionary France, and into our own time through documents like the United Nations Universal Declaration of Human Rights. Global acceptance of this ethic, he argues, is what we need to enter into a new period of peace in which human beings will be guided by a deep understanding of our common humanity. Unlike Nussbaum, Appiah favors a "rooted cosmopolitanism" in which people's connections with their local situations are also important in mediating global relations and identities, although it is not clear how he proposes that this balance be struck in practical terms.

3.2 The Kantian project of the constitutionalization of international law: Does it still have a chance?

Jürgen Habermas

With his conception of a "cosmopolitan condition" (*weltbürgeriche Zustand*), Kant took a decisive step beyond an international law, which remained orientated exclusively to states. Only in the wake of two world wars has the constitutionalization of international law evolved towards cosmopolitan law along the lines prefigured by Kant. However, since the end of the bipolar world order and the emergence of the USA as the predominant world power, an alternative vision for ordering the world has emerged. In this situation the Kantian project of cosmopolitan order must not only confront the traditional objection of "realists" who affirm the quasi-ontological primacy of brute power over law. Other opponents are currently emerging under the banner of a liberal ethos that they propose as an *alternative* to international law.

On the realist conception, the normative taming of political power through law is possible only *within* the confines of a sovereign state whose existence is based on its capacity to assert itself with force. On this premise, international law must forever lack the cutting edge of a law armed with sanctions. The dispute between Kantian Idealists and Carl Schmittian Realists over the limits to the jurisdiction of international relations is today overlaid by another, even more intense controversy. The project of a new liberal world order under the banner of a *Pax Americana*, advocated by the neoconservative proponents of the current US administration, raises the question of whether the *juridification* of international relations should be replaced by a *moralization* of international politics—a moralization that is defined by the ethos of a superpower. Once the bone of contention between Idealists and Realists was the question of whether justice among nations is at all possible. The new controversy is, by contrast, concerned with the issue whether law remains an appropriate medium for realizing the declared goals of achieving peace and international security and of promoting democracy and human rights worldwide. What is controversial now is the *path* by which these goals can be achieved, whether via the legally established procedures of an inclusive, but often weak and selectively operating world organization, or via the unilaterally imposed decisions of a well-meaning hegemon. At first glance the issues seemed to have been settled by events, as Saddam's statue was knocked down from its pedestal in Baghdad. At that time the US government had twice ignored international law, first with its proclamation of a National Security Doctrine in September 2002, and then with the invasion of Iraq in

2003. In addition it had marginalized the United Nations in order to accord priority to its own, no longer legally, but *ethically* justified national interests.

Hence the question arises whether there is anything wrong, normatively speaking, in this unilateral approach. Let us, for the sake of argument, base this question on the counterfactual premise that the American action would more effectively realize the same goals that hitherto had been pursued half-heartedly, and with scant success, by the United Nations. Or should we rather hold fast to the alternative project of a constitutionalization of international law and recall the world-historical mission, once embraced by Presidents Wilson and Roosevelt? To be sure, the Kantian project can only be continued if the USA returns to the internationalism it embraced after 1918 and 1945 and once again assumes the role of a pace-setter in the development of international law towards a "cosmopolitan condition."

I would like (1) to explain the Kantian project, then (2) briefly check the prospects for a modified cosmopolitanism in the light of the history of international law and finally (3) return to the question just raised: how to choose between the presently competing projects on normative grounds.

(1) For Kant law is not merely a suitable *means* for establishing peace between states; rather, he conceives of peace between nations in terms of legal peace ...

...

The core innovation of the Kantian project consists in the transformation of international law, as a law of *states*, into cosmopolitan law, as a law of states and *individuals*. The latter are no longer legal subjects merely as citizens of their respective states, but at the same time as members of a "cosmopolitan commonwealth." The civil rights of individual persons are now supposed to penetrate even international relations. But for Kant, the price that sovereign states have to pay for the promotion of their citizens to world citizens is submission to a higher state authority.

...

There has been much speculation over why Kant, in his essay "Toward perpetual peace," introduced the weaker conception of a League of Nations. To make a long story brief, let me just summarize the main train of thought: Kant understood permanent world peace as the implication of a complete constitutionalization of international relations. The same principles that so far had taken shape only in the constitutions of single republican states should now structure the cosmopolitan condition. That analogy suggested conceiving this new condition in terms of the constitution of a world republic. Kant felt, however, inhibited in following this idea straight away, because he was troubled by the fear of despotic tendencies that seemed to be inherent in the leveling structure of a complex world republic. It was a kind of Foucauldian fear of repressive "normalization" that motivated Kant to choose the temporary surrogate of a League of Nations. For the time being he saw in a global monopoly of power the only legally institutionalized alternative to the classical competition between sovereign states. Since this alternative appeared to have, at least under present conditions, dangerous implications, it seemed better not to start with the realization of a cosmopolitan condition in the medium of coercive law but instead in the weaker form of a voluntary association of peaceable republics.

However, the alternative that forced Kant to this conclusion is by no means a complete one. If we conceive of the legal domestication of a belligerent international arena in sufficiently abstract terms and do not pack the idea of a cosmopolitan condition with false analogies, a different path to the constitutionalization of international law, one opened by liberal, federalist and pluralist notions, seems at least *conceptually* possible. Taking off from currently existing structure, one can imagine the political constitution of a decentred world society as a multi-level system that for good reasons lacks, as a whole, the character of a state.

On this conception, a suitably reformed world organization would effectively and non-selectively fulfill vital but *strictly circumscribed functions* of securing peace and implementing human rights at the *supranational level*, without having to assume the state-like character of a world republic. At the intermediate or *transnational level* the major powers would address the difficult problems of a global domestic politics. In the framework of permanent conferences and negotiations they would have to cope with the challenges to re-regulate and balance the global economy and ecology. Certainly, apart from the US, there are at present no global players with both a sufficiently representative mandate to negotiate, and with the necessary power to implement, such policies. In the various world-regions nation states would have to come together to form continental regimes on the model, for example, of a future European Union which would have gained the strength for an effective foreign policy of its own. International relations, as we know them, would continue to exist in a modified form at this intermediate level—modified already because, under an effective United Nations peace and security regime, even global players would be forbidden to resort to war as a legitimate means of resolving conflicts.

Thus the model of a constitutional state of global scale is not the only way to meet the demanding requirements of a "cosmopolitan condition." The sketchy outline of a multi-level system, which, at the supranational level, fulfills the worldwide security and human rights goals of the UN Charter and which, at the transnational level, solves problems of global domestic politics through compromises among domesticated major powers, serves here merely as an illustration of a *conceptual* alternative to a world republic …

…

(2) Let us now pursue the traces Kant's project has left in the actual history of international law. If we are able to do justice to the enduring relevance of that project we must look beyond Kant's own historical horizon. He, too, was a child of his time. But the provinciality *vis-à-vis* the future, which all of us share, is no objection to the universalistic programme of Kantian moral and legal theory. With the unearned epistemic advantage of later generations, we can look back from a distance of 200 years over a dialectical development of European international law.

The two world wars of the twentieth century, together with the end of the Cold War, constitute ruptures in this legal development, although the last rupture does not yet present a clear pattern like the previous two. The First and Second World Wars were like watersheds in which our hopes were dashed while new ones arose. The League of Nations and the United Nations are both major, though precarious and reversible, achievements on the long, hard road to a political constitution for world society. However, the League of Nations fell apart as Japan invaded Manchuria, Italy annexed Abyssinia, and Hitler's aggressive military build-up bore its first fruits in the Anschluss with Austria and the annexation of the Sudetenland. The work of the UN has been hampered, though not completely brought to a standstill, by a standoff between the major powers and the blockade of the Security Council. The third rupture, the collapse of the Soviet Union, also inspired hopes for a new world order under the leadership for the world organization. With a sense of humanitarian, peace-keeping and peace-enforcing interventions, with the establishment of war-crimes tribunals and the prosecution of human-rights violations, the UN seemed finally capable of taking independent initiatives. But at the same time the setbacks are mounting, including the terrorist attacks interpreted by the USA and its allies as a "declaration of war" against the West.

The developments that culminated in the invasion of Iraq by coalition troops in 2003 have created an ambiguous situation for which there are no parallels in the history of international law. One the one hand, the most powerful member of the UN disregards its fundamental norm, the prohibition on violence. On the other hand, this manifest violation of standing law did not destroy the world organization, which is emerging from the conflict; it seems, with its international authority enhanced. Such an ambivalent history cannot tell us anything unequivocal about the future prospects of an appropriately modified Kantian project. But it can perhaps shed some light on the normative pros and cons …

...

(3) In view of this obscure situation the question we face is whether we still have the hope that progress in the constitutionalization of international law, after two ruinous setbacks, has nevertheless acquired a self-propelling dynamic. Or does this situation mark the beginning of the end of the whole project of a legal channeling of international relations? An appropriate answer would require a proper empirical analysis of the present transition from a national to a postnational constellation. The weakness of a UN in need of reform is obvious, whereas the new types of privatized violence call on the constructive accomplishments of the international community with increasing urgency. They present merely the most obvious symptoms of the disso-lution of the classical-modern constellation dominated by the interaction of independent nation states. But those trends, which are currently capturing attention under the heading of globalization, not only *run counter* to the Kantian project; some of them also *meet it halfway.* The anticipation of a cosmopolitan condition finds in globalization also a supportive context mitigating the initial appearance that the forces, which resist a political constitution for global society, are insuperable. I cannot go into these complex empirical issues here. In the end I can only return to our normative question: Does the actual inefficiency of the UN provide sufficient reason to break with the premises of the Kantian project in view of the challenges currently facing us?

Since the end of the Cold War a unipolar global order has emerged in which the military, economic and technological superpower enjoys unrivalled dominance. The happy circumstance that the US is at the same time the oldest democracy on earth could inspire a conception different from that of hegemonic liberalism. The neo-conservative and the neo-Kantian projects agree in their goals at an abstract evel. Both claim to promote international security and world-wide human rights, but they obviously differ in the choice of means and in the specification of their goals.

As regards the means, an *ethically grounded* unilateralism no longer feels bound to establish procedures in *international law.* With regard to the concrete form of the new global order, hegemonic liberalism does not aim at a law-governed, politically constituted world society, but instead of such a cosmopolitan condition it aims at an international order of formerly independent liberal states which operate under the protection of a peace-securing superpower and obey the imperatives of perfectly liberalized global markets. On this model, peace would not be granted by law but by the ethical values of an imperial power, and the world society would be integrated, not through the *political* relations among world citizens, but through *systemic* relations, ultimately through the market. I think that neither good empirical nor sound normative considerations support this vision.

The unquestionably acute danger of international terrorism cannot be effectively combatted with the classical instruments of war between states, thus also not by the military superiority of a unilaterally operating super-power. Only the effective coordination of intelligence services, police forces and criminal justice, and the supervision of criminal financial transfers, will strike at the logistics of the adversary; and only the combination of social modernization with a self-critical dialogue between cultures will in the long run reach the roots of terrorism. These means are more readily available to an international community horizontally tied together and effectively obliged to cooperate than to the unilateralism of a major power that either disregards or instrumentalizes international law. The image of a unipolar world accurately mirrors the asymmetrical distribution of political power but misrepresents the fact that the complexity of a differentiated and highly independent world society can no longer be mastered from a centre. Conflicts between cultures and major religions can no more be exclusive controlled with military means than crises on world markets can be with administrative means.

Apart from these empirical reasons, hegemonic liberalism is not supported by *normative reasons* either. Even if we start from a best-case scenario and ascribe the purest motives and most intelligent policies to the hegemonic power, the "well-intentioned hegemon" will encounter insuperable cognitive obstacles. A government that must by itself decide on issues of self-defense, humanitarian interventions or international tribunals can operate as thought-fully as it may; in the unavoidable weighing of goods it can never be sure whether it actually separates its own national interests from the universal-izable interests that could be shared by all the other nations. This inability is a matter of the logic of practical discourse, not of good or bad will. A unilateral anticipation of what would be rationally acceptable to all sides can only be tested by submitting the presumptively unbiased proposal to a discursive procedure of opinion and will-formation.

"Discursive" procedures make egalitarian decisions dependent on prior argumentation (so that only justified decisions are accepted); they are furthermore inclusive (so that all affected parties can participate); and they encourage the participants to assume each other's perspectives (so that a fair assessment of all affected interests is possible). This is the cognitive meaning of an impartial decision-making process. Judged by this standard, the ethical justification of a unilateral undertaking by appeal to presumptive universal values of *one's own* political culture must remain fundamentally biased.

This deficiency cannot be made good by the fact that the hegemonic power has a democratic constitution at home. For its citizens confront the same cognitive dilemma as their government. The citizens of one political community cannot anticipate the outcome of the interpretation and appli-cation of supposedly universal values and principles accomplished by the citizens of another political community from *their* local perspective and in *their* own cultural context. In another respect, however, the fact that the superpower has a liberal constitution is indeed significant. Citizens of a democratic political community sooner or later become aware of cognitive dissonance if universalistic claims cannot be squared with the particularistic character of actual practices and obvious motivations.

3.3 Patriotism and cosmopolitanism

Martha Nussbaum

I

In Rabindranath Tagore's novel, *The Home and the World*, the young wife Bimala, entranced by the patriotic rhetoric of her husband's friend Sandip, becomes an eager devotee of the *Swadeshi* movement, which has organized a boycott of foreign goods. The slogan of the movement is *Bande Mataram*, "Hail Motherland." Bimala complains that her husband, the cosmopolitan Hindu landlord Nikhil, is cool in his devotion to the cause: "And yet it was not that my husband refused to support *Swadeshi*, or was in any way against the Cause. Only he had not been able whole-heartedly to accept the spirit of *Bande Mataram*. 'I am willing,' he said, 'to serve my country; but my worship I reserve for Right which is far greater than my country. To worship my country as a god is to bring a curse upon it.'"

Americans have frequently supported the principle of *Bande Mataram*, giving the fact of being American a special salience in moral and political deliberation, and pride in a specifically American identity and a specifically American citizenship a special power among the motivations to political action. I believe, with Tagore and his character Nikhil, that this emphasis on patriotic pride is both morally dangerous and, ultimately, subversive of some of the worthy goals patriotism sets out to serve—for example, the goal of national unity in devotion to worthy moral ideals of justice and equality. These goals, I shall argue, would be better served by an ideal that is in any case more adequate to our situation in the contemporary world, namely the very old ideal of the cosmopolitan, the person whose primary allegiance is to the community of human beings in the entire world.

My articulation of these issues is motivated, in part, by my experience working on international quality-of-life issues in an institute for development economics connected with the United Nations. It is motivated, as well, by the renewal of appeals to the nation, and national pride, in some recent discussions of American character and American education. In a by now well-known op-ed piece in *The New York Times* (February 13, 1994), philosopher Richard Rorty urges Americans, especially the American left, not to disdain patriotism as a value, and indeed to give central importance to "the emotion of national pride" and "a sense of shared national identity." Rorty argues that we cannot even criticize ourselves well unless we also "rejoice" in our American identity and define ourselves fundamentally in terms of that identity. Rorty seems to hold that the primary alternative to a politics based on patriotism and national identity is what he calls a "politics of difference," one based on internal divisions among America's ethnic, racial, religious, and other sub-groups. He nowhere considers the possibility of a more international basis for political emotion and concern ...

One might wonder, however, how far the politics of nationalism really is from the "politics of difference." *The Home and the World* (better known, perhaps, in Satyajit Ray's haunting film of the same title) is a tragic story of the defeat of a reasonable and principled cosmopolitanism by the forces of nationalism and ethnocentrism. I believe that Tagore sees deeply when he sees that at bottom nationalism and ethnocentric particularism are not alien to one another, but akin—that to give support to nationalist sentiments subverts, ultimately, even the values that hold a nation together, because it substitutes a colorful idol for the substantive universal values of justice and right ... Only the cosmopolitan stance ... asks us to give our first allegiance to what is morally good—and that which, being good, I can commend as such to all human beings. Or so I shall argue.

Proponents of nationalism in politics and in education frequently make a thin concession to cosmopolitanism. They may argue, for example, that although nations should in general base education and political deliberation on shared national values, a commitment to basic human rights should be part of any national educational system, and that this commitment will in a sense serve to hold many nations together. This seems to be a fair comment on practical reality; and the emphasis on human rights is certainly necessary for a world in which nations interact all the time on terms, let us hope, of justice and mutual respect.

But is it sufficient? As students here grow up, is it sufficient for them to learn that they are above all citizens of the United States, but that they ought to respect the basic human rights of citizens of India, Bolivia, Nigeria, and Norway? Or should they—as I think—in addition to giving special attention to the history and current situation of their own nation, learn a good deal more than is frequently the case about the rest of the world in which they live, about India and Bolivia and Nigeria and Norway and their histories, problems, and comparative successes? Should they learn only that citizens of India have equal basic human rights, or should they also learn about the problems of hunger and pollution in India, and the implications of these problems for larger problems of global hunger and global ecology? Most important, should they be taught that they are above all citizens of the United States, or should they instead be taught that they are above all citizens of a world of human beings, and that, while they themselves happen to be situated in the United States, they have to share this world of human beings with the citizens of other countries? I shall shortly suggest four arguments for the second conception of education, which

I shall call *cosmopolitan education*. But first I introduce a historical digression, which will trace cosmopolitanism to its origins, in the process recovering some excellent arguments that originally motivated it as an educational project.

II

Asked where he came from, the ancient Greek Cynic philosopher Diogenes replied, "I am a citizen of the world." He meant by this, it appears, that he refused to be defined by his local origins and local group memberships, so central to the self-image of a conventional Greek male; he insisted on defining himself in terms of more universal aspirations and concerns. The Stoics who followed his lead developed his image of the *kosmou politês* or world citizen more fully, arguing that each of us dwells, in effect, in two communities—the local community of our birth, and the community of human argument and aspiration that "is truly great and truly common, in which we look neither to this corner nor to that, but measure the boundaries of our nation by the sun" (Seneca, *De Otio*). It is this community that is, most fundamentally, the source of our moral obligations. With respect to the most basic moral values such as justice, "we should regard all human beings as our fellow citizens and neighbors" (Plutarch, *On the Fortunes of Alexander*). We should regard our deliberations as, first and foremost, deliberations about human problems of people in particular concrete situations, not problems growing out of a national identity that is altogether unlike that of others. Diogenes knew that the invitation to think as a world citizen was, in a sense, an invitation to be an exile from the comfort of patriotism and its easy sentiments, to see our own ways of life from the point of view of justice and the good. The accident of where one is born is just that, an accident; any human being might have been born in any nation. Recognizing this, his Stoic successors held, we should ... recognize humanity wherever it occurs, and give its fundamental ingredients, reason and moral capacity, our first allegiance and respect.

The American student must learn to recognize humanity wherever she encounters it and be eager to understand humanity in its "strange" guises.

This clearly did not mean that the Stoics were proposing the abolition of local and national forms of political organization and the creation of a world state. The point was more radical still: that we should give our first allegiance to no mere form of government, no temporal power, but to the moral community made up by the humanity of all human beings. The idea of the world citizen is in this way the ancestor and source of Kant's idea of the "kingdom of ends," and has a similar function in inspiring and regulating moral and political conduct. One should always behave so as to treat with equal respect the dignity of reason and moral choice in every human being ...

The Stoics stress that to be a citizen of the world one does not need to give up local identifications, which can frequently be a source of great richness in life. They suggest that we think of ourselves not as devoid of local affiliations, but as surrounded by a series of concentric circles. The first one is drawn around the self; the next takes in one's immediate family; then follows the extended family; then, in order, one's neighbors or local group, one's fellow city-dwellers, one's fellow countrymen—and we can easily add to this list groupings based on ethnic, linguistic, historical, professional, gender and sexual identities. Outside all these circles is the largest one, that of humanity as a whole. Our task as citizens of the world will be to "draw the circles somehow toward the center" (Stoic philosopher Hierocles, 1st–2nd CE), making all human beings more like our fellow city dwellers, and so on. In other words, we need not give up our special affections and identifications, whether ethnic or gender-based or religious … We may and should devote special attention to them in education. But we should work to make all human beings part of our community of dialogue and concern, base our political deliberations on that interlocking commonality, and give the circle that defines our humanity a special attention and respect.

This means, in educational terms, that the student in the United States, for example, may continue to regard herself as in part defined by her particular loves—her family, her religious, ethnic, or racial communities, or even for her country. But she must also, and centrally, learn to recognize humanity wherever she encounters it, undeterred by traits that are strange to her, and be eager to understand humanity in its "strange" guises. She must learn enough about the different to recognize common aims, aspirations, and values, and enough about these common ends to see how variously they are instantiated in the many cultures and many histories. Stoic writers insist that the vivid imagining of the different is an essential task of education; and that requires in turn, of course, a mastery of many facts about the different. Marcus Aurelius gives himself the following advice, which might be called the basis for cosmopolitan education: "Accustom yourself not to be inattentive to what another person says, and as far as possible enter into that person's mind" (VI.53). "Generally," he concludes, "one must first learn many things before one can judge another's action with understanding." …

I would like to see education adopt this cosmopolitan Stoic stance. The organic model could of course be abused—if, for example, it were to be taken to deny the fundamental importance of the separateness of persons and of fundamental personal liberties. Stoics were not always sufficiently attentive to these values and to their political salience; in that sense their thought is not always a good basis for a scheme of democratic deliberation and education. But as the image is primarily intended—as a reminder of the interdependence of all human beings and communities—it has fundamental significance. There is clearly a huge amount to be said about how such ideas might be realized in curricula at many levels. Instead of beginning that more concrete task, however, I shall now return to the present day and offer four arguments for making world citizenship, rather than democratic/national citizenship, education's central focus ...

III

Through cosmopolitan education, we learn more about ourselves

One of the greatest barriers to rational deliberation in politics is the unexamined feeling that one's own current preferences and ways are neutral and natural. An education that takes national boundaries as morally salient too often reinforces this kind of irrationality, by lending to what is an accident of history a false air of moral weight and glory. By looking at ourselves in the lens of the other, we come to see what in our practices is local and non-necessary, what more broadly or deeply shared. Our nation is appallingly ignorant of most of the rest of the world. I think that this means that it is also, in many crucial ways, ignorant of itself.

Why should we think of people from China as our fellows the minute they dwell in the United States, but not when they dwell in a certain other place, namely China?

To give just one example of this—since 1994 is the United Nations' International Year of the Family—if we want to understand our own history and our choices where the structure of the family and of child-rearing are involved, we are immeasurably assisted by looking around the world to see in what configurations families exist, and through what strategies children are in fact being cared for ... Such a study can show us, for example, that the two-parent nuclear family, in which the mother is the primary homemaker and the father the primary breadwinner is by no means a pervasive style of child-rearing in today's world. The extended family, clusters of families, the village, women's associations—all these groups and still others are in various places regarded as having major child-rearing responsibilities. Seeing this, we can begin to ask questions—for example, how much child abuse there is in a family that involves grandparents and other relatives in child-rearing, as compared with the relatively isolated Western-style nuclear family; how many different structures of child care have been found to support women's work, and how well each of these is functioning. If we do not undertake this kind of educational project, we risk assuming that the options familiar to us are the only ones there are, and that they are somehow "normal" and "natural" for the human species as such ...

We make headway solving problems that require international cooperation

The air does not obey national boundaries. This simple fact can be, for children, the beginning of the recognition that, like it or not, we live in a world in which the destinies of nations are closely intertwined with respect to basic goods and survival itself. The pollution of third-world nations who are attempting to attain our high standard of living will, in some cases, end up in our air. No matter what account of these matters we will finally adopt, any intelligent deliberation about ecology—as, also, about the food supply and population—requires global planning, global knowledge, and the recognition of a shared future.

To conduct this sort of global dialogue, we need not only knowledge of the geography and ecology of other nations—something that would already entail much revision in our curricula—but also a great deal about the people with whom we shall be talking, so that in talking with them we may be capable of respecting their traditions and commitments. Cosmopolitan education would supply the background necessary for this type of deliberation.

We recognize moral obligations to the rest of the world that are real, and that otherwise would go unrecognized

What are Americans to make of the fact that the high living standard we enjoy is one that very likely cannot be universalized, at least given the present costs of pollution controls and the present economic situation of developing nations, without ecological disaster? If we take Kantian morality at all seriously, as we should, we need to educate our children to be troubled by this fact. Otherwise we are educating a nation of moral hypocrites, who talk the language of universalizability but whose universe has a selfservingly narrow scope.

This point may appear to presuppose universalism, rather than being an argument in its favor. But here one may note that the values on which Americans may most justly pride themselves are, in a deep sense, Stoic values: respect for human dignity and the opportunity for each person to pursue happiness. If we really do believe that all human beings are created equal and endowed with certain inalienable rights, we are morally required to think about what that conception requires us to do with and for the rest of the world.

Once again, that does not mean that one may not permissibly give one's own sphere a special degree of concern. Politics, like child care, will be poorly done if each thinks herself equally responsible for all, rather than giving the immediate surroundings special attention and care. To give one's own sphere special care is justifiable in universalist terms, and I think that this is its most compelling justification. To take one example, we do not really think that our own children are morally more important than other people's children, even though almost all of us who have children would give our own children far more love and care than we give other people's children. It is good for children, on the whole, that things should work out this way, and that is why our special care is good rather than selfish. Education may and should reflect those special concerns—spending more time, for example, within a given nation, on that nation's history and politics. But my argument does entail that we should not confine our thinking to our own sphere—that in making choices in both political and economic matters we should most seriously consider the right of other human beings to life, liberty, and the pursuit of happiness, and work to acquire the knowledge that will enable us to deliberate well about those rights. I believe that this sort of thinking will have large-scale economic and political consequences.

We make a consistent and coherent argument based on distinctions we are really prepared to defend

Let me now return to the defense of shared values in Richard Rorty's article and Sheldon Hackney's project. In these eloquent appeals to the common there is something that makes me very uneasy. On the one hand Rorty and Hackney seem to argue well when they insist on the centrality to democratic deliberation of certain values that bind all citizens together. But why should these values, which instruct us to join hands across boundaries of ethnicity and class and gender and race, lose steam when they get to the borders of the nation? ...

For one thing, the very same groups exist both outside and inside ... What is it about the national boundary that magically converts people toward whom our education is both incurious and indifferent into people to whom we have duties of mutual respect? I think, in short, that we undercut the very case for multicultural respect within a nation by failing to make a broader world respect central to education. Richard Rorty's patriotism may be a way of bringing all Americans together; but patriotism is very close to jingoism, and I'm afraid I don't see in Rorty's argument any proposal for coping with this very obvious danger.

The life of the cosmopolitan, who puts right before country, and universal reason before the symbols of national belonging, need not be boring, flat, or lacking in love.

Furthermore, the defense of shared national values in both Rorty and Hackney, as I understand it, requires appealing to certain basic features of human personhood that obviously also transcend national boundaries. So if we fail to educate children to cross those boundaries in their minds and imaginations, we are tacitly giving them the message that we don't really mean what we say. We say that respect should be accorded to humanity as such, but we really mean that Americans as such are worthy of special respect …

IV

Becoming a citizen of the world is often a lonely business. It is, in effect, as Diogenes said, a kind of exile—from the comfort of local truths, from the warm nestling feeling of patriotism, from the absorbing drama of pride in oneself and one's own. In the writings of Marcus Aurelius (as in those of his American followers Emerson and Thoreau) one sometimes feels a boundless loneliness, as if the removal of the props of habit and local boundaries had left life bereft of a certain sort of warmth and security. If one begins life as a child who loves and trusts its parents, it is tempting to want to reconstruct citizenship along the same lines, finding in an idealized image of a nation a surrogate parent who will do one's thinking for one. Cosmopolitanism offers no such refuge; it offers only reason and the love of humanity, which may seem at times less colorful than other sources of belonging.

In Tagore's novel, the appeal to world citizenship fails—fails because patriotism is full of color and intensity and passion, whereas cosmopolitanism seems to have a hard time gripping the imagination. And yet in its very failure, Tagore shows, it succeeds. For the novel is a story of education for world citizenship, since the entire tragic story is told by the widowed Bimala, who understands, if too late, that Nikhil's morality was vastly superior to Sandip's empty symbol-mongering, that what looked like passion in Sandip was egocentric self-exaltation, and that what looked like lack of passion in Nikhil contained a truly loving perception of her as a person …

3.4 Cosmopolitan democracy and the global order: A new agenda

David Held

The backdrop of this chapter is the rapid growth in the complex interconnections among states and societies … In the spirit of Kant, I make the case for a new cosmopolitanism, but with a substantially different understanding of the necessary components of law, order, and accountability that can be found in Kant's writings.

The new constellation of global politics

Extraordinary changes have been occurring in international politics since 1989. For almost half a century, a system of geo-governance organized around the bifurcation of East and West dominated the planet. Almost at a stroke, it disintegrated, leaving few clues as to what alternative system might take its place …

While it is still very early to take stock of the advantages and disadvantages of the termination of the Cold War, three crucial issues can be posed to clarify the nature of the current global order:

1   What are the repercussions for domestic regimes of the end of the Cold War?

2   What changes are taking place in the structure of inter-state relations?

3   Which institutions can offer a basis for deliberation over, and action upon, global (i.e., transcontinental and intercontinental) problems?

To clarify the context of this chapter, I will introduce these issues briefly.

i

Among the domestic political changes in recent years has been the remarkable increase in the number of liberal democratic states …

…

Viewed from the perspective of domestic politics, the emerging world order is two-faced. It has fostered the extension of democracy; however, it has revealed (and, in some cases, detonated) tensions in nation states. By imposing a form of limited autonomy on the vast majority of states, the Cold War suppressed many forms of domestic conflict—at least in Europe. When the Cold War ended, some of the wounds provoked by domestic discord reopened.

ii

The current historical juncture has posed new problems not only for domestic politics but also for the organization of interstate relations ...

...

Generally speaking, however, it is striking that the increase in the number of democratic states has not been accompanied by a corresponding increase in democracy *among* states. Policy making in the UN Security Council and the International Monetary Fund, and in less formal settings such as the Group of Seven summits, has changed little since the collapse of the Berlin Wall. National governments, both the powerful and less powerful ones, have continued to act on the basis of their own reasons of state. The explanation for this has partly to do with uncertainty about the rules, values, and institutions necessary to establish greater accountability among nations. But it has also to do with the reluctance of democracies to extend their model of governance to inter-state relations—that is, with their reluctance to be called to account in matters of security involving foreign and international affairs.

iii

The most conspicuous feature of the new international situation is the mergence of issues that transcend national frontiers. Processes of economic internationalization, the problem of the environment, and the protection of the rights of minorities are, increasingly, matters for the world community as a whole. The limits on national autonomy imposed by the balance of terror have now been supplanted by a much subtler, more structural form of erosion caused by the processes of environmental, social, and economic globalization—that is, by shifts in the transcontinental or inter-regional scale of human social organization and the exercise of social power.

...

Now that the old confrontation between East and West has ended, regional and global problems such as the environment, the spread of AIDS, the debt-burden of the so-called Third World, the flow of financial resources that escape national jurisdiction, the drug trade, and international crime have been placed on the international political agenda. Nonetheless, profound ambiguity still reigns as to which institutions should take supranational decisions and according to what criteria.

...

The questions posed by the rapid growth of complex connections and relations between states and societies and by the evident intersection of national and international forces and processes remain largely unexplored.

The limits of democratic theory

Throughout the nineteenth and twentieth centuries there has been an assumption at the heart of liberal democratic thought concerning a "symmetric" and "congruent" relationship between political decision makers and the recipients of political decisions. In fact, symmetry and congruence are assumed at two crucial points: between citizen-voters and the decision makers whom they are (in principle) able to hold to account, and between the "output" (decisions, policies, etc.) of decision makers and their constituents (ultimately, "the people" in a delimited territory). It has been assumed, in other words, by democratic theorists, orthodox and radical, that "the fate of the national community" is largely in its own hands, and that a satisfactory theory of democracy can be developed by examining the interplay between "actors" and "structures" in the nation state.

At the center of this approach to democratic politics is a taken-for-granted conception of sovereignty and an uncritically appropriated concept of political community. The difficulty here is that political communities have rarely, if ever, existed in isolation as bounded geographic totalities, and they are better thought of as multiple overlapping networks of interaction. These networks of interaction crystalize around different sites and forms of power (economic, political, military, and cultural, among others), producing patterns of activity that do not correspond in any straightforward way to territorial boundaries. The spatial reach of the modern nation state did not fix impermeable borders for other networks, the scope and reach of which have been as much local as international or global. Political communities are locked into a variety of processes and structures that range in and through them, linking and fragmenting them in complex constellations. It is no surprise, then, that national communities by no means make and determine decisions and policies exclusively for themselves, and that governments by no means determine what is right or appropriate exclusively for their own citizens.

The assumption that one can understand the nature and possibilities of political community by referring merely to national structures and mechanisms of political power is not justified ... If the agent at the heart of modern political discourse (be it a person, a group, or a collectivity) is locked into a variety of overlapping communities, "domestic" and "international," then the proper "home" of politics and democracy becomes a puzzling matter.

The requirement of the democratic good: Cosmopolitan democracy

If freedom is threatened by the behaviors of other nations and states, what is right for a political community, Kant argued, cannot prevail. In contrast, "right" can prevail, Kant held, if the rule of law is sustained in all states as well as in international relations. Within the terms of the argument presented here, this is an important contention, but it must be recast to meet the conditions of democracy in the context of national, regional, and global interconnectedness. Accordingly, it can be maintained, democracy can prevail in a political community if and only if it is not impeded by threats arising from the action (or nonaction) of other political communities or from the networks of interaction that cut across community boundaries.

Although the threats to freedom derive, in Kant's view, from many forms of violence, they stem primarily from war and the preparation for war ...

While the threats to autonomy from war and direct coercion are hard to overestimate, they constitute only one element in the challenge to self-government or self-determination in the political community. Such challenges can come from any of the sources of power and domination—economic, political, cultural, military. Power in any one of these spheres can erode the effective entrenchment of democracy. And challenges to democracy can arise not only from within the power domains of particular communities but also from power domains that cut across communities. Sites of power can be national, transnational, and international. Accordingly, democracy within a political community requires democracy in the international sphere ...

Cosmopolitan democratic law is most appropriately conceived as a domain of law different in kind from the law of states and the law made between one state and another (that is, international law). For Kant, the foremost interpreter of the idea of a cosmopolitan law, cosmopolitan law is neither a fantastic nor a utopian way of conceiving law; it is a "necessary complement" to the unwritten code of existing national and international law, and a means of transforming the latter into a public law of humanity. Kant limited the form and scope of cosmopolitan law to the conditions of universal hospitality, by which he meant the right of a stranger or a foreigner "not to be treated with hostility" when arriving in someone else's country. He emphasized that this right extended to the circumstances that allow people to enjoy an exchange of ideas and good with the inhabitants of another country, but it did not extend as far as the right of citizenship ...

Cosmopolitan law, thus understood, transcends the particular claims of nations and states and extends to all in the "universal community." It connotes a right and a duty that must be accepted if people are to learn to tolerate one another's company and to coexist peacefully ...

The pursuit in diverse locales of individual of collective projects, within the context of a commitment to universal "good neighborliness," requites that the anatomy of power and domination be grasped in order that the legitimate boundaries of one's own autonomy and that of others can be appreciated ... Universal hospitality is not achieved if, for economic, cultural, or other reasons, the quality of the lives of others is shaped and determined in near or far-off lands without their participation, agreement, or consent. The condition of universal hospitality (or, as I would rather put it, of a cosmopolitan orientation) is not cosmopolitan law narrowly conceived—following Kant—but rather a cosmopolitan democratic public law in which power is, in principle, accountable wherever it is located and however far removed its sources are from those whom it significantly affects.

...

Kant argued firmly on behalf of confederalism in international affairs, on the ground that a single state of all peoples—a state of nations or an international state—is an impractical and potentially dangerous objective. Nonetheless, the idea of a democratic cosmopolitan order is not simply compatible with the idea of confederalism. It is the case that the establishment of a cosmopolitan democracy requires the active consent of peoples and nations: initial membership can only be voluntary ... Thereafter, however, in circumstances in which individuals are not directly engaged in the process of governance, consent ought to follow from the majority decision of their representatives, so long as the latter—the trustees of the governed—uphold cosmopolitan democratic law and its covenants.

The institutional program of cosmopolitan democracy

Against the background of these arguments, how should democracy be understood? The problem of democracy in our times is to specify how it can be secured in a series of interconnected power and authority centers. Democracy involves not only the implementation of a cluster of civil, political, and social rights (freedom of speech, press, and assembly, the right to vote in free and fair elections, universal education, and so on) but also the pursuit and the enactment of these rights in a transnational and inter-governmental power structure. Democracy can only be fully sustained in and through the agencies and organizations that form an element of, and yet cut across, the territorial boundaries of the nation state ...

To begin with, the cosmopolitan model requires, as a transitional measure, that the UN system actually live up to its charter. Among other things, this would involve pursuing measures to implement key elements of rights conventions, enforcing the prohibition on the discretionary right to use force, and activating the collective security system envisaged in the UN charter ...

However, while each move in this direction would be significant, particularly in enhancing the prospects of a more enduring peace, it would still represent, at best, a move toward a very partial or incomplete form of democracy in international life ...

Thus, hand in hand with the changes already described, the cosmopolitan model of democracy would seek the creation of regional parliaments (for example, in Latin America and in Africa) and the enhancement of the role of such bodies where they already exist (as in Europe) in order that their decisions become recognized, in principle, as legitimate independent sources of law ...

Furthermore, alongside these developments, the cosmopolitan model of democracy would seek the [entrenchment of a cluster of rights, including civil, political, economic, and social rights, in order to provide shape and limits to democratic decision making. This requires that such rights be enshrined within the constitutions of parliaments and assemblies (at the national and international level) and that the influence of international courts be extended so that groups and individuals have an effective means of suing political authorities for the enactment and enforcement of key rights, within and beyond political associations.]

In the final analysis, the formation of an authoritative assembly of all democratic states and agencies—a reformed General Assembly of the United Nations, or a complement to it—would be an objective. Agreement on the terms of reference of an international democratic assembly would be difficult, to say the least. Among the difficulties to be faced would be the rules determining the assembly's representative base. (Should one country get one vote? Could major international functional organizations be represented?) But if its operating rules could be settled—in an international constitutional convention, for example—the new assembly would become an authoritative international center for the consideration and examination of pressing global issues such as health and disease, food supply and distribution, the debt burden of the Third World, the instability of the hundreds of billions of dollars that circulate the globe daily, ozone depletion, and reducing the risks of nuclear and chemical warfare.

...

The cosmopolitan conception of democracy is a means of strengthening democracy "within" communities and civil associations by elaborating and reinforcing democracy from "outside" through a network of regional and international agencies and assemblies that cut across spatially delimited locales. The impetus to the pursuit of this network can be found in a number of processes and forces, including the development of transnational grass-roots movements with clear regional or global objectives, such as the protection of natural resources and the environment, and the alleviation of disease and ill health; the elaboration of new legal rights and duties affecting states and individuals in connection with the "common heritage of mankind," the protection of the "global commons," the defence of human rights, and the deployment of force; and the emergence and proliferation in the twentieth century of international institutions to coordinate transnational forces and problems, from the UN and its agencies to regional political networks and organizations. Accordingly, it can be argued, a political basis exists upon which to build a more systematic democratic future.

This future ought to be conceived in cosmopolitan terms—a new institutional complex with global scope, given shape and form by reference to a basic democratic law, that takes on the character of government to the extent, and only to the extent, that it promulgates, implements, and enforces this law. But however its institutions are precisely envisaged, it is a future built on the recognition that democracy within a single community and democratic relations among communities are deeply interconnected, and that new organizational and legal mechanisms must be established if democracy is to survive and prosper.

3.5 The case for contamination

Kwame Anthony Appiah

1

I'm seated, with my mother, on a palace veranda, cooled by a breeze from the royal garden. Before us, on a dais, is an empty throne, its arms and legs embossed with polished brass, the back and seat covered in black-and-gold silk. In front of the steps to the dais, there are two columns of people, mostly men, facing one another, seated on carved wooden stools, the cloths they wear wrapped around their chests, leaving their shoulders bare. There is a quiet buzz of conversation. Outside in the garden, peacocks screech. At last, the blowing of a ram's horn announces the arrival of the king of Asante, its tones sounding his honorific, *kotokohene*, "porcupine chief." (Each quill of the porcupine, according to custom, signifies a warrior ready to kill and to die for the kingdom.) Everyone stands until the king has settled on the throne. Then, when we sit, a chorus sings songs in praise of him, which are interspersed with the playing of a flute. It is a Wednesday festival day in Kumasi, the town in Ghana where I grew up.

Unless you're one of a few million Ghanaians, this will probably seem a relatively unfamiliar world, perhaps even an exotic one. You might suppose that this Wednesday festival belongs quaintly to an African past. But before the king arrived, people were taking calls on cellphones, and among those passing the time in quiet conversation were a dozen men in suits, representatives of an insurance company. And the meetings in the office next to the veranda are about contemporary issues: H.I.V./AIDS, the educational needs of 21st century children, the teaching of science and technology at the local university. When my turn comes to be formally presented, the king asks me about Princeton, where I teach. I ask him when he'll next be in the States. In a few weeks, he says cheerfully. He's got a meeting with the head of the World Bank.

Anywhere you travel in the world—today as always—you can find ceremonies like these, many of them rooted in centuries-old traditions. But you will also find everywhere—and this is something new—many intimate connections with places far away: Washington, Moscow, Mexico City, Beijing …

What are we to make of this? On Kumasi's Wednesday festival day, I've seen visitors from England and the United States wince at what they regard as the intrusion of modernity on timeless, traditional rituals—more evidence, they think, of a pressure in the modern world toward uniformity. They react like the assistant on the film set who's supposed to check that the extras in a sword-and-sandals movie aren't wearing wristwatches. And such purists are not alone. In the past couple of years, Unesco's members have spent a great deal of time trying to hammer out a convention on the "protection and promotion" of cultural diversity. (It was finally approved at the Unesco General Conference in October 2005.) The drafters worried that "the processes of globalization ... represent a challenge for cultural diversity, namely in view of risks of imbalances between rich and poor countries." The fear is that the values and images of Western mass culture, like some invasive weed, are threatening to choke out the world's native flora.

The contradictions in this argument aren't hard to find. This same Unesco document is careful to affirm the importance of the free flow of ideas, the freedom of thought and expression and human rights—values that, we know, will become universal only if we make them so. What's really important, then, cultures or people? In a world where Kumasi and New York—and Cairo and Leeds and Istanbul—are being drawn ever closer together, an ethics of globalization has proved elusive.

The right approach, I think, starts by taking individuals—not nations, tribes or "peoples"—as the proper object of moral concern. It doesn't much matter what we call such a creed, but in homage to Diogenes, the fourth-century Greek Cynic and the first philosopher to call himself a "citizen of the world," we could call it cosmopolitan. Cosmopolitans take cultural difference seriously, because they take the choices individual people make seriously. But because cultural difference is not the only thing that concerns them, they suspect that many of globalization's cultural critics are aiming at the wrong targets.

Yes, globalization can produce homogeneity. But globalization is also a threat to homogeneity ...

[T]he enclaves of homogeneity you find these days—in Asante as in Pennsylvania—are less distinctive than they were a century ago, but mostly in good ways. More of them have access to effective medicines. More of them have access to clean drinking water, and more of them have schools. Where, as is still too common, they don't have these things, it's something not to celebrate but to deplore. And whatever loss of difference there has been, they are constantly inventing new forms of difference: new hairstyles, new slang, even, from time to time, new religions. No one could say that the world's villages are becoming anything like the same.

So why do people in these places sometimes feel that their identities are threatened? Because the world, their world, is changing, and some of them don't like it. The pull of the global economy—witness those cocoa trees, whose chocolate is eaten all around the world—created some of the life they now live. If chocolate prices were to collapse again, as they did in the early 1990's, Asante farmers might have to find new crops or new forms of livelihood. That prospect is unsettling for some people (just as it is exciting for others). Missionaries came awhile ago, so many of these villagers will be Christian, even if they have also kept some of the rites from earlier days. But new Pentecostal messengers are challenging the churches they know and condemning the old rites as idolatrous. Again, some like it; some don't.

Above all, relationships are changing. When my father was young, a man in a village would farm some land that a chief had granted him, and his maternal clan (including his younger brothers) would work it with him. When a new house needed building, he would organize it. He would also make sure his dependants were fed and clothed, the children educated, marriages and funerals arranged and paid for. He could expect to pass the farm and the responsibilities along to the next generation.

Nowadays, everything is different. Cocoa prices have not kept pace with the cost of living. Gas prices have made the transportation of the crop more expensive. And there are new possibilities for the young in the towns, in other parts of the country and in other parts of the world. Once, perhaps, you could have commanded the young ones to stay. Now they have the right to leave—perhaps to seek work at one of the new data-processing centers down south in the nation's capital—and, anyway, you may not make enough to feed and clothe and educate them all. So the time of the successful farming family is passing, and those who were settled in that way of life are as sad to see it go as American family farmers are whose lands are accumulated by giant agribusinesses. We can sympathize with them. But we cannot force their children to stay in the name of protecting their authentic culture, and we cannot afford to subsidize indefinitely thousands of distinct islands of homogeneity that no longer make economic sense.

Nor should we want to. Human variety matters, cosmopolitans think, because people are entitled to options. What John Stuart Mill said more than a century ago in "On Liberty" about diversity within a society serves just as well as an argument for variety across the globe: "If it were only that people have diversities of taste, that is reason enough for not attempting to shape them all after one model. But different persons also require different conditions for their spiritual development; and can no more exist healthily in the same moral, than all the variety of plants can exist in the same physical, atmosphere and climate. The same things which are helps to one person towards the cultivation of his higher nature, are hindrances to another ... Unless there is a corresponding diversity in their modes of life, they neither obtain their fair share of happiness, nor grow up to the mental, moral, and aesthetic stature of which their nature is capable." If we want to preserve a wide range of human conditions because it allows free people the best chance to make their own lives, we can't enforce diversity by trapping people within differences they long to escape …

The preservationists often make their case by invoking the evil of "cultural imperialism." Their underlying picture, in broad strokes, is this: There is a world system of capitalism. It has a center and a periphery. At the center—in Europe and the United States—is a set of multinational corporations. Some of these are in the media business. The products they sell around the world promote the creation of desires that can be fulfilled only by the purchase and use of their products. They do this explicitly through advertising, but more insidiously, they also do so through the messages implicit in movies and in television drama. Herbert Schiller, a leading critic of "media-cultural imperialism," claimed that "it is the imagery and cultural perspectives of the ruling sector in the center that shape and structure consciousness throughout the system at large."

That's the theory, anyway. But the evidence doesn't bear it out. Researchers have actually gone out into the world and explored the responses to the hit television series "Dallas" in Holland and among Israeli Arabs, Moroccan Jewish immigrants, kibbutzniks and new Russian immigrants to Israel. They have examined the actual content of the television media—whose penetration of everyday life far exceeds that of film—in Australia, Brazil, Canada, India and Mexico. They have looked at how American popular culture was taken up by the artists of Sophiatown, in South Africa. They have discussed "Days of Our Lives" and "The Bold and the Beautiful" with Zulu college students from traditional backgrounds.

And one thing they've found is that how people respond to these cultural imports depends on their existing cultural context. When the media scholar Larry Strelitz spoke to students from KwaZulu-Natal, he found that they were anything but passive vessels. One of them, Sipho—a self-described "very, very strong Zulu man"—reported that he had drawn lessons from watching the American soap opera "Days of Our Lives," "especially relationship-wise." It fortified his view that "if a guy can tell a woman that he loves her, she should be able to do the same." What's more, after watching the show, Sipho "realized that I should be allowed to speak to my father. He should be my friend rather than just my father." It seems doubtful that that was the intended message of multinational capitalism's ruling sector.

But Sipho's response also confirmed that cultural consumers are not dupes. They can adapt products to suit their own needs, and they can decide for themselves what they do and do not approve of …

In fact, one way that people sometimes respond to the onslaught of ideas from the West is to turn them against their originators. It's no accident that the West's fiercest adversaries among other societies tend to come from among the most Westernized of the group …

Sometimes, though, people react to the incursions of the modern world not by appropriating the values espoused by the liberal democracies but by inverting them. One recent result has been a new worldwide fraternity that presents cosmopolitanism with something of a sinister mirror image. Indeed, you could think of its members as counter-cosmopolitans. They believe in human dignity across the nations, and they live their creed. They share these ideals with people in many countries, speaking many languages. As thorough-going globalists, they make full use of the World Wide Web. They resist the crass consumerism of modern Western society and deplore its influence in the rest of the world. But they also resist the temptations of the narrow nationalisms of the countries where they were born, along with the humble allegiances of kith and kin. They resist such humdrum loyalties because they get in the way of the one thing that matters: building a community of enlightened men and women across the world. That is one reason they reject traditional religious authorities (though they disapprove, too, of their obscurantism and temporizing). Sometimes they agonize in their discussions about whether they can reverse the world's evils or whether their struggle is hopeless. But mostly they soldier on in their efforts to make the world a better place.

These are not the heirs of Diogenes the Cynic. The community these comrades are building is not a polis; it's what they call the ummah, the global community of Muslims, and it is open to all who share their faith. They are young, global Muslim fundamentalists. The ummah's new globalists consider that they have returned to the fundamentals of Islam; much of what passes for Islam in the world, much of what has passed as Islam for centuries, they think a sham ...

Unlike cosmopolitanism, of course, it is universalist without being tolerant ...

Yet tolerance by itself is not what distinguishes the cosmopolitan from the neofundamentalist. There are plenty of things that the heroes of radical Islam are happy to tolerate. They don't care if you eat kebabs or meatballs or kung pao chicken, as long as the meat is halal; your hijab can be silk or linen or viscose. At the same time, there are plenty of things that cosmopolitans will not tolerate. We will sometimes want to intervene in other places because what is going on there violates our principles so deeply. We, too, can see moral error. And when it is serious enough—genocide is the least-contro-versial case—we will not stop with conversation. Toleration has its limits.

Nor can you tell us apart by saying that the neofundamentalists believe in universal truth. Cosmopolitans believe in universal truth, too, though we are less certain that we already have all of it. It is not skepticism about the very idea of truth that guides us; it is realism about how hard the truth is to find. One tenet we hold to, however, is that every human being has obligations to every other. Everybody matters: that is our central idea. And again, it sharply limits the scope of our tolerance.

To say what, in principle, distinguishes the cosmopolitan from competing universalisms, we plainly need to go beyond talk of truth and tolerance. One distinctively cosmopolitan commitment is to pluralism. Cosmopolitans think that there are many values worth living by and that you cannot live by all of them. So we hope and expect that different people and different societies will embody different values. Another aspect of cosmopolitanism is what philosophers call fallibilism—the sense that our knowledge is imperfect, provisional, subject to revision in the face of new evidence.

The neofundamentalist conception of a global ummah, by contrast, admits of local variations—but only in matters that don't matter. These counter-cosmopolitans, like many Christian fundamentalists, do think that there is one right way for all human beings to live; that all the differences must be in the details …

That liberal pluralists are hostile to certain authoritarian ways of life—that they're intolerant of radical intolerance—is sometimes seen as kind of self-refutation. That's a mistake: you can care about individual freedom and still understand that the contours of that freedom will vary considerably from place to place. But we might as well admit that a concern for individual freedom isn't something that will appeal to every individual. In politics, including cultural politics, there are winners and losers—which is worth remembering when we think about international human rights treaties. When we seek to embody our concern for strangers in human rights law, and when we urge our government to enforce it, we are seeking to change the world of law in every nation on the planet. We have declared slavery a violation of international law. And, in so doing, we have committed ourselves, at a minimum, to the desirability of its eradication everywhere. This is no longer controversial in the capitals of the world. No one defends enslavement. But international treaties define slavery in ways that arguably include debt bondage, and debt bondage is a significant economic institution in parts of South Asia. I hold no brief for debt bondage. Still, we shouldn't be surprised if people whose incomes and style of life depend upon it are angry …

So liberty and diversity may well be at odds, and the tensions between them aren't always easily resolved …

A tenable global ethics has to temper a respect for difference with a respect for the freedom of actual human beings to make their own choices. That's why cosmopolitans don't insist that everyone become cosmopolitan. They know they don't have all the answers. They're humble enough to think that they might learn from strangers; not too humble to think that strangers can't learn from them. Few remember what Chremes says after his "I am human" line, but it is equally suggestive: "If you're right, I'll do what you do. If you're wrong, I'll set you straight."

Part 3

Conventional cosmopolitanism visions generally seek to create ethical structures that are grounded in Western philosophy but that can nevertheless be universally adopted. While continuing to employ the term cosmopolitanism, the readings we will now consider suggest that a universal ethic is a remote possibility, not to mention an undesirable one for cultures that have weathered the imposition of the West for centuries already. These essays raise an important issue to consider here: cosmopolitanism as it was presented in the readings above might best be regarded as a local ethical framework for approaching the world. Its claims to universality, however, may well mark it as another (arguably kinder and gentler) articulation of Western imperialism.

We broach this subject immediately with the first essay written by American sociologist Craig Calhoun. Calhoun argues, contra Nussbaum and Held for example, that a global secular ethic is not a realistic expectation in our era: a universally shared sense of morality and solidarity cannot be a straightforward mediator between uncontrolled capitalism and traditionalism. He believes that global perspectives are always idiosyncratic, that they are based on local bonds forged in terms of national, ethnic, and religious variables. Furthermore, he suggests that cosmopolitan ethics are no less idiosyncratic than any others: "Cosmopolitanism is not universalism; it is belonging to a social class able to identify itself with the universal."

The essays following Calhoun's are written by two Indian intellectuals: Ashis Nandy, a Bengali political and social psychologist, and literary theorist Srinivas Aravamudan who was born in Madras and now lives in the United States. Nandy proposes a form of cosmopolitanism that has an entirely different point of departure from those we considered in Part 2. Whereas none of the previous readings explored the tangible ways in which late modernity has been shaped by its history of contact with the imperializing West, Nandy embarks on a search for cosmopolitan meanings that focuses on the fall-out of this history. The West, he writes, has unavoidably and indelibly altered Asian societies. The troubling side of this is that non-western cultural discourses are too often filtered through Western conceptual categories. But he also contends that Asia, Africa and South America may be the only places on the planet where multiculturalism truly thrives. He suggests that a viable global ethic can be one only that draws its resources from the "subjugated West"—the cultural spaces where modern people have been forced to survive within multiple overlapping cultural orders in which there have been imbalances of power.

Srinivas Aravamudan picks up on the term cosmopolitanism and in some ways he turns it on its head. Here we find a trenchant critique of Western cosmopolitanism as a secular ethical construct, one that requires the death of the gods in the interest of creating a universal ethical philosophy. It is, he writes, "a bourgeois, Western, or delocalized aesthetic aspiration." In its place, Aravamudan describes a cosmopolitanism he dubs guru English— the religious vocabulary of the subcontinent that was translated by Indian scholars over two centuries into English. These transcriptions were created to ensure scholars' ongoing role in colonial structures of power by providing British colonials with information they wanted to better understand the population they were seeking to control. However, these transcriptions influenced not only colonial administrators but moved out into a global marketplace where their influence was felt both within the British Empire and throughout the modern West. Thus they have created an entirely different set of cosmopolitan discourses and practices whose genesis was in religious texts and political contingencies specific to colonial India.

3.6 Cosmopolitanism and nationalism

Craig Calhoun

Cosmopolitanism has become an enormously popular rhetorical vehicle for claiming at once to be already global and to have the highest ethical aspirations for what globalization can offer. It names a virtue of considerable importance. But, and these are my themes, it is not at all clear (a) that cosmopolitanism is quite so different from nationalism as sometimes supposed, (b) whether cosmopolitanism is really supplanting nationalism in global politics, and (c) whether cosmopolitanism is an ethical complement to politics, or in some usages a substitution of ethics for politics.

Cosmopolitanism in the modern social imaginary

Salman Rushdie writes that "among the great struggles of man—good/evil, reason/unreason, etc.—there is also this mighty conflict between the fantasy of Home and the fantasy of Away, the dream of roots and the mirage of the journey." Cosmopolitanism is a central way in which the modern era has organised "the fantasy of Away." The term is operative in culture and commerce, ethics and politics. Whether as the fashionable man of the world or the responsible (and gender neutral) citizen of the world, the cosmopolitan inhabits the world.

...

Paris is more cosmopolitan than Lille, one might argue, and New York more cosmopolitan than Cleveland (and neither Lille nor Cleveland is at the opposite end of the spectrum). The meaning is primarily that the city's diversity reflects that of the world—without denying that many inhabitants of Paris and New York are in fact quite parochial in their perspectives ...

Sometimes cosmopolitan is used loosely simply to mean transnational. Often it denotes a more rigorous stress on the truly universal. This is crucial to most systematic uses of the term in ethics and political philosophy ... Most ethical thinking approaches the whole, the universal, as a complete set of all human individuals (usually those alive at one time, though occasionally ancestors and more often those yet to be born are also given consideration) ... But thinking in terms of a set or category of human individuals misses part of what makes cosmopolitanism a compelling concern today: the extraordinary growth of connections among human beings and variously organised social groups, relationships mediated by markets and media, migrations and infectious diseases.

Precisely because the world is so intensively connected today, cosmopolitanism has become an important theme in politics and social science, not only ethics. It figures in practical affairs and public debates as well as intellectual explorations. Interest in cosmopolitanism has also been fueled by anxieties over identity politics and multiculturalism. Many commentators are worried that efforts to support different ways of life undermine the common culture required by democracy. They think that too much respect for ethnic and cultural differences among nations undermines attempts to enforce universal human rights.

...

Globalization can lead to renewed nationalism or strengthening of borders—as has often been the case since the 2001 terrorist attacks ... Globalization requires an ethics not only because ordinary people find themselves interacting more often with people from other countries, cultures, and religions but because they are implicated in relationships with others around the world whom they will never meet. Through trade and foreign aid and wars and diplomacy and the tourist industry and the global organization of religion, people on every continent are joined to others through indirect relationships. These are mediated by information technology, business corporations, governments, and NGOs. But they remain human relationships and therefore demand ethical evaluation ...

[But] globalization demands more than ethics. Precisely because so many of the crucial relationships that drive and shape it are indirect, they do not resolve easily into interpersonal norms. They require action aimed at states, corporations, markets, and media—systems and technologies in short. They require politics. And politics is required in another sense as well, the sense of political speech that constitutes social organisation, not only interpersonal relationships.

Mixing fashion, commerce, ethics, and politics

... [C]osmopolitanism lives a double life as a pop cultural evocation of openness to a larger world and a sometimes more systematic and academic claim about the moral significance of transcending the local, even achieving the universal. Both have flourished especially in good times and amid optimism about globalization ...

...

Cosmopolitanism signals a direct connection between the individual and the world as a whole. But if this is sometimes given ethical emphasis, equally often the world appears simply as an object of consumption, there for individuals' pleasure ...

...

The issue is not just one of consumerism versus ethics, or the coexistence of stylistic cosmopolitanism with political nationalism. It is the tendency to substitute ethics or style for deeper senses of politics. Cosmopolitan typically suggests an attitude or virtue that can be assumed without change in basic political or economic structures—which are external to the individual. Much of its appeal comes from the notion that cosmopolitanism (a version of ethical goodness) can be achieved without such deeper change. But therein lies a key problem in an otherwise attractive concept.

Cosmopolitanism is not simply a free-floating cultural taste, personal attitude or political choice, however; it is a matter of institutions. What seems like free individual choice is often made possible by capital—social and cultural as well as economic. Take the slogan in Sony's recent computer advertisements: "C is for Choice, Color, and Cosmopolitanism" (Business Wire 2006). Surely C is also for capital.

...

The markets, the migrations, and the media that encourage and shape cosmopolitanism are not simply responses to individual taste or morality but creatures of capitalism. This does not determine every detail of their operation nor does it make them necessarily bad. But it does mean that cosmopolitanism is not free-floating, not equally available to everyone, not equally empowering for everyone. The material globalization on which cosmopolitanism rests is strikingly unequal as well as uprooting. This is one of the reasons why the cosmopolitanism of some sparks the resentments of others. But it would be a mistake to identify anxieties about cosmopolitanism simply with resentment or indeed with ethnic prejudice or benighted localism. In the first place localism is not always benighted. More basically, belonging to specific social groups is an important source of collective strength for many; the solidarity of these groups is a basis for action to redress many ills and sometimes even to mitigate inequality; communities, nations, and religions motivate many in ways that abstract membership of the human race does not. We need not simply oppose cosmopolitanism and belonging, as universalism and particularism are opposed in logic and in Parsonsian theory. They can be complements to each other.

The melting pot

The cosmopolitan critique of particularistic belonging is a sort of global revision of the older idea of a melting pot. This was proposed most famously as a description of the United States in the early twentieth century. An era of high immigration had brought together speakers of different languages, followers of different religions, people raised in different cultures ...

But the phrase had much older roots. Emerson, for example, referred in 1845 to racial and cultural mixture through the metaphor of "the smelting pot" ...

By the 1970s, some worried patriots were writing of "the rise of the unmeltable ethnics" (Novak 1973). And some happier patriots were celebrating the salad bowl or the mosaic instead of the melting pot, mixture without loss of distinction. In other words, America remained diverse and maintaining cultural distinctions and ethnic solidarities—rather than melting them away in the assimilationist pot—became a positive goal ...

... [T]he terrorist attacks of 2001 made the issue feel newly acute. Samuel Huntington, as often, caught an aspect of the national mood and framed an issue on the minds of many who hesitated to name it so bluntly. His recent book, *Who Are We?* (2004), is shaped by a deep anxiety that Hispanic immigrants do not want to become Americans in the same sense as did his WASP ancestors (it is perhaps no accident that he traces descent to immigrants who came on the Mayflower and is a descendant of several generations of Harvard men). Indeed, Huntington suspects, Latin American immigrants not only don't want to assimilate, they can't. It is not clear to what extent Huntington thinks that the problem is the strength of Hispanic-Catholic identity or the unanticipated weakness of American nationalism as a culture of assimilation. Either way, he articulates a sense of threat among many in the US analogous to that which many Europeans feel over Islamic immigrants.

Yet this new anxiety over unmeltable immigrants has risen at the same time as a widespread celebration of the melting pot ideal in the form of mixed race identities. In the US this is symbolised by Barack Obama and the golfer Tiger Woods—who describes himself as "Cablinàsian": simultaneously Caucasian, Black, Indian, and Asian ...

...

Imagining a world without nations, a world in which ethnicity is simply a consumer taste, a world in which each individual simply and directly inhabits the whole, is like imagining the melting pot in which all ethnicities vanish into the formation of a new kind of individual. In each case this produces an ideology especially attractive to some. It neglects the reasons why many others need and reproduce ethnic or national distinctions. And perhaps most importantly it obscures the issues of inequality that make ethnically unmarked national identities accessible mainly to elites, and make an easy sense of being a citizen of the world contingent on having the right passports, credit cards, and cultural credentials.

...

Cosmopolitanism is most often invoked by those who see identity politics as a sort of mistake—like lingering ethnonationalism, rather than citizenship of the world. But the issues haven't gone away. European politics is rife with struggles over whether national identities or the common claim of "European" should be primary. There are few African countries where claims for religious, or ethnic, or regional or "tribal" identities aren't sometimes as powerful as projects of national integration. Latin American countries find themselves in common identity in the struggle against US domination, but internally are split by movements deriving significant force from indigenous resentment against elites defined in part by European ancestry (as well as cosmopolitan property). The economic rise of China both masks identity struggles within the People's Republic and intensifies others around Asia. And from the Middle East through South and Southeast Asia (and indeed in Europe, Africa, and the US) Islamic renewal generates both struggles over identity and struggles defined by religious identities that modernisation theorists had pronounced permanently fading.

Universalism as style

As a social condition, cosmopolitanism is not universalism; it is belonging to a social class able to identify itself with the universal. Belonging to the global cosmopolitan class is structured by social institutions just as surely as belonging to a local caste in India or a Parisian quartier anxious about Arab neighbors or European unification. We should be accordingly cautious about following earlier modernisation theories in identifying cosmopolitan unambiguously with progress or following individualistic philosophical traditions that approach such cosmopolitanism overwhelmingly as a matter of individual ethical judgment ...

...

Contemporary cosmopolitanism commonly reflects the experience and perspective of elites and obscures the social foundations on which that experience and perspective rests. Thinking about cosmopolitanism as ethical universalism reinforces the lack of attention to the social foundations on which it rests—even when ethical universalism might be a basis for egalitarian critique.

Whether in the Roman Empire for the Stoics, or the (temporary) post-Westphalian pacification and growth of European states for Kant, or the great trading and imperial cities of high modernity, or global capitalism today, cosmopolitanism always depends on social foundations. Transnational institutions can be developed that offer ordinary people greater voice. Emerging global elite culture and mass for-profit consumer culture can both be contested. International law and regulation can limit both capitalist rapacity and state violence. But cosmopolitanism alone commonly focuses attention away from these political, economic, and social questions and towards apparently free-floating ethics and culture.

Thinking about cosmopolitanism as taste or even intellectual orientation reinforces its association with elites and makes it harder to understand the actually existing cosmopolitanism of multicultural cities (which involves not only stylish consumption or the gaze of *flâneurs* but soccer matches, ethnic jokes and grudging accommodation of neighbors). This connects to a tendency to imagine cosmopolitanism more as escape from the constraints of cultural prejudice than the production of cultural capacities for interaction and integration. If we look more at the material and institutional underpinnings of actual cosmopolitanism we will see less rational planning and more historical production of varied practical ways of organising life across, not only in, communities. Thinking about cosmopolitanism as a political idea demands attention to whether it is a corrective and complement to national and other solidarities or itself grounded in some other global solidarity.

Cosmopolitan style and taste and ethics and politics can reinforce each other but also contend with each other. I want to raise questions about the tendency for cosmopolitan ethics to substitute for transnational politics, about the tendency for abstract thinking about the potential global whole to undermine appreciation for actual if incomplete and imperfect integration in cities, nations, and religions. Integrating only part of humanity, I will suggest, doesn't mean merely being particularistic or parochial.

...

Some writers identify cosmopolitanism with a reflexive, open, inclusive normative consciousness. Martha Nussbaum (1996), for example, sees cosmopolitanism in terms of individual selves, located amid concentric circles of potential connections—and sees cosmopolitanism as the ethically superior identification with and sense of obligation to the widest, maximally universal circle of humans as a whole. Anthony Appiah (2006) has argued for a "rooted cosmopolitanism" in which local ties still matter even amid far-flung connections and with a global ethical consciousness. If his is the perspective of postcolonial cultural elites, and more generally those who came from somewhere but went to Princeton (and Harvard and Oxford), others stress the extent to which a range of different occupations, even warfare, may bring recognition of the larger world beyond local (or national) cultural roots. But in all these cases, cosmopolitanism is an "outlook." It is about either ethical obligations or cultural openness.

Cosmopolitanism may be a cultural orientation, but it is never the absence of culture. It is produced and reinforced by belonging to transnational networks and to a community of fellow-cosmopolitans. There are different such communities—academic and corporate and NGO, religious and secular. One may participate in multiple such networks, but it is an illusion—an ideological illusion—to imagine citizenship of the world as simply freedom from belonging to more sectional groupings.

...

It is impossible not to belong to social groups, relations, or culture. The idea of individuals abstract enough to be able to choose all their "identifications" is deeply misleading. Versions of this idea are, however, widespread in liberal cosmopolitanism. They reflect the attractive illusion of escaping from social determinations into a realm of greater freedom, and from cultural particularity into greater universalism. But they are remarkably unrealistic, and so abstract as to provide little purchase on what the next steps of actual social action might be for real people who are necessarily situated in particular webs of belonging, with access to particular others but not to humanity in general. Treating ethnicity as essentially (rather than partially) a choice of identifications, they neglect the omnipresence of ascription (and discrimination) as determinations of social identities. They neglect the huge inequalities in the supports available to individuals to enter cosmopolitan intercourse as individuals (and also the ways in which certain socially distributed supports like wealth, education, and command of the English language are understood as personal achievements or attributes). And they neglect the extent to which people are implicated in social actions which they are not entirely free to choose (as, for example, I remain an American and share responsibility for the invasion of Iraq despite my opposition to it and distaste for the US administration that launched it). Whether blame or benefit follow from such implications, they are not altogether optional.

Cosmopolitanism seems to signal both the identity (and therefore unity) of all human beings despite their differences, and appreciation for and ability to feel at home among the actual differences among people and peoples. We focus sometimes on the essential similarity of people and sometimes on their diversity.

We should be careful not to imagine that either sort of cosmopolitanism is an immediately useful example for democracy. Modern democracy grew in close relationship to nationalism, as the ideal of self-determination demanded a strong notion of the collective self in question. Nationalism was also (at least often) an attempt to reconcile liberty and ethical universalism with felt community. This doesn't mean that we should not seek more cosmopolitan values, cultural knowledge, and styles of interpersonal relations in modern national democracies. It certainly doesn't mean that we should embrace reactionary versions of nationalism which have often been antidemocratic as well as anticosmopolitan. But it does mean that we need to ask some hard questions about how cosmopolitanism relates to the construction of political and social solidarities. Does cosmopolitanism actually underpin effective political solidarity, or only offer an attractive counterbalance to nationalism? How can we reconcile the important potential of multiple and hybrid cultural and social identities with political participation and rights? What is the relationship between valuing difference and having a strong enough commitment to specific others to sacrifice in collective struggle or accept democracy's difficult challenge of living in a minority and attempting only to persuade and not simply dominate others with whom one does not agree? It will not do simply to substitute ethics for politics, no matter how cosmopolitan and otherwise attractive the ethics. It will not do to imagine democratic politics without paying serious attention to the production of strong solidarity among the subjects of struggles for greater self-determination.

Many forms and visions of belonging are also responses to globalization, not merely inheritances from time immemorial. Nations and national identities, for example, have been forged in international relations from wars to trade, in international migrations and among those who traveled as well as those who feared their arrival, and in pursuit of popular sovereignty against traditional rulers. Nationalism has often grown stronger when globalization has intensified. Islam, Christianity, Buddhism and other religions arose in the contexts of empires and conflicts but also have been remade as frames of identity crossing nations and yet locating believers in a multireligious world. Religion has shaped globalization not only as a source of conflict but of peace-making. The significance of local community has repeatedly been changed by incorporation into broader structures of trade and association. And communal values have been articulated both to defend havens in a seemingly heartless world and to set examples for global imitation. While structures of belonging may be shaped by tradition, thus, we need to understand them not merely as traditional alternatives to modernity or cosmopolitanism but as important ways in which ordinary people have tried to take hold of modernity and to locate themselves in a globalising world.

In a broad, general sense cosmopolitanism is unexceptionable. Who—at least what sophisticated intellectual—could argue for parochialism over a broader perspective, for narrow sectarian loyalties over recognition of global responsibilities? Who could be against citizenship of the world? But the word "citizenship" is a clue to the difficulty. Cosmopolitanism means something very different as a political project—or as the project of substituting universalistic ethics for politics—from what it means as a general orientation to difference in the world. And a central strand of political theory is now invested in hopes for cosmopolitan democracy, democracy not limited by nation-states. In the spirit of Kant as well as Diogenes, many say, people should see themselves as citizens of the world, not just of their countries. This requires escape from the dominance of a nationalist social imaginary (that is, a nationalist way of understanding what society is and constituting new political communities).

It is an escape that carries the risk of throwing the baby out with the bathwater. We should, I think, join in recognizing the importance of transnational relations and therefore transnational politics, movements, and ethics. We should try to belong to the world as a whole and help it thrive, and be more just and better organized. But we should not imagine we can do so very well by ignoring or wishing away national and local solidarities. This is something I think the work of Ernest Gellner affirms. We need to be global in part through how we are national. And we need to recognize the ways national—and ethnic and religious—solidarities work for others. If we are among those privileged to transcend national identities and limits in our travel and academic conferences and reading and friendships we should nonetheless be attentive to the social conditions of our outlook and the situations of those who do not share our privileges.

3.7 Defining a new cosmopolitanism: Towards a dialogue of Asian civilizations

Ashis Nandy

Asia has known the West for about two millennia and has interacted with the West seriously for over six hundred years. But it began to have a third kind of close encounter with the West starting from the eighteenth century, when the industrial revolution and the discovery and colonization of the Americas gave the West a new self confidence *vis-à-vis* its eastern neighbour. Asia no longer remained a depository of ancient riches-philosophies, sciences or religions that had crucially shaped the European civilisation, including its two core constituents: Christianity and modern science. Nor did it remain solely the depository of the exotic and the esoteric-rare spices, perfumes, silks and particularly potent mystics and shamans. Asia was now redefined as another arena where the fates of the competing nation-states of Europe were going to be decided.

It is at the fag end of this phase of Europe's world domination that we stand today, ready to pick up the fragments of our lives and cultures that have survived two centuries of European hegemony and intrusion. For while some Asians have become rich and others powerful during these two hundred years, none has emerged from the experience culturally unscathed.

Asian cultures never responded to the European encroachment passively, even though many Asian nationalists of earlier generations felt that that was exactly what their cultures had done. While that sentiment is not absent today among Asia's ruling élite and young Asians charged with nationalist fervour, it is now pretty obvious that Asian civilisations, whatever else they may or may not have done, have certainly not been passive spectators of their own humiliation and subjugation. They coped with the West in diverse ways—sometimes aggressively resisting its intrusiveness, sometimes trying to neutralise it by giving it indigenous meanings, sometimes even incorporating the West as an insulated module within their traditional cultural selves.

However, all Asian cultures have gradually found out during the last two hundred years that—unlike the European Christendom or the traditional West—the modern West finds it difficult to coexist with other cultures. It may have a well-developed language of coexistence and tolerance and well-honed tools for conversing with other civilisations. It may even have the cognitive riches to study, understand or decode the non-West. But, culturally, it has an exceeding poor capacity to live with strangers. It has to try to either overwhelm or proselytise them. Is this a trait derived from the urban-industrial vision and global capitalism which, not satiated even after winning over every major country in the world, have to penetrate the smallest of villages and the most private areas of our personal lives? Is it a contribution of the ideologues of development, who after all their successes, still feel defeated if some remote community somewhere does not fall in line or some eccentric individual attacks them? I do not know, but I do find that even most dissenting westerners, who have genuinely identified with the colonised societies and fought for their cause, sometimes at some personal cost, have usually supported the `right' causes without any empathy with native categories or languages of dissent, without even a semblance of respect for the indigenous modes of resistance, philosophical or practical. It will not be too uncharitable to say that they, too, have struggled to retain the capital of dissent in the West and to remain flamboyant spokespersons of the oppressed of the world—whether the oppressed are the proverbial proletariat or the not-so-proverbial women, working children or victims of environmental depredations. Even decolonization demands western texts and academic leadership, they believe. And many Asians, especially the expatriate Asians in the first world, enthusiastically agree.

As the West has been partly internalised during the colonial period, its cultural stratarchy and arrogance, too, have been introjected by important sections of the colonised societies and by societies not colonised but living with fears of being colonised. They all have learnt to live with this internalised West-the feared intimate enemy, simultaneously a target of love and hate—as I have elsewhere described it. Psychoanalysts should be happy to identify the process as a copybook instance of the ego defence called "identification with the aggressor." For this adored enemy is a silent spectator in even our most intimate moments and the uninvited guest at our most culturally typical events and behaviour. For even our religions and festivities, our birth, marriage and death rituals, our food and clothing, our concepts of traditional learning and wisdom have all been deeply affected by the modern West. Even return to traditions in Asia often means a return to traditions as they have been redefined under western hegemony. Even our pasts do not belong to us entirely.

This is not an unmitigated disaster. It is possible to argue that Asia, Africa and South America are the only cultural regions that are truly multi-cultural today. Because in these parts of the world, living simultaneously in two cultures—the modern western and the vernacular—is no longer a matter of cognitive choice, but a matter of day-to-day survival for the humble, the unexposed and the ill-educated. Compared to that multicultural sensitivity, the fashionable contemporary ideologies of multiculturalism and post-coloniality in our times look both shallow and provincial.

One of the most damaging legacies of colonialism, however, lies in a domain that attracts little attention. The West's centrality in all intercultural dialogues of our times has been ensured by its dominance of the cultural language in which dialogue among nonwestern cultures takes place. Even when we talk to our neighbours, it is mediated by western categories, western assumptions and western frameworks. We have learnt to talk to even our closest neighbours through the West.

This inner demon that haunts us has managed to subvert most forms of cultural dialogue among the non-western cultures. All such dialogues today are mediated by the West as an unrecognised third participant. For each culture in Asia today, while trying to talk to another Asian culture, uses as its reference point not merely the West outside, but also its own version of an ahistorical, internalised West, which may or may not have anything to do with the empirical or geographical West. One can no longer converse with one's neighbour without conversing with its alienated self, its internalised West, and without involving one's own internalised West.

Is another model of cultural exchange—I almost said multiculturalism —possible? In the space available to me I cannot hope to give a complete answer to this question. Nor can I hope to fully defend any tentative answer that I give. Instead, I shall offer you, as a part-answer to the question, a few propositions, hoping that at least some of them you will find sensible.

First, all dialogues of civilisations and cultures today constitute a new politics of knowledge and politics of cultures. For, whether we recognize it or not, there is a major, powerful, ongoing, official dialogue of cultures in the world. The format of that ongoing dialogue has been standardized, incorporated within the dominant global structure of awareness, and institutionalized through international organizations. It can be even seen as a format that has been refined and enshrined as part of commonsense in the global mass culture. In this dialogue, the key player naturally is the modern West, but it also has a series of translators in the form of persons and institutions whose primary function is to either interpret the modern West for the benefit of other cultures or interpret other cultures for the benefit of the modern West, both under the auspices of the West. The dominant dialogue is woven around these twin sets of translations.

As a result, all proposals for alternative forms of dialogue are both a defiance of the dominant mode of dialogue and an attempt to question its hegemony, legitimacy, format or organizing principles. Even a symposium or scholarly volume on the possibilities of such a dialogue can be read as a form of dissent.

Second, the presently dominant mode of dialogue is hierarchical, unequal and oppressive because it disowns or negates the organizing principles of the self-definitions of all cultures except the modern West; it is designed to specially protect the popularized versions of the western self-definition in the global mass culture. The mode ensures that only those parts of self of other cultures are considered valuable or noteworthy in the global citadels of knowledge which conform to the ideals of western modernity and the values of the European Enlightenment. As if the Enlightenment in seventeenth-century Europe said the last word on all problems of the humanity for all times to come and subsequent generations had been left only with the right to reinterpret or update the Enlightenment vision! The other parts of nonwestern selves are seen as disposable superstitions or useless encumbrances.

The European Enlightenment's concept of history has been complicit with this process. That history has as its goal nothing less than the decomposition of all uncomfortable pasts either into sanitized texts meant for academic historians and archeologists or into a set of tamed trivia or ethnic chic meant for the tourists. In countries like China, Japan and India, it is likely that the coming generations will know Chinese, Japanese or Indian pasts mainly in terms of processes that have led to the modernization of these countries. The rest of their pasts will look like useless esoterica meant for the practitioners of disciplines such as anthropology, history of religions, fine arts or literature. The process is analogous to the way the global pharmaceutical industry systematically scans the ingredients of many traditional healing systems, to extract their active principles and, after dis-embedding them from their earlier context, incorporate them in the modern knowledge system as commercially viable constituents.

My argument is that, however apparently open and non-hierarchical the dominant mode of dialogue might look, its very organisation ensures that, within its format, all other cultures are set up to lose. They cannot bring to the dialogue their entire selves. They have to hide parts of their selves not only from others but also from their own westernised or modernized selves. These hidden or repressed part-selves have increasingly become recessive and many cultures are now defined not by the voices or lifestyles of a majority of those living in the culture but by the authoritative voices of the anthropologists, cultural historians and other area specialists speaking about these cultures in global fora. These hidden or disowned selves can now usually re-enter the public domain only in pathological forms—as ultra-nationalism, fundamentalism and defensive ethnic chauvinism. They have become the nucleus of the paradigmatic contradiction in our public life, the one between democratic participation and democratic values. Democratic participation is valued but not the conventions, world-images and philosophies of life the participants bring into public life.

Third, the dominant mode of dialogue also excludes the dissenting or the repressed West. Over the last four hundred years, the western society in its mad rush for total modernisation and total development, has lost track of its own pre-modern or non-modern traditions, at least as far as public affairs are concerned. Hans-Georg Gadamer, I am told, believes that Europe's main contribution to the world civilisation is, contrary to what Europeans now think, its rich cultural plurality. Gadamer may well be right, but any such formulation has a very short shelf life in contemporary European public life itself. In practice, Europe and North America have been re-defined as cultures of hyper-consumption and mega-technology which have nothing to learn from the rest of the world.

Fortunately, the dissenting Europe and North America I am talking about, however small and powerless, are not dead. And they do sense what their cultural dominance is doing to them. They sense that the dominance, apart from the devastation it has brought to other parts of the world, has increasingly reduced the western imperium to a provincial, monocultural existence. European and North American cultures have increasingly lost their cosmopolitanism, paradoxically because of a concept of cosmopolitanism that declares the western culture to be definitionally universal and therefore automatically cosmopolitan. Believe it or not, there is a cost of dominance, and that cost can sometimes be heavy.

Any alternative form of dialogue between cultures cannot but try to rediscover the subjugated West and make it an ally. I consider the effort to do so an important marker of the new cosmopolitanism that uses as its base the experience of suffering in Asia, Africa and South America during the last two hundred years. These parts of the world can claim today that they have learnt to live with two sets of truly internalised cultural codes—their own and, for the sake of sheer survival, that of the West. From colonialism and large-scale deculturation we may have learnt something about what is authentic dissent even in the West and what is merely a well-intentioned but narcissistic effort to ensure that the worldview of the modern West does not collapse. The first identifier of a post-colonial consciousness cannot but be an attempt to develop a language of dissent which will not make much sense—and will not try to make any sense—in the capitals of the global knowledge industry. Such a language cannot be fitted in the available moulds of dissent as an Asian, African or South American subsidiary of a grand, multinational venture in radical dissent.

A dialogue of civilisations in the coming century will, I suspect, demand adherence to at least four cardinal methodological principles: First, it will demand for the participating cultures equal rights to interpretation. If elaborate hermeneutic strategies are brought to bear upon the writings of Thomas Jefferson on democracy and Karl Marx on equality, to suggest that Jefferson's ownership of slaves did not really contaminate his commitment to human freedom or to explain away Marx's blatantly Eurocentric, often racist interpretations of Africa and Asia, the least one can do is to grant at least some consideration to Afro-Asian thinkers and social activists who were as much shaped by the loves and hates of their times. We do not have to gulp the prejudices and stereotypes of their times, but we can certainly show them the consideration we show to Plato when we discuss his thought independently of his comments on the beauties of homosexuality.

Second, the new dialogue we are envisioning will insist that we jettison the nineteenth-century evangelist legacy of comparative studies which offset the practices of one civilisation against the philosophical or normative concerns of another. Colonial literature is full of comparisons between the obscenities of the caste system in practice in South Asia and the superior humanistic values of Europe articulated in the Biblical texts or, for that matter, even in the rules of cricket. In reaction, many defensive Indians compared the moral universe of the Vedas and the Upanishads with the violence, greed and ruthless statecraft practised by the Europeans in the Southern world, to establish the moral bankruptcy of the West. The time has come for us to take a less reactive position, one that will allow us to enrich ourselves through a cultural conversation of equals. Cultures, I have argued elsewhere, do not learn from each other directly; they use new insights to reprioritise their own selves, revaluing some cultural elements and devaluing others. Every such conversation is also an invitation to self-confrontation. It allows us to arrive at new insights into the management of social pathologies to which we have become culturally inure.

Third, an authentic conversation of cultures presumes that the participants have the inner resources to own up the pathologies of their cultures and bear witness to them on behalf of other particpants in the dialogue. Such a frame of dialogue cannot but reject any explanation of such pathologies as the handiwork of marginal persons and groups who have misused their own cultures. A dialogue is no guarantee against future aberrations, but it at least ensures self-reflexivity and self-criticism. It thus keeps open the possibility of resistance. This is particularly important in our times, when entire communities, states or cultures have sometimes gone rabid. If Europe has produced Nazism and Stalinism in our times, Asia has also produced much militarism and blood-thirsty sadism in the name of revolution, nationalism and social engineering. Not long ago, Cambodia lost one-third of its people, killed by their own leaders, who believed that only thus could they ensure prosperity, freedom and justice to the remaining two-third. The birth of India and Pakistan was accompanied by the murder of a million people and the displacement of another ten million.

Finally, a conversation of cultures subverts itself when its goal becomes a culturally integrated world, not a pluricultural universe where each culture can hope to live in dignity with its own distinctiveness. The nineteenth-century dream of one world and global governance has made this century the most violent in human experience and the coming century is likely to be very sceptical towards all ideas of cultural co-existence and tolerance that seek to cope with mutual hostilities and intolerance through further homogenisation of an increasingly uniform world or within the format of nineteenth-century theories of progress or social evolutionism.

The idea of Asia carries an ambivalent load in our times. It was for two centuries converted artificially into a backyard of Europe, where the fate of the world's first super-powers were determined. It is for our generation to negotiate the responsibility of redefining Asia where some of the greatest cultural experiments of the coming century may take place. For by chance or by default, Asia has now a place for even the West. Asia once held in trusteeship even Hellenic philosophy and for a few hundred years European scholars went to the Arab world to study Plato and Aristotle. We might be holding as part of a cultural gene bank even aspects of traditional western concepts of nature (as in St Francis of Assissi or William Blake) and social relationships (as in Ralph Emerson and Henry David Thoreau) to which the West itself might some day have to return through Asia.

3.8 Guru English

Srinivas Aravamudan

The disavowal of cosmopolitanism after 1968 could be explained in the context of the global Left's repudiation of Stalinism and the decline of internationalism following decolonization. The postcolonial state, from which the gospel of diverse collectivity could have been preached (whether universalism, nonsectarian uniformitarianism, or multiculturalism), was exposed as ideologically bankrupt. Hijacked by local elites for their financial betterment and ethnic domination, the postcolonial state survives as a homeostasis between global powers and internal contradictions.

Responses to the failure of modernization theses and developmental agendas took several routes. One tendency was the repudiation of cosmopolitanism itself as a bourgeois, Western, or delocalized aesthetic aspiration, outmoded and tone-deaf to contemporary realities. A more tolerant (if patronizing) downgrading of cosmopolitanism represented it as a noble but idealist goal that could not respond to, or correspond with, the rootedness of local politics, interests, cultures, and perturbations. Thus cosmopolitanism was seen as politically ineffective but nonetheless tolerable in manifestos, mission statements, and party congresses. However, after these reactions reached the dead end of extreme particularity with the fragmentary positions of subnationalisms, radical relativism, and the micropolitics of location, it appears that several thinkers have taken a step back in the direction of the general. This is not total retreat but a shuffle between globalization and localization that leads to a "glocalization" of uncertain consequence. Such a newly cautious cosmopolitanism attempts to rebuild and pluralize cosmopolitanism from below. Its theorists thereby describe the new *cosmopolitanisms* as "discrepant," "vernacular," and "actually existing" in place of the older forms, which were preformed, normative, and universalistic. This grassroots version of cosmopolitanism—one that migrant workers, tourists, and refugees participate in as equally as transnational executives, academics, and diplomats—exists alongside die-hard cosmopolitanisms of the old kind, featuring Kantian projectors, World Bank economists, and religious universalists. For every James Clifford, Homi Bhabha, or Bruce Robbins, each of whom insists on the careful reconstruction of cosmopolitanism as an efficacious (but always provisional) lingua franca that dissolves the reifications of particularity, there are also apologists for the grand normative scaffolding of Western liberalism and universalism, in the manner of Martha Nussbaum, Tzvetan Todorov, or Julia Kristeva …

There is no easy answer to these debates, as Rabindranath Tagore realized in his lectures on nationalism: "Neither the colourless vagueness of cosmopolitanism, nor the fierce self-idolatry of nation-worship is the goal of human history." In the spirit of identifying a discrepant cosmopolitanism, I turn to the global impact of South Asian English rather than the simple abstraction of English-in-general ...

English as a South Asian vernacular first acquired recognition, paradoxically, when representatives of high Victorian imperialism dismissed it as a bureaucratic cant of the native functionaries of the Raj, a *baboo English*. As early as 1874, *Mukherjee's Magazine* in Calcutta published an article entitled "Where Shall the Baboo Go?" Baboo (or babu) English eventually became the butt of Kipling's satire and the object of colonial lexicographies, such as Col. Henry Yule's famous *Hobson Jobson*; post-independence writers from G.V. Desani to Salman Rushdie have expanded the vibrancies of baboo English into an Anglophone fiction that has gone global in its quest for new markets and audiences. However, this article explores *guru English* as a variant but equally modernized cant of South Asian origin. In guru English, the indeterminacy of the modifier is visible: there is no possessive finality of the definite article, as there is with *the* King's (or Queen's) English. Gurus are many, even if at any time there is just one British monarch. The Sanskrit etymology of guru presents this figure as "a dispeller of darkness," but a parallel etymology of guru as "heavy" may be just as relevant, even if ironically so, when we think of guru English. For these reasons, before we assume too readily the spread of English as lingua franca across the globe, we have to ask such questions as whose (South Asian) English? What are the goals of this language's users? What links various aspects of (South Asian) English, whether as international lingua franca or national official language, or even more as precise acrolects, sociolects, and idiolects? ...

I see the evolution of guru English occurring in three distinct phases: (a) 1757–1857, the period of Company to Empire, itself consisting of two parts: (i) 1757–1805, when the work of the first-wave Orientalists was consolidated; and (ii) 1805–57, when the rise of utilitarianism repudiated or sidelined Orientalist agendas, with the Anglicists triumphing over the Orientalists by 1835; (b) 1858–1947, the period of the British Raj proper, consisting of two parts: (i) 1858–1919, when first-wave nationalism as well as cosmopolitan syncretisms such as Theosophy reinterpreted and modernized South Asian religions in English, even as Orientalism was revived as high Indo-European philology under scholars such as Max Müller; and (ii) 1919–47, when the nationalist sway overwhelmed other religious-cosmopolitan agendas even though they continued to exist below the surface; and (c) 1947–the present, the post-independence phase, again in two parts: (i) 1947–65, a period of religious intensification in South Asia and the preparatory phase for South Asian proselytization of the rest of the world alongside state-sponsored explorations of secularism; and (ii) 1965 –the present, when the guru phenomenon exploded worldwide, after first forming a beachhead in the United States and becoming one accepted component of so-called New Age religions ...

... Rammohun Roy had been read outside South Asia, and the American Transcendentalists avidly followed Eastern religious literature, but more time had to elapse before Anglophone South Asian religious leaders could be showcased on a genuinely global scale. Undoubtedly the first spectacular instance of that was the textual feast that commenced as a result of the founding by Helena Petrovna Blavatsky of the Theosophical Society in New York in 1875; the second, more ecumenical, party commenced with the convening of the World Parliament of Religions in Chicago in 1893.

Theosophy, by speaking in proxy for both the Buddhist and the Hindu aspects of the Indian spiritual tradition, was a great alternative cosmopolitanism to the parochial nature of the Raj, even though, as Gauri Viswanathan has recently suggested, its aim was a decentering of Empire into Commonwealth rather than a dissolution of it. British imperial race theory was creatively transfigured and reapplied in benevolent ways that could rationalize spiritual evolution without compromising the political structure that sustained such reflections. I have also discussed elsewhere the complex affiliations between Theosophy and both Irish and Indian Anglophone literature, especially in such novels as Joyce's *Ulysses*, Desani's *All about H. Hatterr*, and Rushdie's *The Satanic Verses* and *The Moor's Last Sigh*. Blavatsky's entertaining charlatanry involved the frequent telekinesis of letters from the Masters into her study and claims of astral travel to the Himalayas to confer with these teachers. The brilliance of Blavatsky's innovation lay in her invention of a pseudo-spiritualism, bringing Eastern spiritualism back to the West in popular format. The quotidian nature of these gurus' visitations to Blavatsky are remarkable: she claimed to have first met the Master Morya in that most cosmopolitan and commercial of events, London's Great Exhibition of July 1851.

Despite Blavatsky's amusing claim, the World Parliament of Religions was most likely the first occasion when South Asian religious leaders were actually showcased in a Western context, or at least in a manner that can be historically reconfirmed. The great attention gained by Swami Vivekananda's uninvited performance shot him into prominence both in India and elsewhere and resulted in the establishment of the Ramakrishna-Vedanta movement in the United States as well as in other countries. However, there were also papers presented by several other exponents of South Asian religion, including Nara Sima Charyar (Narasimhachari), S. Parthasarathy Ayyangar, and Mani Lal Dwivedi, whom we can call "Hindus"; Virchand R. Gandhi, a Jain; Protop Chunder Mozoomdar, a Brahmo; Jeanne Sorabji, a Christian convert who nevertheless read a paper on Zoroastrianism; Alexander Russell "Mohammed" Webb, a Theosophical convert to Islam; and G. N. Chakravarti, an Indian Theosophist.

Vivekananda's inception of "practical Vedanta" over two trips to the United States in the 1890s was most lastingly successful. Ecumenical and almost Unitarian during his sojourn in the United States, Vivekananda revealed some more chauvinist colors on his return to India, where he began to attack Brahmos and Theosophists. As Carl T. Jackson suggests, the Ramakrishna-Vedanta movement was the first Hindu organization to establish itself lastingly on American soil for the following reasons: some of its success results from the religious flexibility revealed along with its organizational adeptness, whereby authority was negotiated and divided between local devotees and the headquarters at Belur, near Calcutta. Much oscillation took place on questions of message (for instance, whether to promote the abstract religious philosophy of Vedanta or the personal cult of Ramakrishna), and manners of raising money had to be sorted out. But Jackson's scholarship confirms that the Ramakrishna Mission as one of the first U.S.-based neo-Hindu movements that used a number of newer techniques of garnering followers, using a combination of personal instruction, newspaper advertisements, regular religious services, and the sale of devotional and religious literature to gain prominence.

While movements such as the Ramakrishna Mission showed the expansion of middle-class reform Hinduism in India and abroad, they form the next phase of guru English's global glut. Picking up on such techniques, but taking them much further through aggressive marketing, Yogananda of the Yogoda Satsang or the Self-Realization Fellowship worked the mass media and produced testimonials of miracle-working, healing, and magical cures in his journals. In retrospect, it is easier to see how these kinds of techniques eventually led to the huge expansion of a number of religious organizations, such as Maharishi Mahesh Yogi's, in the post-1965 moment. Different techniques of direct marketing, word-of-mouth endorsement, and product testing made guru English into an especially persuasive form of rhetoric. Several observers have rightly pointed out that despite the earlier instances I have discussed, such as the Theosophists, Vedantists, and Transcendentalists, the real guru glut, and also its saturation of global media, can perhaps be related to the relaxation of U.S. immigration laws in 1965 and the parallel phenomena of increased international air travel and migration ...

... [T]he third example of guru English highlighted here is that of workaday charismatic corporate entrepreneurship. It is, to date, perhaps as fully integrated into mainstream business culture as one can conceive. Deepak Chopra is a medically trained, highly successful, media-savvy Indian guru who has penetrated several genres of mass-market publishing, including the self-help, diet, alternative medicine, and management markets. The telegenic Chopra has obvious New Age appeal. His followers (sometimes called Chopriites—it is tempting to call them "Shoprights," as many of his clients are reportedly just as well-accessoried as well-heeled) are middle-aged baby boomers with considerable disposable income. Many of them, it seems, can afford to spend thousands of dollars for a weekend therapy session with the great man himself. Within the spectrum of available gurus, Chopra stands for TM Lite. Chopra gave up his medical practice for this even more lucrative career that blends naturopathy, Ayurvedic principles, large amounts of guidance counseling, and pep talk. Several of his best-sellers, including *Ageless Body, Timeless Mind* and *Seven Spiritual Laws of Success*, have been read by millions. He counts among his clients such Hollywood celebrities as Demi Moore, Liz Taylor, and George Harrison. Translated into twenty-five different languages, his books have sales figures recorded in several millions. Chopra was featured on the cover of the journal *Sales and Marketing Management* and was profiled in *Far Eastern Economic Review*. According to *Forbes*, his income averages around $11 million a year; some of this income derives from the lecture circuit, where he can command $25,000 to $30,000 per gig, five to six times a month.

As much as it shows cosmopolitanism at work in the marketplace, Chopra's itinerary reveals savvy consumerist product differentiation. Giving up his earlier career as an endocrinologist in Boston, Chopra joined the Maharishi, setting up the Ayurveda Health Center for Stress Management and Behavioural Medicine in Massachusetts. However, he broke from the SCI organization in 1991 and established other institutions. One of these is the Chopra Center for Well Being in La Jolla, California, which advertises alternative therapies and spiritual renewal, as well as Ayurvedic creams and herbal essences at inflated prices. Chopra is a truly North American guru, on a first-name basis with all his disciples. Holding weekend seminars named "Seduction of the Spirit" that run $1,595 per person, Deepak offers a message barely distinguishable from the marketing hype that surrounds him. Reassuring his followers that "poverty is a reflection of an impoverished spirit," Chopra sells everything he can, including authorized books, audio- and videotapes, teas, vitamins, massage oils, and even silver tongue cleaners to remove undigested toxic materials. He has even tried to set his message to rap music and is frequently on television talk shows promoting his latest book. According to one report, sales of his featured book jumped by 173,000 copies the day after Chopra was featured on the Oprah Winfrey show. Chopra's television special for the Public Broadcasting Service, *Body, Mind, and Soul: The Mystery and the Magic*, aired during a funding drive, garnered PBS $2.5 million in pledges of support.

Interviewed in *Psychology Today*, Chopra rationalizes his upbeat account of how everything, and especially age, is only in the mind. Cancer victims are responsible for their disease, and if they cannot be blamed, society should be held collectively responsible for it. If bad genes have led to individuals' susceptibility to certain diseases, this is because "what I inherit is genetically there because it is an end-product of how my ancestors metabolized their own experience." Slowly it begins to dawn on the reader that such a statement resembles a postgenetics rationalization of the doctrine of karma. Reading through his work, one can see secularized and Western transcreations of Hindu universalist themes and concepts. All societies, according to Chopra, are naturally composed of the intellectuals, the warriors, the business class, and the working people, and such divisions are natural and normal parts of the social body. Indeed, this is a gross simplification of the *varna* or *jati* or caste system in South Asia, but it is a classification that translates and substitutes universalistically for the more difficult task of social analysis.

Chopra's "Wellness Program on Interactive CD-ROM," entitled *The Wisdom Within*, was released by Randomsoft (a division of the publisher Random House). The software unveils a "three-level program, incorporating all of the best elements from Dr. Chopra's writings, seminars, audio and video tapes in an easy-to-use and highly customizable environment." The three sections are entitled "Living in Balance," an Ayurvedic guide for nutrition, exercise, meditation, and massage; "The Field of Infinite Possibilities," where users can journey through three layers of being: body, mind, and spirit (which correspond to TM's objective, subjective, and transcendental existence); and "The Sacred Space," where four background environments—mountains, sea, desert, and forest—can be explored and where the user can keep a personal journal, reach the Pool of Affirmations, and go through a list of recommended daily activities. The CD-ROM lists for $29.95, with a companion book thrown in for the price. Chopra shows us that guru English will not lag too far behind in telemarketing, televangelism, or being able to go virtual.

In conclusion, there remain many questions of a sociological and historical bent about the spread of guru English that may always go unanswered. Why are both Sai Baba and Rajneesh very popular in Italy? Why is Vedanta so much more popular with Jewish Americans than with any other U.S. ethnic or religious group? How does the charisma of the traveling guru operate in a number of disparate media-saturated contexts, as compared to the guru in a single location who attracts clientele from many locales? However, while the sociology of gurus is incomplete (and a new traveling theory may well be needed to complete it), guru English is clearly a phenomenon that merits analysis of a kind that literary criticism does best. It appears that guru English is a site not just for desultory cosmopolitanism but also for engaged criticism, perhaps precisely because of the fact of guru English's evanescent nature. Publishing categories (and even university disciplines) such as management, marketing, self-help, and motivational psychology have differentiated themselves from their earlier unity, which was found in the field of rhetoric, a field that predated what is now the field of literary study and cultural analysis.

While one part of the job of literary critic as rhetorician would be to play the role of a debunker, exposing the naive use of rhetoric as marketing tool and manipulation, a more lasting advantage may be that of understanding rhetoric at work rather than ceding the field entirely to marketers, healers, and professional inspirers. When South Asian gurus turn into marketing versions of Dr. Feelgood, it is high time that postcolonial theory goes in search of material in the airport bookshops. If gurus go global, speak English, and generate a new literature because that's where the money is, scholars of English can rediscover the literature in the fictional boomlet and the religious cant.

Cosmopolitanism as a political and rhetorical position is not divorced from the phenomenon of its commodification. As Deepak declares, "Action generates memory, which generates the possibility of desire, which creates action again. This is the software of the soul." Is it fanciful to suggest that this doctrine alludes to one-click virtual shopping? But in the same vein, this guru needs to be told that some of us may soon want an upgrade.

Questions for discussion

1   How does Immanuel Kant's geography, in which places—actual geographical locations occupied by actual people—disrupt the purity of his rational and universalizing thought on cosmopolitanism? Are there echoes of this disruption in contemporary cosmopolitan theory?

2   It has been suggested that cosmopolitanism, separated as it often seems to be from the realities of global cultural and ethnic diversity and struggle, proposes an ethical program that buttresses existing disequilibriums of wealth and power, especially those of the United States.[4] Is this a fair criticism?

3   A problem with which Kant saddled later advocates of cosmopolitanism is one of balancing the idea of cosmopolitan right with those of the sovereign state. Jürgen Habermas is wedded to the democratic model of governance, a system predominantly found in certain regions of the northern hemisphere in which personal and political freedoms are said to be sacrosanct. But these rights are specific to the sovereign nation state, promoted and protected by state apparatus. Is it possible to extend these into an international situation determined largely by neoliberalism capitalist impulses? Can

such a project be anything more than, as Habermas says, "conceptually possible?"

4   While citizens of affluent states may have the option of imagining themselves to be "citizens of the world" as Martha Nussbaum suggests, is this a viable option for economically and politically marginalized communities? Is it possible that in these latter situations, group solidarity or even ethnic nationalism might provide needed bases of critique and resistance to destructive globalizing forces?

5   David Held's basic assumption is that Western liberal democracy is the most morally sound political system that exists and that it should consequently be the guiding principle in creating global governance. Taken to its logical conclusion, can such a view remain compatible with respect for national political identities and state sovereignty (both of which Held wishes to maintain)?

6   Kwame Anthony Appiah's cosmopolitanism is meant to foster a less bifurcated understanding of the world by transcending conventional dichotomies of West vs. rest, us vs. them etc. Does his differentiation between cosmopolitanism and "competing universalisms" (especially Islamic neo-fundamentalism) further this goal? Appiah further writes, "[T]he right approach starts by taking individuals—not nations, tribes or 'peoples'—as the proper object of moral concern." Can this valuation of individuals over communities, rooted as it is in Western European philosophy and history, be a viable ethical framework for nations and cultures in which the individual is not the primary unit of moral concern?

7   Bengali Historian Dipesh Chakrabarty has famously written that to understand the modern world it is imperative that we "contemplate the necessarily fragmentary histories of human belonging that never constitute a one or a whole."[5] Calhoun's critique of cosmopolitanism invites us to consider this further. What does this perspective offer us in terms of forging transnational relationships and ethical action?

8   Ashis Nandy writes: "the modern West finds it difficult to coexist with other cultures. It may have a well-developed language of coexistence and tolerance ... [b]ut culturally it has

an exceedingly poor capacity to live with strangers." How might we relate this statement to our readings on cosmopolitanism in the first part of this section?

9 Srinivas Aravamudan's cosmopolitanism takes as its starting point colonial adjudications and sacred texts. What are the implications of this argument for (i) our Western distinction between the sacred and the secular and (ii) the broader idea of a secular modernity?

Suggestions for further reading

Kwame Anthony Appiah, *Cosmopolitanism: Ethics in a World of Strangers*, New York: W. W. Norton & Co., 2006.

Srinivas Aravamudan, *Guru English: South Asian Religion in a Cosmopolitan Language*, Princeton, NJ: Princeton University Press, 2005.

James Bohman and Matthia Lutz-Bachmann (eds), *Perpetual Peace: Essays on Kant's Cosmopolitan Ideal*, Cambridge, MA: The MIT Press, 1997.

Craig Calhoun, "Secularism, citizenship, and the modern social imaginary," in C. Calhoun, M. Juergensmeyer, and J. Van Anterwerpen (eds), *Rethinking Secularism*, Oxford: Oxford University Press, 2011, pp. 75–91.

Dipesh Chakrabarty, *Provincializing Europe: Postcolonial Thought and Historical Difference*, Princeton, NJ: Princeton University Press, 2000.

Jacques Derrida, *On Cosmopolitanism and Forgiveness*, New York: Routledge, 2001.

Martha Nussbaum, *For Love of Country*, Boston, MA: Beacon Press, 2002.

R. Radhakrishnan, *Theory in an Uneven World*, Malden, MA: Wiley-Blackwell, 2003.

Joanne Punzo Waghorne, *Diaspora of the Gods: Modern Hindu Temples in an Urban Middle-Class World*, New York: Oxford University Press, 2004.

Section IV

Before and beyond the discourse of globalization

Part 1

In a sense, this section brings us full circle in this Sourcebook. The readings in this section present us with alternative visions of globalization. Each, from its own vantage point, contextualizes the universalizing aspirations of Western intellectuals and Western economic interests. Each arises out of a specific experience of a global world and each is mediated by place. In this sense each is also a map of the world. But these maps are different from the early ones we explored in Section I. These later maps define worlds in which a disregard for reciprocity is a human malaise. And each, importantly, is enmeshed in the transcendent and religious—powerful defining resources that seem to emerge as the surpluses, so to speak, of the exchanges that have taken place between persons coexisting in a politically, economically, and socially lopsided global world. In such a world human meanings (individual and social) must be negotiated in relation to powers that seek to dominate. These cannot be avoided. African American historian and civil rights advocate W.E.B. Du Bois famously articulated this reality at the beginning of the twentieth century as a sort of "double-consciousness":

> One ever feels his two-ness,—an American, a Negro; two souls, two thoughts, two unreconciled strivings; two warring ideals in one dark body, whose dogged strength alone keeps it from being torn asunder.[1]

In the closing paragraphs of *The Protestant Ethic and the Spirit of Capitalism* Max Weber writes:

> [T]he pursuit of wealth stripped of its religious and ethical meaning,

tends to become associated with purely mundane passions, which often actually give it the character of sport.

No one knows who will live in this cage in the future, or whether at the end of this tremendous development, entirely new prophets will arise …

In a sense these final readings offer a rejoinder to this reflection. We begin the section in the sixteenth century with an excerpt from Garcilaso de la Vega's *Royal Commentaries of the Incas and General History of Peru*. Garcilaso was born in 1539 just a few years after the Spanish occupation of Cuzco (in modern-day Peru). He was the son of a Spanish captain and an Incan princess. His early years were spent with his mother's family but in later childhood he received a Spanish education. The *Commentaries* are concerned with chronicling the history both of pre-contact Incan society and of the Spanish conquest in order to demonstrate to the Spanish that Incan traditions equipped them to have a voice in the governance of their now globalized society. In the excerpt from the *Commentaries* included here Garcilaso, in a most politically adroit manner, highlights a history of competent Incan rule through the narration of a story he has learned from an elder. In it we learn that the Sun (the Inca's father) chose the Inca to peacefully unite all the indigenous peoples of the Cuzco region long before the arrival of Spaniards. Garcilaso was thrust into a historical situation that was in the throes of profound transition. The Inca had commanded the largest empire in the Americas when the Spaniards arrived on their shores. Centered at Cuzco, the empire had come into its own in the early thirteenth century, and would ultimately fall to the Spanish 300 years later. Garcilaso found himself situated in the last days of a brilliant empire.

Our second reading, the "Manifesto of the Second Pan-African Congress" was written for a second set of meetings held in London, Paris and Brussels under the banner of the Pan-African Congress in 1922. The first had been held in Paris and was organized by W.E.B. Du Bois to coincide with the Paris Peace Conference where, in the wake of WWI, allied nations were busy allocating among themselves territories in Africa that had been claimed by enemy forces. The Congress was convened to press for the return of these territories to indigenous African peoples to whom they rightfully belonged. The focus of all the Pan-African Congresses was African nationalist aspirations and the struggle for an end to discrimination of diasporic Africans in whatever state they found themselves. The Congresses were thus concerned with globalization from the perspective of Africans and diasporic Africans throughout the world. From this perspective the slave trade and the carving up of Africa into colonial holdings was an encompassing global reality that required a universal vision and response in the form of pan-

Africanism—a specifically black experience in which the entire colonial and postcolonial worlds were implicated.

The "Manifesto" was written by Du Bois and appeared first in the November 1921 issue of *The Crisis*, the magazine of the National Association for the Advancement of Colored People (NAACP). It asserts that world peace depends upon social and political equality of all persons. Democracy, it says, is a fundamental right and global imperative. But it is incompatible with unbridled capitalism, which undermines political autonomy, land rights, and cultural and religious freedoms. The document contains deep resonances with Western Enlightenment values and early twentieth-century economic goals (and particularly with those of the United States): individual liberty, equality, justice, and free trade. But the Manifesto is cast entirely in a transcendent frame. In it we read of God and demi-gods, the Prince of Peace, of salvation and souls, and of meanings of human community that are "written in the stars." These are all invoked like a prayer for a world in which the color line might not be the defining political, social and economic property, where there can be a recognition by dominant powers of mutuality and a desire for fairness and reciprocity.

In the next reading, Bernard Nietschmann, an American geographer, invites us to think about a different kind of globalization by focusing on the Fourth World. Unlike the concepts of the First, Second, and Third Worlds, he points out that the Fourth World is not geographically bound. Indeed it can, and does, exist simultaneously within any or all of these other worlds wherever "spiritually-based" indigenous societies find themselves facing oppression and exploitation.

A few words of explanation here will help us in understanding who in fact populates this Fourth World. The term was popularized by George Manuel who was Chief of the National Indian Brotherhood in Canada in the 1970s, and it was essentially intended to pose a critique of the development model in economics that had relegated "underdeveloped" nations to Third World status. Manuel's hope was that the idea of a Fourth World could provide a rubric for bringing indigenous peoples together and creating a unified voice in the struggle for recognition of their rights. We should be clear, too, on what is meant by the term indigenous. Essentially it refers to persons and groups who share a set of experiences: (i) economies, religious frameworks, languages, and claims to territories that predate European settler cultures which have all been variously assailed in modernity and (ii) a commitment to seeking and achieving justice in the wake of this global assault. Thus it signifies the people of communities and nations (both rural and urban) who are economically, politically, and socially marginalized by industrial states and their technologies; whose territorial rights are not recognized; and whose claims to national sovereignty within larger states are ignored or suppressed.

is this racist? To define a group of people as marginalized?

From Nietschmann we turn to the "United League of Indigenous Nations Treaty." In 2007 representatives of 11 indigenous nations met in Denver, Colorado to establish the United League of Indigenous Nations and to ratify the ULIN Treaty. By the Treaty these indigenous nations imbedded in other states—Canada, the United States, New Zealand, and Australia—created an alliance to fight in an international forum for recognition of their common economic and political rights. We might note that the Treaty was ratified the same year that the United Nations General Assembly adopted the Declaration on the Rights of Indigenous Peoples, an aspirational document endorsed by 144 countries. Only four countries voted against the UN Declaration: Canada, the United States, New Zealand and Australia (under pressure from indigenous peoples and the United Nations, all four would ultimately sign on over the next few years). From the ULIN Treaty's original 11 signatory nations of 2007, the number grew to include 90 nations by 2014. The Treaty deals with issues relating to climate change, commercial trade between individual nations, the legitimacy of indigenous legal systems, and the protection of indigenous rights and cultures. The document articulates a shared political, economic, and ethical vision based on a common history of living in a postcolonial world. Eleven vastly different societies drew on this shared experience to create an ethical framework that reflects that experience, while remaining open enough to allow for differences. It begins with an affirmation of the sacrality of humans and landscape. It goes on to affirm that self-governance and self-determination—both of which have been assailed in modernity—are foundational rights that are based in the work of the Creator.

The following essay is provided by Makere Harawira, a Maori educational theorist who now resides in Canada. Harawira, in similar fashion, provides the outlines of an ethical system that reflects the confrontation of Western imperialism with strong local traditions among Maori people. This tradition does not begin in a global village, a global economy, or liberal ideology. Rather its foundation is in recognition of the interdependence of Maori people and divinities of the earth, sea, and sky, an interdependence that requires equality of persons, mutual responsibility, and a just distribution of resources and wealth.

Assuming a broader geographical basis as a foundation the Afro-Cuban poet and journalist Pedro Sarduy proposes a transnational ethical framework that takes the specific history and legacy of the transatlantic slave trade as its starting point. The stories he learns from his great-grandmother and grandmother bridge "time and distance," placing him in a global frame that starts with the slave trade and runs through Cuba's wars of independence to the present day. There is a deeply religious side to this frame. He writes of standing on a beach on the Ivory Coast and finding his thoughts transported to the suffering of Africans destined for slavery, as well as to a deep realization of the relationship between that horror and neocolonialism. He makes a point of noting that he has this realization on the same day that Cubans back home are celebrating Changó, a Yoruba Orisha who figures centrally in Cuban Santeria.

4.1 Royal commentaries of the Incas and general history of Peru: Part one

Garcilaso de la Vega

"Who was the first of our Incas? What was he called? What was the origin of his line? How did he begin to reign? With what men and arms did he conquer this great empire? How did our heroic deeds begin?"

The Inca was delighted to hear these questions, since it gave him great pleasure to reply to them, and turned to me (who had already often heard him tell the tale, but had never paid as much attention as then) saying:

"Nephew, I will tell you these things with pleasure: indeed it is right that you should hear them and keep them in our heart (this is their phrase for 'in the memory'). You should know that in olden times the whole of this region before you was covered with brush and heath, and people lived in those times like wild beasts, with no religion or government and no towns or houses, and without tilling or sowing the soil, or clothing or covering their flesh, for they did not know how to weave cotton or wool to make clothes. They lived in twos and threes as chance brought them together in caves and crannies in rocks and underground caverns. Like wild beasts they ate the herbs of the field and roots of trees and fruits growing wild and also human flesh. They covered their bodies with leaves and the bark of trees and animals' skins. Others went naked. In short, they lived like deer or other game, and even in their intercourse with women they behaved like beasts, for they knew nothing of having separate wives."

I must remark, in order to avoid many repetitions of the words "our father the Sun," that the phrase was used by the Incas to express respect whenever they mentioned the sun, for they boasted of descending from it, and none but Incas were allowed to utter the words: it would have been blasphemy and the speaker would have been stoned. The Inca said:

"Our father the Sun, seeing men in the state I have mentioned, took pity and was sorry for them, and sent from heaven to earth a son and a daughter of his to indoctrinate them in the knowledge of our father the Sun that they might worship him and adopt him as their god, and to give them precepts and laws by which they would live as reasonable and civilized men, and dwell in houses and settled towns, and learn to till the soil, and grow plants and crops, and breed flocks, and use the fruits of the earth like rational beings and not like beasts. With this order and mandate our father the Sun set these two children of his in Lake Titicaca, eighty leagues from here, and bade them go where they would, and wherever they stopped to eat or sleep to try to thrust into the ground a golden wand half a yard long and two fingers in thickness which he gave them as a sign and token: when this wand should sink into the ground at a single thrust, there our father the Sun wished them to stop and set up their court."

"Finally he told them: 'When you have reduced these people to our service, you shall maintain them in reason and justice, showing mercy, clemency, and mildness, and always treating them as a merciful father treats his beloved and tender children. Imitate my example in this. I do good to all the world. I give them my light and brightness that they may see and go about their business; I warm them when they are cold; and I grow their pastures and crops, and bring fruit to their trees, and multiply their flocks. I bring rain and calm weather in turn, and I take care to go round the world once a day to observe the wants that exist in the world and to fill and supply them as the sustainer and benefactor of men. I wish you as children of mine to follow this example sent down to earth to teach and benefit those men who live like beasts. And henceforward I establish and nominate you as kings and lords over all the people you may thus instruct with your reason, government, and good works'."

"When our father the Sun had thus made manifest his will to his two children he bade them farewell. They left Titicaca and travelled northwards, and wherever they stopped on the way they thrust the golden wand into the earth, but it never sank in. Thus they reached a small inn or resthouse seven or eight leagues south of this city. Today it is called Pacárec Tampu, 'inn or resthouse of the dawn.' The Inca gave it this name because he set out from it about daybreak. It is one of the towns the prince later ordered to be founded, and its inhabitants to this day boast greatly of its name because our first Inca bestowed it. From this place he and his wife, our queen, reached the valley of Cuzco which was then a wilderness."

"The first settlement they made in this valley," said the Inca, "was in the hill called Huanacauri, to the south of this city. There they tried to thrust the golden wand into the earth and it easily sank in at the first blow and they saw it no more." Then our Inca said to his wife: "Our father the Sun bids us remain in this valley and make it our dwelling place and home in fulfilment of his will. It is therefore right, queen and sister, that each of us should go out and call together these people so as to instruct them and benefit them as our father the Sun has ordained." Our first rulers set out from the hill of Huanacauri, each in a different direction, to call the people together, and as that was the first place we know they trod with their feet and because they went out from it to do good to mankind, we made there, as you know, a temple for the worship of our father the Sun, in memory of his merciful beneficence towards the world. The prince went northwards, and the princess south. They spoke to all the men and women they found in that wilderness and said that their father the Sun had sent them from the sky to be teachers and benefactors to the dwellers in all that land, delivering them from the wild lives they led and in obedience to the commands given by the Sun, their father, calling them together and removing them from those heaths and moors, bringing them to dwell in settled valleys and giving them the food of men instead of that of beasts to eat. Our king and queen said these and similar things to the first savages they found in those mountains and heaths, and as the savages beheld two persons clad and adorned with the ornaments our father the Sun had given them—and a very different dress from their own—with their ears pierced and opened in the way we their descendants have, and saw that their words and countenances showed them to be children of the Sun, and that they came to mankind to give them towns to dwell in and food to eat, they wondered at what they saw and were at the same time attracted by the promises that were held out to them. Thus they fully credited all they were told and worshipped and venerated the strangers as children of the Sun and obeyed them as kings. These savages gathered others and repeated the wonders they had seen and heard, and a great number of men and women collected and set out to follow our king and queen wherever they might lead.

"When our princes saw the great crowd that had formed there, they ordered that some should set about supplying open-air meals for them all, so that they should not be driven by hunger to disperse again across the heaths. Others were ordered to work on building huts and houses according to plans made by the Inca. Thus our imperial city began to be settled: it was divided into two halves called Hanan Cuzco, which as you know, means upper Cuzco, and Hurin Cuzco, or lower Cuzco. The king wished those he had brought to people Hanan Cuzco, therefore called the upper, and those the queen had brought to people Hurin Cuzco, which was therefore called the lower. The distinction did not imply that the inhabitants of one half should excel those of the other in privileges and exemptions. All were equal like brothers, the children of one father and one mother. The Inca only wished that there should be this division of the people and distinction of name, so that the fact that some had been gathered by the king and others by the queen might have a perpetual memorial. And he ordered that there should be only one difference and acknowledgment of superiority among them, that those of upper Cuzco be considered and respected as first-born and elder brothers, and those of lower Cuzco be as younger children. In short they were to be as the right side and the left in any question of precedence of place and office, since those of the upper town had been gathered by the men and those of the lower by the women. In imitation of this, there was later the same division in all the towns, great or small, of our empire, which were divided by wards or by lineages, known as *hanan aillu* and *hurin aillu*, the upper and lower lineage, or *hanan suyu* and *hurin suyu*, the upper and lower district.

"At the same time, in peopling the city, our Inca showed the male Indians which tasks were proper to men: breaking and tilling the land, sowing crops, seeds, and vegetables which he showed to be good to eat and fruitful, and for which purpose he taught them how to make ploughs and other necessary instruments, and bade them and showed them how to draw irrigation channels from the streams that run through the valley of Cuzco, and even showed them how to make the footwear we use. On her side the queen trained the Indian women in all the feminine occupations: spinning and weaving cotton and wool, and making clothes for themselves and their husbands and children. She told them how to do these and other duties of domestic service. In short, there was nothing relating to human life that our princes failed to teach their first vassals, the Inca king acting as master for the men and the Coya queen, mistress of the women." The peoples subdued by the first Inca Manco Cápac. The very Indians who had thus been recently subdued, discovering themselves to be quite changed and realizing the benefits they had received, willingly and joyfully betook themselves to the sierras, moors, and heaths to seek their inhabitants and give them news about the children of the Sun. They recounted the many benefits they had brought them, and proved it by showing their new clothes they wore and the new foods they ate, and telling how they lived in houses and towns. When the wild people heard all this, great numbers of them came to behold the wonders that were told and reported of our first fathers, kings, and lords. Once they had verified this with their own eyes, they remained to serve and obey them. Thus some called others and these passed the word to more, and so many gathered in a few years that after six or seven, the Inca had a force of men armed and equipped to defend themselves against any attackers and even to bring by force those who would not come willingly. He taught them how to make offensive weapons such as bows and arrows, lances, clubs, and others now in use.

"And to cut short the deeds of our first Inca, I can tell you that he subdued the region to the east as far as the river called Paucartampu, and to the west eight leagues up to the river Apurímac, and to the south for nine leagues to Quequesana. Within this area our Inca ordered more than a hundred villages to be settled, the biggest with a hundred houses and others with less, according to what the land could support. These were the first beginnings of our city toward being established and settled as you now see it. They were also the beginnings of our great, rich, and famous empire that your father and his friends deprived us of. These were our first Incas and kings, who appeared in the first ages of the world; and from them descend all the other kings we have had, and from these again we are all descended. I cannot inform you exactly how many years it is since our father the Sun sent us his first children, for it is so long no one has been able to remember: we believe it is above four hundred years. Our Inca was called Manco Cápac and our Coya Mama Ocllo Huaco. They were, as I have told you, brother and sister, children of the

Sun and the Moon, our parents. I think I have expatiated at length on your enquiry and answered your questions, and in order to spare your tears, I have not recited this story with tears of blood flowing from my eyes as they flow from my heart from the grief I feel at seeing the line of our Incas ended and our empire lost."

This long account of the origin of our kings was given me by the Inca, my mother's uncle, of whom I asked it. I have tried to translate it faithfully from my mother tongue, that of the Inca, into a foreign speech, Castilian, though I have not written it in such majestic language as the Inca used, nor with the full significance the words of that language have. If I had given the whole significance, the tale would have been much more extensive than it is. On the contrary, I have shortened it, and left out a few things that might have been odious. However, it is enough to have conveyed its true meaning, which is what is required for our history. The Inca told me a few similar things, though not many, during the visits he paid to my mother's house; these I will include in their places later on, giving their source. I much regret not having asked many more questions so that I might now have information about them from so excellent an archive and write them here.

4.2 Manifesto of the second Pan-African Congress

W.E.B. Du Bois

The absolute equality of races—physical, political and social—is the founding stone of world peace and human advancement. No one denies great differences of gift, capacity, and attainment among individuals of all races, but the voice of science, religion, and practical politics is one in denying the God-appointed existence of super-races, or of races naturally and inevitably and eternally inferior.

That in the vast range of time, one group should in its industrial technique, or social organization, or spiritual vision, lag a few hundred years behind another, or forge fitfully ahead, or come to differ decidedly in thought, deed and ideal, is proof of the essential richness and variety of human nature, rather than proof of the coexistence of demi-gods and apes in human form. The doctrine of racial equality does not interfere with individual liberty, rather, it fulfils it. And of all the various criteria by which masses of men have in the past been prejudged and classified, that of the color of the skin and texture of the hair, is surely the most adventitious {accidental} and idiotic.

It is the duty of the world to assist in every way the advance of the backward and suppressed groups of mankind. The rise of all men is a menace to no one and is the highest human ideal; it is not an altruistic benevolence, but the one road to world salvation.

For the purpose of raising such peoples to intelligence, self-knowledge, and self-control, their intelligentsia of right ought to be recognized as the natural leaders of their groups.

The insidious and dishonorable propaganda, which, for selfish ends, so distorts and denies facts as to represent the advancement and development of certain races of men as impossible and undesirable, should be met with widespread dissemination of the truth …

If it be proven that absolute world segregation by group, color, or historic infinity is best for the future, let the white race leave the dark world and the darker races will gladly leave the white. But the proposition is absurd. This is a world of men, of men whose likenesses far outweigh their differences; who mutually need each other in labor and thought and dream, but who can successfully have each other only on terms of equality, justice, and mutual respect. They are the real and only peacemakers who i work sincerely and peacefully to this end.

The beginnings of wisdom in interracial contact is the establishment of Political institutions among suppressed peoples. The habit of democracy must be made to encircle the earth. Despite the attempt to prove that its practice is the secret and divine gift of the few, no habit is more natural or more widely spread among primitive people, or more easily capable of development among masses ...

Surely in the twentieth century of the Prince of Peace [Jesus] ... there can be found in the civilized world enough of altruism, learning, and benevolence to develop native institutions for the native's good, rather than continue to allow the majority of mankind to be brutalized and enslaved by ignorant and selfish agents of commercial institutions, whose one aim is profit and power for the few.

And this brings us to the crux of the matter: It is the shame of the world that today the relation between the main groups of mankind and their mutual estimate and respect is determined chiefly by the degree in which one can subject the other to its service, enslaving labor, making ignorance compulsory, uprooting ruthlessly religion and customs, and destroying government, so that the favored Few may luxuriate in the toil of the tortured many ...

The day of such world organization is past and whatever excuse be made for it in other ages, the twentieth century must come to judge men as men and not as material and labor ...

What do those wish who see these evils of the color line and racial discrimination and who believe in the divine right of suppressed and backward peoples to learn and aspire and be free?

The Negro race through its thinking intelligentsia is demanding:

1   The recognition of civilized men as civilized despite their race or color

2   Local self-government for backward groups, deliberately rising as experience and knowledge grow to complete self-government under the limitations of a self-governed world

3   Education in self-knowledge, in scientific truth and in industrial technique, undivorced from the art of beauty

4   Freedom in their own religion and social customs, and with the right to be different and non-conformist

5   Co-operation with the rest of the world in government, industry, and art on the basis of Justice, Freedom, and Peace

6   The ancient common ownership of the land and its natural fruits and defense against the unrestrained greed of invested capital

7   The establishment under the League of Nations of an international institution for the study of Negro problems

8   The establishment of an international section in the Labor Bureau of the League of Nations, charged with the protection of native labor.

The world must face two eventualities: either the complete assimilation of Africa with two or three of the great world states, with political, civil, and social power and privileges absolutely equal for its black and white citizens, or the rise of a great black African state founded in Peace and Good Will, based on popular education, natural art, and industry and freedom of trade; autonomous and sovereign in its internal policy, but from its beginning a part of a great society of peoples in which it takes its place with others as co-rulers of the world.

In some such words and thoughts as these we seek to express our will and ideal, and the end of our untiring effort. To our aid we call all men of the Earth who love Justice and Mercy. Out of the depths we have cried unto the deaf and dumb masters of the world. Out of the depths we cry to our own sleeping souls.

The answer is written in the stars.

4.3 The Fourth World: Nations without a state

Bernard Q. Nietschmann

Non state conflicts

Most of the world's conflicts are between states and nations, yet almost all international efforts to prevent and contain war and to promote peace are directed to state against state conflicts. With 168 states asserting the right and power to impose sovereignty and allegiance upon more than 3000 nations, conflicts occur that cannot be contained or hidden, nor resolved on a state-to-state basis. More than one-half of the world's 45 hot wars involve Fourth World nations against invading First, Second and Third World states (some put the numbers at 32 of 58). And Fourth World nations are also engaged in hundreds of warm and cold wars against expanding states.

The nature of conflicts has changed, yet the means to understand and resolve them have not. Most hot and cold wars since 1945 have not been state against state, but states against indigenous nations and ethnic groups that are fielding resistance forces to protect sovereignty, to gain greater autonomy, to restore national boundaries erased by colonial powers, and to end economic exploitation and political oppression. Many Fourth World nations are promoting or practicing separate rights to their own territory, not as minorities, but as distinct sovereign peoples.

Considerable international effort is directed towards controlling and containing state against state conflicts. Yet when Fourth World nations attempt to defend or regain territory and sovereignty usurped by a settler state, these conflicts are labeled "domestic" by the international community of the Brotherhood of States.

From the domestic perspective, indigenous combatants are seen as "rebels," terrorists,' "bandits," "separatists," and "extremists." But most Fourth World nation combatants see themselves engaged in an international conflict, nation against state; and thus they may call themselves soldiers, fighters, warriors. The view of international states is that states declare war, nations declare terrorism.

By treating conflicts between states and nations as but an internal matter of the state, the conflict may be masked but not understood, nor resolved.

For one thing, it is quite likely that the combatant and civilian base in an embattled Fourth World nation do not identify as citizens or minorities of the state, or as rebels or insurgents against it. They identify as a people with their own nation that has its own territory and sovereignty. This means that most of the international agreements and forces (diplomatic, economic, military, etc.) are not agreed to by people doing the fighting on the other side of the frontier.

The other side of the frontier

The settler states of First, Second, and Third World countries encircle and encroach upon Fourth World nations. What is termed nation-building, economic development, population resettlement, and integration is seen by indigenous peoples on the other side of the frontier as simply attempts to dispossess and to incorporate indigenous lands and resources. While some 168 internationally recognized states attempt to expand political control and to use energy-intensive technology to exploit annexed environments, across the frontier, some 3000 indigenous nations persist in their efforts to defend their own land—and spiritually-based societies and economies.

The term Fourth World includes indigenous enclave nations and peoples and designates identities and sovereignties masked by the ready acceptance of the sanctity of international states.

The Fourth World and the persistence and continuing defense of indigenous nations have remained largely hidden to the outside because of the widespread acceptance of myths that all indigenous peoples are disappearing, their absorption by state systems is inevitable, and they have no sovereignty, territory, or rights except those given to them by states.

Anthropologists focus on dying cultures, political scientists chronicle the decline of "tribalism," and human rights organizations admonish governments for abuses and reductions of tribal minorities. These all reinforce the dominant idea that indigenous peoples are on the way out. However, if one crosses to the other side of the frontier, the perspectives are vastly amplified: regionally and worldwide indigenous peoples are actively engaged in political, military, legal and economic solutions to defend and promote their interests.

Fourth World hot and cold wars will increase in number and intensity as central state governments continue to expand to integrate and assimilate indigenous peoples and their lands and resources.

The hot wars will be fought against the developing countries, and the cold wars will be carried on against the developed countries. Most of the Fourth World wars are being waged against Third World colonialist states that seek to incorporate lands and peoples that formerly were autonomous small nations. Third World colonialism is a principal factor behind Fourth World wars.

Increasingly, the Fourth World is emerging as a new force in international politics because in the common defense of their nations, many indigenous peoples do not accept being mere subjects of international law and state sovereignty and trusteeship bureaucracies. Instead, they are organizing and exerting their own participation and policies as sovereign peoples and nations.

States and nations, minorities and peoples

It is critical to note the distinctions made by indigenous leaders and movements between states and nations, minorities and peoples. States are the political apparatuses that unite (sometimes forcibly) different peoples and nations into one internationally recognized political and territorial entity. Nations, conversely, are made up of a self-identifying people, often united by a common language, religion and political consensus, who occupy all or part of an ancestral territory. Although they are often referred to as minorities (tribal minorities, ethnic minorities), indigenous peoples reject this label as it automatically infers membership in a state which may be the issue that is in dispute. To identify a people as a minority often sacrifices their claimed national identity to state sovereignty.

For example, the UN Human Rights Sub-Commission's definition of a minority is "A group numerically smaller than the rest of the population of a State, in a non-dominant position, whose members—being citizens of the State—possess ethnic, religious, or linguistic characteristics differing from those of others of the population and show, if only implicitly, a sense of solidarity directed towards preserving their culture, traditions, religion and language."

While these may very well be important, even critical, to preserve and protect, the significant geographical and material base for the survival of a people is conspicuously absent: nothing is said about land and resources. This is not only typical, it is symptomatic of common terminology, perspectives, and policies that attempt to negate the root cause of state-nation conflicts. A people, rather than a minority, is a concept widely recognized and accepted to include rights to territory, self-determination, and sovereignty. One of the ironies in the current status of international legislation on rights is that individuals have more rights than does a people in a nation unless that people forms a state.

One-nationality states [the nation-state] are rare (Iceland), while the drive to create one territory and one people out of many nations and peoples (ironically termed "nation building") is a primary cause of half the world's conflicts.

Reversing the frontiers

The Fourth World is trying to stabilize and push back the frontiers imposed by colonialism and expanded by modern states that seek to politically and economically develop their own peoples. The essential conflict is centuries old, but it is indigenous peoples who are creating new situations through the worldwide movement for self-determination, and territorial and political sovereignty. This is leading to new political, military, economic and legal entities that are separate and distinct from traditional East-West, North-South, and left-right alliances and conflicts.

The accompanying sketch map indicates some of the Fourth World hot wars. Defense of indigenous land, resources, people and identity appear to be the common roots of most if not all of these conflicts, not East-West, or North-South geopolitics. These wars have an apparent tenacity and grass-roots strength that make them difficult to suppress. Central to many of these indigenous peoples' defensive wars is the belief that their ability to resist will outlive the invaders ability to oppress. Some armed conflicts have been going on for several decades.

For example, the Eritrean-Ethiopian conflict is Africa's longest war; the Karen-Burmese war is Southeast Asia's longest; and the Naga have been fighting the government of India since the early 1950s. Fourth World hot wars are imbedded in communal land and identity which provide the potential to be longlived and tenacious. Most of the wars don't seek to overthrow but to remove the invading or settler governments from indigenous nations, and to achieve recognition of indigenous peoples' rights to self-determination.

To deal with an indigenous war a settler state may choose one or more strategies:

1   attempt to militarily defeat the resistance (East Timor, West Papua, Western Sahara, Afghanistan, Eritrea, Tigray, Indian Nicaragua);

2   begin a long-term program to relocate and assimilate the indigenous population (Guatemala, Nicaragua, Indonesia, etc.);

3   stay out of the indigenous territory (no known examples); and

4   negotiate (at present, India and the Mizo National Front, Nicaragua and the Miskito, Sumo and Rama, The Tamils and Sri Lanka). [written in 1985]

Indigenous cold wars occur worldwide and involve claims and disputes over political jurisdiction, self-determination, rights to land, fishing, and compensation demands for expropriated lands and resources. Many of these conflicts are being fought in the courts; for example, Sami grazing lands in Sweden and Norway, and Aboriginal homelands and sacred sites in Australia. Indigenous cold wars involve the Micmac, Cree, Shuswap and Bella Coola (Canada); the Quinault, Hopi, Navajo, Lakota, Iroquois, Inuit Athapaskans, and Aleuts (United States); Tibetans and indigenous Taiwanese (China); Ainu (Japan); Meo, Akha,

Karen, Lahu, etc. (Thailand); Maori (New Zealand); Pitjantjatjara, Yirrkala, Gurindji, and Warlpiri (Australia); Shaba, Luba, and Kasai (Zaire); Catalonians and Basques (Spain); Corsicans and Sardinians (Italy); Flemish and Walloons (Belgium); Mapuches (Chile); Aymara and Quechua-speaking peoples (Peru); Guaymi and Chocó (Panama); Baruca, Cabecares and Bribris (Costa Rica); and Zapotec, Mixe and Mayans (Mexico). There are many, many more.

Negotiated resolutions of a hot war or a settlement of a cold war, generally requires a bilateral agreement between the state and nation over political and territorial autonomy or sovereignty. Many examples exist worldwide although they are not widely known. And each of the examples provide alternatives to the current state of affairs based on no solution or a final solution.

Indigenous peoples and nations have made many advances toward self-determination and new relations with adjacent or encircling states, such as the San Blas Kuna and Panama; the Basques and Spain; the Inuit of Greenland and Denmark; the Six Nations and the United States and Canada; the Otavalo, Shuar and Ecuador; and the Faroe Islanders and Denmark. And the Miskitos, Mizos, and Tamils are in the process of negotiations with settler states. Some indigenous nations have become recognized states such as Papua New Guinea, Solomon Islands, Vanuatu, Kiribati, Qatar, and Nauru.

4.4 United League of Indigenous Nations Treaty, 2007

Preamble

We, the signatory Indigenous Nations and Peoples, hereby pledge mutual recognition of our inherent rights and power to govern ourselves and our ancestral homelands and traditional territories. Each signatory nation, having provided evidence that their respective governing body has taken action in accordance with their own custom, law or tradition to knowingly agree to and adopt the terms of this treaty, hereby establish the political, social, cultural and economic relations contemplated herein.

Principles

Recognizing each other as self-governing Indigenous Nations, we subscribe to the following principles:

1   The Creator has made us part of and inseparable from the natural world around us. This truth binds us together and gives rise to a shared commitment to care for, conserve, and protect the land, air, water and animal life within our usual, customary and traditional territories.

2   Our inherent customary rights to self-governance and self-determination has existed since time immemorial, have been bestowed by the Creator and are defined in accordance with our own laws, values, customs and mores.

3   Political, social, cultural and economic relationships between our Indigenous Nations have existed since time immemorial and our right to continue such relationships are inseparable from our inherent Indigenous rights of nationhood. Indigenous Peoples have the right of self-determination and, by virtue of that right, our Peoples freely determine our political status and freely pursue our social, cultural and economic development.

4   No other political jurisdiction, including nation-states and their governmental agencies or subdivisions, possess governmental power over any of our Indigenous Nations, our people and our usual, customary and traditional territories.

5   Our inherent, aboriginal control and enjoyment of our territories

includes our collective rights over the environment consisting of the air, lands, inland waters, oceans, seas, sea ice, flora, fauna and all other surface and sub-surface resources.

6   Our Indigenous rights include all traditional and ecological knowledge derived from our relationship with our lands, air and waters from time immemorial, the exercise of conservation practices, traditional ceremonies, medicinal and healing practices, and all other expressions of art and culture.

Goals

This Treaty is for the purpose of achieving the following goals:

1   To establish supportive bonds among signatory Indigenous Nations in order to secure, recover, and promote, through political, social, cultural and economic unity, the rights of all our peoples, the protection and recovery of our homelands and for the well-being of all our future generations.

2   To establish a foundation for the exercise of contemporary Indigenous nation sovereignty, without regard to existing or future international political boundaries of non-Indigenous nations, for the following purposes: (a) protecting our cultural properties, including but not limited to sacred songs, signs and symbols, traditional ecological knowledge and other forms of cultural heritage rights by collectively affirming the principle that our own Indigenous laws and customs regarding our cultural properties are prior and paramount to the assertion that any other laws or jurisdiction including international bodies and agencies, (b) protecting our Indigenous lands, air and waters from environmental destruction through exercising our rights of political representation as Indigenous nations before all national and international bodies that have been charged, through international treaties, agreements and conventions, with environmental protection responsibilities, (c) engaging in mutually beneficial trade and commerce between Indigenous nations and the economic enterprises owned and operated collectively by Indigenous peoples and by individual citizens of our Indigenous nations, and (d) preserving and protecting the human rights of our Indigenous peoples from such violations as involuntary servitude, human trafficking, or any other form of oppression.

3 To develop an effective and meaningful process to promote communication and cooperation among the Indigenous Nations on all other common issues, concerns, pursuits, and initiatives.

4 To ensure that scholarly exchanges and joint study on strategies of self-determination are undertaken by Indigenous scholars.

Mutual Covenants

We, the signatory Indigenous Nations, are committed to providing the following mutual aid and assistance, to the best of our ability and in accordance with our own prior and paramount Indigenous laws, customs and traditions:

1 Exchanging economic, legal, political, traditional and technical knowledge regarding the protection of Indigenous cultural properties.

2 Collaborating on research on environmental issues that impact Indigenous homelands, including baseline studies and socio-economic assessments that consider the cultural, social and sustainable uses of Indigenous Peoples' territories and resources.

3 Participating in trade and commerce missions to lay a foundation for business relations and the development of an international, integrated Indigenous economy, and

Each signatory Indigenous Nation shall:

1 Appoint a coordinator or responsible official for Treaty matters;

2 identify and establish an inter-Nation coordination office and communication network to assist in assembling data, information, knowledge and research needed to effectively address substantial issues of common concern;

3 Coordinate statements of policy and information on Treaty matters, especially information to be disseminated to the media;

4 Participate in periodic reviews and strategy planning sessions as needed.

Effective Date

The effective date of this Treaty is August 1, 2007.

Ratification

Following the effective date of the Treaty, any other Indigenous Nation may ratify this Treaty at a meeting of the United League of Indigenous Nations. Ratifying Indigenous Nations may attach explanations or clarifications expressing their respective cultural understandings associated with the provisions of the Treaty through a Statement of Understandings which must be consistent with the spirit and intent of the Treaty.

4.5 Economic globalization, indigenous peoples, and the role of indigenous women

Makere Harawira

Although there is a great deal of rhetoric about the evils of globalization, generally speaking, it remains a poorly defined concept. At one level, the term "globalization" refers to the processes by which the world is becoming more interdependent. Interdependence is a concept that is extremely well understood by indigenous peoples because it is embedded in our psyche. Our geneology or whakapapa, which to Maori is everything, connects us to first Papatuanuku, (Earth Mother) and to all her children, to Tangaora (God of the Sea) and his children, to Ranginui, (Sky Father) and beyond that to the stars and to other planets of the solar system. These concepts are at the heart of Maori cosmologies and Maori ways of being in the world. By being embedded in our whakapapa (genealogy), they have been passed down through generations and are at the heart of how we see ourselves in relation to the world.

Globalization also refers to other processes—for example the notion of the global village, to the way in which we are becoming politically and socially more and more interdependent. However it also and primarily these days, is used to refer to the creation of a single global economy ... Embedded within this new single global economy is a set of liberal European epistemologies which define human beings as economic units and the free market as a rationally operating framework within which perfect competition exists, which has its roots in the mercantilism of the earliest forms of imperialism, and which is deeply ideologically flawed. Economic liberalism and free trade are the lynch pins of the new economic order designed to carry humankind on a wave of economic triumph into the new millennium.

Extending this line of thought, the problem is not just economic globalization nor even the notion of the market. To explain, Adam Smith's theory of a self-regulating market efficiency depended upon small, locally-owned enterprises that compete in local markets on the basis of price and quality, not globalised free trade and footloose capital. What we are in fact witnessing is the assertion of a new form of global capitalism that are more dangerous than ever. The popular concept of nation-states exercising sovereignty on behalf of national interest and of the interests of the various groups residing within their borders is being heavily challenged by the locating [of] economic power within transnational corporations whose wealth exceeds that of many countries ...

Human rights, foreign policy, military engagements, are selectively responded to by states on the basis of economic interest, be it defined as political or strategic. Underneath every encounter of war, every humanitarian intervention by the US and its allies, including the interventions in Kosovo, is an economically defined set of interests or agendas. The United Nations, that body created following World War 2 as guardian of the new world order of the time, within which human rights instruments, regulations circumscribing the rights of multinational companies and ensuring the ability of states to provide for the rights of citizens, and within whose framework the draft declaration of the rights of indigenous peoples has been struggled over inch by inch, which declared 1993 as the Year of Indigenous Peoples and the beginning of a new partnership with indigenous peoples, now has a new set of partners within the UNDP. They are the heads of multinational companies. Development within the UNDP is now defined and determined by this group of multinational business interests. We are witnessing the assertion of new forms of capitalism, of a new global capitalist order in which the resources, the wealth, the assets of the world are increasingly concentrated in the hands of a few, while the vast majority are increasingly dispossessed.

Arguably the most disenfranchised, disempowered and dispossessed groups within this new global economic order are indigenous peoples and minorities all over the world. This is well documented. The object of deliberate genocide, tens of thousands, hundreds of thousands of indigenous people have died during our time in the struggle to retain the right to live on and care for their territories to which they not only depend for survival but have ancient, deeply-held spiritual and genealogical connection. Despite the documented evidence, these facts determinedly ignored by mainstream reporting, ignored by governments, ignored by the majority of people who either don't know due to a well-controlled media, or simply are occupied with their own daily struggle. And … while righteous indignation can be freely generated over ethnic cleansing in Kosovo, that same righteous indignation is largely absent regarding the plight of thousands of indigenous peoples.

Multilateral economic and trade agreements

The framework of this global capitalist economic order is sustained and regulated by a series of multilateral agreements whose function is to protect the interests of business over that of governments, civil society and most certainly indigenous peoples … These agreements are enforceable in courts of law both nationally and internationally.

One of the central pillars of this global economic order is the World Trade Organization which came into existence in 1993 due to the inadequacy of the GATT agreement as an enforcer of the international regulations that provide the structure for the global capitalist order. New regional economic agreements such as NAFTA and APEC are also designed to reinforce this economic order. Built into these international and regional agreements are legally enforceable clauses protecting the rights of trade and investment—for which read transnational business interests—over those of local communities and countries ...

The impact on indigenous peoples of economic agreements designed to remove the few remaining trade protections and barriers to market liberalisation is devastating. For Maori, the implications are enormous. Aotearoa/New Zealand has led the way in participating in international agreements with less protection barriers than any other participant. With the GATT negotiations for instance, Aotearoa/New Zealand put in place the least amount of protections whereas the initiating country, the United States, put in place carefully calculated protections to protect its own industry while reaping the benefits of less astute bargaining from other countries. The fact that such agreements enable the sale of or trade in almost all such resources, assets and enterprises as remain in New Zealand ownership, when they privilege foreign investors without requiring any return to this country, caused Maori as well as many other New Zealanders great concern ...

In Aotearoa/New Zealand, Maori led the way in raising awareness of and resistance to the Multilateral Agreement on Investment, in fact, when the multilateral agreement on investment negotiations became known, Maori women were in the forefront of highly successful mobilisation against the MAI. Despite this, in regards to APEC, determined efforts by the Crown to coopt Maori business leaders as part of the APEC process appears to be successfully fragmenting any cohesive efforts at challenging the APEC model of open regionalism as the pathway to fortune and happiness.

Removal of environment and resource protections

The provisions of these regional and international agreements override nation-state regulations including environmental regulations, genetically modified or hormone treated foodstuffs, labor laws and all citizenship rights. The loss of nation-states ability to regulate environmental and other protections within their own borders has enormous implications for indigenous peoples' lands and resources including intellectual and cultural property rights over which the battle being waged in Aotearoa/New Zealand for some years now has been led Maori women and fiercely resisted by the government. Economic globalization has fostered the rape and plunder of indigenous intellectual and cultural knowledge by multinational pharmaceutical companies who collect and study plant materials which have been used by particular indigenous groups for often thousands of years for very specific uses, and then patent the results of their research so that firstly, they own the property rights and therefore also the profits and secondly, so that in many cases, this plant can no longer be freely used by those who have traditionally used it ...

In Aotearoa/New Zealand, Maori women were the initiators of a claim before the Waitangi Tribunal which seeks to protect Maori intellectual and cultural rights over flora and fauna. The most noticeable aspect of this case which is a landmark case and which has implications for indigenous people everywhere, is the way that the Crown has consistently put obstacles in the way of the case because of its implications for foreign investment. The significance of this claim is wider than might at first be realised by non-Maori in that it represents the strongest case for protecting New Zealand's flora and fauna from pillaging and exploitation by overseas-owned multinational companies.

Structural adjustment and the global economic order

Structural adjustment programs such as those imposed in Yugoslavia, Russia, Brazil, Mexico, Aotearoa, to name just a few, are an integral part of the development of the new global economic order as they are the means by which the assets and resources of countries are made available, often at rock bottom prices to the same groups of creditors whose debts are paid off by loans through the IMF. Because of the size of its population (less than four million with an indigenous population of 15 percent) and its isolation, Aotearoa has been regarded as ideally placed to be the experimental model for pushing the limits of New Right-driven economic structural adjustment. The embracing of these ideologies in the 1980's saw Aotearoa develop what the OECD promotes as a model open economy, one which is driven by free market ideologies. For the past 15 years this has entailed a steady move towards a minimalist form of governance that functions to increase the influence of power brokers and undermine democracy as we know it. A key principle of this restructuring is the separation of economics from social issues. At the international level, at the regional level ... and at the local level—policy and decision-making is based on the notion of economic gain without counting the cost in human terms. Here in Aotearoa this has been reflected in the wholesale privatisation of a range of provisions including health and education, the sale of state owned enterprises including power and recent attempts by the government to remove itself from its own obligations under the human rights act. All of these policy directions are underpinned by the same economic agenda—that of making Aotearoa even more attractive to foreign investment by opening up these areas to private enterprise. Far from resulting in increased employment and the promised reduction of our overseas debt, the privatisation and structural adjustment program of these

15 years has resulted in not only in a record overseas debt of $102 billion but also an enormous increase in unemployment. This has been coupled with economic rationalisation applied to public policies for health, welfare and education, for all of which Maori statistics are the worst in the country ... The human cost has been enormous.

Included in these costs has been:

- the unnecessary and premature death of a Maori man refused dialysis on the basis of economic rationalisation;

- the lingering painful death of a 21 year old Maori youth who was refused proper examination of his extreme head pain for two months due to an assumption that he was a street kid looking for easy drugs;

- the suicide of record numbers of people—the majority of them aged between 14 and 24, the majority of them Maori and Pacific Island youth. Some of them are my own nieces and nephews. The youth suicide rate in Aotearoa is the highest in the world, the majority Maori and Pacific Island ...

Global economic capitalism: Ongoing colonization

For indigenous peoples, these new forms of economic globalization are a continuation of the colonization which has been perpetrated on them since the beginnings of capitalist expansion. Nevertheless the experience of globalization is not the same for all people within groups. Economic globalization has enormously increased the hardship and despair of many groups of women. Indigenous women's experience of globalization is one of multiple layers of oppression. From the very beginning, colonization turned indigenous societies on their head. In the case of Aotearoa/New Zealand, colonization has reversed the form and structure of our societies, rewritten our histories, redefined who we are and our relationships with one another as with the experience of my own *iwi*.

As was the case with some other tangata whenua groups in Aotearoa, Waitaha were a matriarchal people. Waitaha women had great mana, and were the holders of knowledge that was highly tapu, or sacred. They held the knowledge of whakapapa (genealogy), they held the knowledge of medicines, of plants, and of the stars that our whakapapa connects us to. With the advent of colonization much of our whakapapa and particularly the whakapapa of many of our women and the knowledge that they held, was displaced and almost lost. The histories of many iwi are replete with famous and outstanding female rangatira. The systematic rewriting of Maori histories and the sustained and deliberate attack on Maori social structures and values of collectivity which has continued to this day has not only fragmented our people and dispossessed them of their lands but also removed the status of Maori women and relegated them to the lowest level of society ...

The influence of western liberal patriarchal values has been one of the most significant contributions to the oppression of Maori women. The cooptation of indigenous leaders by neoliberal ideologies of individualism, competitiveness and consumerism is increasing the levels of oppression experienced by many indigenous peoples. The most significant and disruptive effect of colonization which is being reiterated in the current forms of economic liberalism and globalization of the economy has been the theft of long and deeply-held traditional values and understandings of collectivity, of manakitanga (caring for one another), of kaitiakitanga (Caring for Earth Mother), for Tangaroa (god of the sea) and for their children and in the further redefining of our social structures as corporate tribes.

The notion that Maori were a tribal people is highly arguable, certainly my own people were not. While Waitaha as a whole was composed of at least three distinctly different groups, our social structure consisted of large extended family groupings within which roles were distinctly defined. Today, the infiltration of neoliberal ideologies into Maori leadership can be interpreted as yet another level of oppression particularly of Maori women whose voice the male elite leadership often try to silence. Far from enabling a revival of traditionally-held beliefs and practices, self-determination for Maori is being reinterpreted in terms of an economic base. The attraction of economic wealth as the means to achieving tino rangatiratanga or self-determination for Maori is further displacing and fragmenting traditional social structures of whanau and hapu. It undermines the core values and whakapapa relationships which connect indigenous peoples to the land and to the spirituality and values which are the core of cultural identity. The whenua (land) with which we have deep spiritual connections and whose loss so traumatised our people has become a commodity to be traded, symbolising the theft of the deep spiritual beliefs and values which locate us within the universe and in relationship to each other in particular defined ways.

Much of the current practice being constructed as iwi or tribal development is in direct opposition to the deep cultural values and philosophies that underpin Maori social and spiritual life. One example is the trading of resource consents for activities such as mining. Another is hapu consents for experimental GMO farms within their rohe in exchange for the short-term benefits of employment and training is another ...

Conclusion

The world order that is being currently created is terminally ill. It cannot be worked with. It cannot be fixed from inside. It is embedded in epistemologies that are counterproductive to any form of sane and genuinely sustainable and peaceful world order. It needs replacing with a completely new model. As indigenous peoples who are experiencing a further wave of colonization through global economic capitalism, and who as a result are hugely over-represented in all negative indices, the challenge is to seek ways of transforming these outcomes not only for Maori but for all who live within Aotearoa. Outstanding whaea such as Whina Cooper, Eva Rickard, Mira Szaszy, Sana Murray to name but a few, have led the way for the current endeavours by Maori women to combat the loss of Maori traditional values and the insidious forms of colonization being asserted by economic globalization. Within indigenous peoples and in particular, indigenous women are the seeds for a new world order based on traditional values of manakitanga, kaitiakitanga, wairuatanga …

It has been said that when women regain their rightful place within the world, wars will cease. It has also been said that women will refuse to give up their sons and daughters to war, wars will cease. Perhaps we could add that when women refuse to participate in or otherwise support power over politics, when women refuse to participate in the currently asserted global capitalist economic order and themselves begin the creation of a new order within which Papatuanuku and the traditional values of nurturance, equality, spirituality and just distribution are central, wars will cease and peace will finally begin.

4.6 In living memory

Pedro Pérez Sarduy

I loved my Great-gran Sabue, my mother's gran, a lot. She wasn't really called Sabue, that's what I called her because she didn't like Cunduna, her real name, and to call her Great-gran didn't seem affectionate enough to me. She said she wasn't called Cunduna either, but she couldn't remember her real name. That's why, rather than Cunduna or Great-gran, I preferred to call her Sabue, and she seemed to like it, and because I was the only one who called her that. Sabue lived down by the marsh, on the outskirts of Quemado de Güines, a small rural town in the north of Las Villas province which had big sugar cane plantations, and we lived in the provincial capital Santa Clara.

When my mother and I went for the end-of-year festivities—December 24, Christmas Eve, and December 26, "Quemadense Ausente," a day to honour those who had been born there and gone off to the capital—Sabue would come to fetch me early in the morning and I'd spend most of the day with her, in her shack. I'd help her make wood charcoal to sell, or doing anything else. We always had some excuse for being together. I learnt a lot on those visits. At the beginning, it was once a year, but after my parents separated and my mother had to go to Havana to work as a servant and I had to go to live with Aunt Nena, the oldest of my mother's nine sisters, who lived in Quemado, I was happy we could be together two or three times a month. Sabue didn't much like going into town, because people made fun of her, called her names because she wore clothes of many colors and a white turban. I remember how she'd say people had to respect her because she was "negra de nación," a black African nation woman. She'd repeat this with great authority, but gently and in syncopated cadence.

We all knew from her that she had come as a small child with her mother as a slave, from a far-off place called Africa. She never mentioned dates, but maybe some natural happening: "Mama died of typhoid in the slave quarters, during the rains before the harvest." When her mind was clear, Sabue, with her stock of many years of life, told me "black slave things," so I'd know, about colonial times when there were many slaves in Cuba and blacks wanted an end to slavery once and for all, but there was no end to the overseer's whip. Of course, she had her own way of telling. If anyone or anything crossed her, Sabue would stand tall and thin, one hand raising her old carved ebony stick, the other on her waist, and declare in a serious tone, in her Bantu manner, if not language: "Don't mess with Cunduna, I'm 'negra gangá de nación' [a black African nation gangá woman], damn it."

Sabue's only daughter was my grandmother Alberta, who I called Tata. It was overhearing my mother and some of her many sisters talking that years later I learnt that Sabue had made a papaya seed remedy to have no more children. Sabue told me, without much of an explanation, that she'd had to work hard for my gran not to be a slave. It so happens Tata was born around 1875, five years after the Spanish authorities declared the "free belly" law of 1870, whereby the children of slave mothers were no longer considered captive.

I was never a naughty child, but, like all children, got in trouble now and then—I'd throw stones at the mango trees, I'd go hunting snakes and hutias in neighbours' yards, looking for snails, scorpions and all kinds of strange bugs to play with my cousins. When I'd get into mischief, Sabue would tell me off: "You little devil … you're worse than Aponte." She'd say it kindly, because she knew José Antonio Aponte hadn't been a bad black, on the contrary. First the Spaniards and later many Hispanic-descent Cubans might have concluded that the Havana-born free black carpenter who planned the 1812 slave uprising didn't set the best example; but, for the great majority of African-descent Cubans, Aponte has always been a symbol of resistance and heroism. That I learnt from Sabue, who in turn learnt it from her mother. Trying to make sure I got the message, Sabue, the only great-grandmother I knew alive, talked to me about Aponte as if she'd actually known him: "Aponte was a handsome 'nengre' [black], loved and handsome as they come", and a man of great exploits.

When Sabue finally tired of life, I was all night at her wake, where the drums never stopped in her palm thatch hut down in the bush. I wasn't afraid to accompany her to the cemetery. I really felt her death.

Like my maternal grandmother Alberta, my other grandmother on my father's side, who everyone revered with the grand name of Mama, had 14 children, but in inverse gender: four females and ten males. One of them was my father. My grandfather died before I was born, but Mama had also been born free in the last quarter of the nineteenth century and was of Yoruba descent.

The memories of our grandparents and great grandparents were filled with stories recreated between reality and imagination, which became one and the same. Time and distance didn't seem beyond reach, but on the contrary was brought closer by Mama who always had another story to tell of black generals in the wars of independence against Spain and how she collaborated in the Mambí insurrection.

I didn't go around boasting my two grandmothers had been born free in the last quarter of the nineteenth century, but I felt very proud of them, for all they had inculcated in me. One way or another, this has kept me, and my children, going, to confront, wherever it surfaces, the bitter legacy of slavery which is the racism that has prevailed throughout the twentieth century, and is unending.

Slavery lasted 360 years in Cuba. Between 1526 and 1886, over a million Africans of different ethnic groups were transported across the Atlantic to work in the mines, the sugar plantations, coffee, tobacco, domestic service, and the construction of housing and forts. They were only able to bring with them their cultures and their religious beliefs, some instruments they reproduced in the new lands, and the power of memory which remains to this day.

That's why, on my first visit to Africa, in early December 1998, my thoughts were inevitably with my "viejas." Together with men and women from 27 countries of the Americas, Europe and Africa, I was taking part in a colloquium of Afro-Ibero-American studies in Grand Bassam, close to Abidjan, capital of the Ivory Coast—only a few hours' journey from Elmina Castle, in Ghana, one of the infamous slaving port-cities on the coast of West Africa.

I don't know whether by chance, but on the hot, clear afternoon of December 4, a group of us were at the beach. I walked alone for a while on the terracotta-color sand, like that of Cuba's Caribbean beaches. There was only one thing I could think about on such an occasion. I tried to imagine the suffering of the crossing, capture and the complicity of Africans on the continent who went along with the European slavers trading in human cargo— one of the themes of the symposium—and reflect on the extent to which the legacy of slavery linked to colonialism and neocolonialism continued to weigh on Africans in their own lands as well as all of us in the African diaspora.

The date was special, for me and the others from Cuba. Back on our Caribbean island, it was the day when thousands of drum rituals celebrated Changó, an important orisha or divinity in the Yoruba pantheon, and the name by which one of the most popular religions of African origin continues in Cuba, also known as Regla de Ocha or Santería.

The African cultural heritage has been preserved on the island up until our day thanks to the oral tradition passed down to us by those Afro-Cuban gatekeepers who have been our parents, grandparents and great-grandparents; rituals are the communicating vessels with our origins.

Despite this, until recently there had been no monument to commemorate slavery, until the recent totemic sculpture of Alberto Lescay in the hills surrounding El Cobre, near Santiago de Cuba. There have, in different periods of the twentieth century, been sculptures, museums and monuments that have been allegoric, including the many sculptures dedicated to Major General Antonio Maceo y Grajales, the man who symbolizes and synthesizes the rebellion of all Cubans because, among other things, in 1878 he rejected the truce proposed by Spain for a negotiated end to the Ten Years' War, because Spain refused to include the abolition of slavery in the talks.

One of the sculptures in memory of the Bronze Titan (as Maceo, a great mulatto warrior and man of great ideals, was also called) is in Cacahual, on the outskirts of Havana, the country's capital. Another is in the park that bears his name on the Havana seafront, where he is riding horseback facing the centre of the island, not North. Busts and statues have gone up to his mother, Mariana Grajales, who from the early 20th century, has been considered the mother of the nation. The most outstanding of these is in the eastern town of Guantánamo.

In the early 1990s, a sculpture to Maceo was unveiled in Revolution Square in his birth city Santiago de Cuba, which was the most allegorical of its time. The work of black Cuban sculptor Alberto Lescay, it represented the most impressive mausoleum to be put up in Cuba since the 1959 Revolution. The warrior figure of Maceo, also on horseback, can be seen from all angles surrounded by 23 huge structures rising to the sky which represent machetes, the feared tool-turned-weapon used by Cuban Creoles and freed blacks when they rose up in arms on October 10, 1868. That day, planter Carlos Manuel de Céspedes set an example to his class and liberated the slaves on his La Demajagua plantation. With the cry of independence from Spanish rule and the involvement of blacks in that struggle, a nation was in the making. Patriotic homage to a legendary national hero, the sculpture, according to Lescay, also carries within it a strong redemption.

Maceo was born into a Santiago de Cuba free colored family in 1845. My grandmother Mama, who was particularly fascinated by his imposing figure, told me that when Maceo was little there were times he'd be seen talking to slaves in the slave depot close to his home and there first heard the word freedom. When he was 23, he had joined the struggle for Cuba's independence; and, in 1896, he died fighting, as had his father Marcos Maceo and his brothers before him.

Despite the fact that the slave trade was officially abolished in Cuba in 1865, the clandestine trade continued and slavery was not abolished up until 1886. In 1873, during the war, what is thought to be the last slave cargo of African slaves arrived in Cuba. Possibly amongst them were some of my own ancestors.

Like my two grandfathers, many soldiers and officers in the first war of independence were black. When the veterans tried to resuscitate the independence movement in the 1879–80 Little War, the colonial press led a virulent campaign painting the patriotic struggle as a race uprising. But they were struggling for a republic "with all and for the good of all," as in the rallying call of José Martí, a Cuban of Spanish origin who, in exile in the United States at the end of the 19th century, founded the Cuban Revolutionary Party. Martí fell in battle in 1895, in his first and last attempt to turn his words of redemption into deeds. With the fall of Maceo a year later, the aspirations of those who envisioned a united Cuba for all Cubans were frustrated as the United States entered the war and negotiated a treaty with Spain, without Cuba.

And so, it was not until a few years ago, 1997 to be exact, that Cuba commemorated specifically the slave past, in the form of the Monument to the Runaway Slave. Part of UNESCO's international project on the route of the slave, there will also be a museum given over to slavery and the copper mines, considered to be the oldest in the Americas. The town, Santiago del Prado de El Cobre, took its name from "el cobre," the copper, discovered by the Spaniards in the 16th century. The monument took a year of intense labor to complete. The idea was that of sculptor Alberto Lescay and the director of Casa del Caribe in Santiago de Cuba, Joel James. Lescay describes the piece as a "song to the spirituality of the hills charged with the energy of men and women who sweated and toiled over the centuries, working the land for its metal ..."

In addition to geographical, cultural and spiritual considerations, one of the key motivating factors in selecting the spot was historical. Between 1731 and 1800, slaves working the mines successively took on Spanish troops until finally they were defeated them, forcing the king of Spain to concede their freedom. This has gone down in history as the first victorious slave rebellion in the Caribbean, which makes it important on the slave route.

The vertical bronze figure, forged in workshops of the Caguayo Foundation, which Lescay heads, is just over 9 meters high. It is set in an iron piece, which is one of the huge pots used for boiling the sugar juice taken from a nineteenth century sugar mill. The pot symbolizes the "Nganga," the receptacle for the attributes of the spirits in the Afro-Cuban religion of Congo, called Regla de Palo, or Palo Monte, originated in Angola.

For many Cubans, however, the most colossal monument against slavery has been the blood shed by Cubans on successive internationalist missions against colonialism, starting in the Congo in 1965. Ten years later, Cuba's military involvement in Angola became a southern African epic, fitting contribution to the overthrow of apartheid in South Africa by the sons and daughters of a people through whose veins flows African blood. Such sentiments were to be found in the words of Cuban President Fidel Castro in 1976 when he said: "Those who one day captured and sent slaves to the Americas, perhaps could never have imagined that one of those peoples to have received slaves would send its combatants to fight for the freedom of Africa."

To this day, Cuba has no museum on slavery and the slave trade such as those in Hull or Liverpool, in England. The first bears the name of Hull's illustrious British abolitionist William Wilberforce. The second is the Maritime Museum of the Slave Trade, in Liverpool, one of the two great British slave ports. Bristol is the other, but has no equivalent museum to its slave trading past.

Though there are statues in the Caribbean in memory of the region's maroons, or runaway slaves, I do not believe any one is eloquently symbolic enough to reflect the atrocities and legacy of that triangular trade between Africa, Europe and the Americas. The media of today all too frequently remind us that the scourge of slavery continues through Africa, wracked by ethnic civil wars, famines, epidemics, forced displacement, endemic racism, economic hyper-dependence, systematic over-exploitation of its natural resources, political corruption, and countless other calamities tending towards the mass extinction of its people.

A simple monument, not a great monument but a simple one, could be an initiative on the part of countries that, in one form or another, took part in the triangular trade to provide systematic aid to the African continent to eradicate at least some of that legacy.

In January 2001, the University of Havana conferred an Honorary Doctorate on Nigerian writer of Yoruba origin, Wole Soyinka, Nobel Prize for Literature in 1986 (coincidentally the year marking the centenary of the abolition of slavery in Cuba). Soyinka spoke of the ties of friendship between Cubans and Africans and declared that the many young Africans studying in Cuba carried with them a seal of development and success. He referred to Cuba's aid to Africa in the struggle against colonialism, followed by an army of teachers and doctors helping develop the region—all of which Nelson Mandela had singled out on multiple occasions.

What better monument than that?

At the start of the 21st century, with galloping globalization, such a gesture should be neither a pipe dream nor difficult to undertake. If a poor, small country like Cuba could build its own solidarity with Africa in the form of free scholarships for thousands of students from Africa and other parts of the so-called Third World, it should not be too much to ask of the rich nations in question an altruistic gesture of this nature. In the final analysis, many of their economies were grounded on slave labor and the fruits of colonialism. At the same time, each and every country in Europe and the Americas which benefited from or suffered the consequences of the slave trade and slavery should also have even a modest mausoleum as lasting testimony. Africa records its role in the triangular trade with two historic sites: Elmina, in Ghana, and Gorée island, two miles outside Dakar, capital of Senegal. A place of pilgrimage for Africans of the diaspora and declared UNESCO World Patrimony, the isle preserves the trace of that terrible past, including the gate of no return through which the human cargo passed for export to the New World.

Putting up monuments recording the facts would not be designed to inflict greater wounds into human memory but rather cleanse them for them to heal one day. In the final analysis, it's about paying a debt. Others have been paid. This one remains.

Part 2

As we all well know, while globalization refers to a human process at work on our planet, its effects are hardly uniform. The ways that persons, communities, and nations have engaged with this phenomenon have been idiosyncratic both in terms of time frame and style—ranging anywhere from 100 to 500 years, and experienced variously as, for example, economic gain, cultural cross-pollination, dispossession of land, enslavement, exile or sweatshops. Globalization has thus of necessity been adjudicated at local levels making the possibility of a uniform narrative about it—let alone a common ethical framework for dealing with it—highly unlikely.

What we can confidently say, perhaps, is that modernity and late modernity have been periods of intense mapping and remapping of the planet and its human constituents. In the process everyone has had to find some framework (practical and ethical) for dealing with this situation. And every one of these frameworks, even those of Western intellectuals, is merely a local mode of approaching something that is experienced as universal. While the West may have eliminated the gods from its notion of a transnational and transcultural marketplace, many others have found themselves unmistakably open to ultimate forces capable of re-sancitfying this profane meaning of exchange. Their task has been, as the American anthropologist Marshal Sahlins puts it, to "integrate their experience of the world system into something that is logically and ontologically more inclusive: their own system of the world."[2] In this sense religion and globalization are not discreet entities. Our global world is, in fact, a world infused with religious significance.

These issues come to the fore in two final selections in this Reader. The first is the poem "EarthChild" by Ghanaian poet and scholar Kofi Anyidoho. The world that is mapped in the poem begins in imperialism, the slave trade, and the colonization of Africa, and stretches to the "Voudoun Haitian shores" of today. Employing self-consciously religious language, Anyidoho describes a world that is populated with false gods, priests, devotees, and Souls variously protected in granite walls and the "cross rhythms of jazz." In the cosmopolitan centers of the Atlantic world, languages that have been assailed by modern history erupt in music: wailing saxophones and "God's Trombones" that link London, Paris, Lisbon, New York, Chicago, Havana, and Kingston with a footpath reaching back over the deadly middle passage to the dust of Africa. Souls withstand and reshape this global cosmopolitan world with Song that myth-making pawnbrokers "couldn't take away."

The final selection is an essay by the Tibetan poet Tenzin Tsundue, who writes of being a Tibetan exile, a person with his feet in an intensely transcultural world. He is, however, no cosmopolitan. In a fitting closure to the Reader, Tsundue begins with an invocation of maps. Rather than being a citizen of the world, at home everywhere, he is legally designated in his country of residence as a citizen of another state that does not appear on any political map. He is a man with nowhere to call home. With his fellow exiles he lives in a globalized world—in a multicultural environment where refugees compete for work in technological industries, and where one can speak Tibetan, write in English, and sing in Hindi. In this situation re/creating transcultural spaces is not a priority. As refugees Tenzin and his community in exile simply want to go home. And Exile is not simply a political and cultural state of being. It is fraught with ultimate significance. For the older generations, continuity with home is created through shared memories, butter tea, and the motion of prayer wheels. For the generation born in exile dislocation redefines the meaning of "eternity."

4.7 EarthChild

Kofi Anyidoho

And still we stand so tall among the cannonades
We smell of mists and of powdered memories ...
Born to Earth and of the Earth
we grew like infant corn among the Locust Clan
we gathered at dawn in armfuls of dust
we blew brainstorms in the night of our birth.
Termites came and ate away our Voice
ate away our rainbow's gown of flames
soiled memories with banquets of blood.
And still we stand so tall among the fields of thorn
We smell of mists and of scented memories ...
There once were gods who came at dawn
and took away our Voice
leaving here the howls of storm
the screams of devotees
the rancid breaths of priest.
And still we stand so tall among the cannonades
We smell of mists and of powdered memories ...
EarthChild EarthChild EarthChild
SeyamSinaj SinajSinaj SeyamSinaj
EarthChild EarthChild EarthChild
your Songs traverse this land of hostile winds
you blow brainstorms into banquet halls of MoonChildren
you die you live in Song
you hate you love in Song
you measure our joy in interplay of polyrhythmic Sounds.
SinajSinaj SeyamSinaj SinajSeyam
EarthChild EarthChild EarthChild
SinajSinaj SeyamSinaj SinajSeyam
I am you are my Song our dream my love
our Hope
You sought my Soul I sought your Soul so long
in cross rhythms of Jazz in polyrhythmic miles of Jazz
till Miles our Davis led us through the rumbling weight of
Drums
I found I lost you again in wails of Saxophones
lost found you again in booming hopes of God's Trombones.

And still we stand so tall among the cannonades
We smell of mists and of powdered memories ...
But come next fall EarthChild EarthChild EarthChild
I may lose you again to pampered dreams of history's pawnbrokers
and all I have is
A Song for you
A Song for you
A Song for you ...
You will walk away with all our history braided on your head
all woven into cross rhythms of hair each strand
so linked to every other strand each path
so linked to every other path each destiny
the destiny of every other single destiny.
And in all alleyways of old London and Paris and
Lisbon
And in all Harlemways of New York Chicago New
Orleans
in Kingston-Jamaica Havana in Cuba Atlanta in
Georgia
on Voudun shores of Haiti our Haiti Oh Haiti!
on Voudun shores of Haiti Oh Haiti our Haiti!
on Voudun shores of Haiti our Haiti Oh Haiti!
you will find footprints running backways
into lives once lost to sharp rhythms of Panther's greed
lives all lost to cold embrace of Atlantic waves.
SeyamSinaj SinajSeyam SeyamSinaj
EarthChild EarthChild EarthChild
SinajSeyam SeyamSinaj SinajSeyam
I am you are my Song our dream your dawn
our Love
You sought my Soul I sought your Soul so long
in cross rhythms of Jazz in polyrhythmic miles of Jazz
till Miles our Davis took us through the agonies of Joys
so good
walking off with all his stuff with almost all our Song.
I lost I found you again in wails of Saxophones
found lost you again in rumbling weight of Drums
lost found you again in hopeful booms of God's
Trombones
your voice so strained against the pains of ecstacies.
And still we stand so tall among the Locust Clan
We smell of mists and of scented memories ...

and yet such menace in casual glance of friends
so much fear in eyes of mythmakers.
Some swear there will be mountains washed away to sea
seagulls flying through out whispered dreams
pains so deep in granite walls of Souls
corncobs left half-burnt from blazes in our mind.
But those who took away our voice
Are now surprised
They couldn't take away our Song.
EarthChild EarthChild EarthChild
SeyamSinaj SinajSeyam SeyamSinaj
EarthChild EarthChild EarthChild
I Sing I Sing I Sing
A Song A Hope A Love
a Song for you
a Song for you
a Song for you …
And still we stand so tall among the cannonades
We smell of mists and of powdered memories …
And those who took away our Voice
Are now surprised
They couldn't take away our Song.

4.8 My kind of exile

Tenzin Tsundue

"I am more of an Indian.
Except for my chinky Tibetan face"

Ask me where I'm from and I won't have an answer. I feel I never really belonged anywhere, never really had a home. I was born in Manali, but my parents live in Karnataka. Finishing my schooling in two different schools in Himachal Pradesh, my further studies took me to Madras, Ladakh and Mumbai. My sisters are in Varanasi but my brothers are in Dharamsala. My Registration Certificate (my permit to stay in India) states that I'm a foreigner residing in India and my nationality is Tibetan. But Tibet as a nation does not feature anywhere on the world political map. I like to speak in Tibetan, but prefer to write in English, I like to sing in Hindi but my tune and accent are all wrong. Every once in a while, someone walks up and demands to know where I come from ... My defiant answer "Tibetan" raises more than just their eyebrows ... I'm bombarded with questions and statements and doubts and sympathy. But none of them can ever empathise with the plain simple fact that I have nowhere to call home and in the world at large all I'll ever be is a "political refugee."

When we were children in a Tibetan school in Himachal Pradesh, our teachers used to regale us with tales of Tibetans suffering in Tibet. We were often told that we were refugees and that we all bore a big "R" on our foreheads. It didn't make much sense to us, we only wished the teacher would hurry up and finish his talk and not keep us standing in the hot sun, with our oiled hair. For a very long time I sincerely believed that we were a special kind of people with an "R" on our foreheads. We did look different from the local Indian families who lived around our school campus; the butcher family who killed twenty-one sheep and goats every morning (when the goats bleated with half-cut throats from behind the slaughterhouse, we used to throw stones at the tin roof). There were five other families who lived nearby; they owned apple orchards and seemed to eat only apples in different forms! In school we never saw many people other than ourselves and a few *Injis* (westerners), who visited from time to time. Perhaps the first thing I learned at school was that we were refugees and we didn't belong to this country.

I am still to read Jhumpa Lahiri's *Interpreter of Maladies*. When she spoke about her book in a magazine, she said that her exile grew with her and that seems to be happening with me too. From the whole gamut of recent Hindi films, I was eagerly waiting for one particular film, *Refugee*, produced and directed by JP Dutta. There is a scene in the movie that so eloquently puts forth our plight—a father had brought his family from across the border into the neighbouring country and is living far from comfortably but is a survivor. Events follow one after another and there comes a scene where the authorities hold him captive and question his identity. He breaks down: "*Wahan hamara jena mushkil ho gaya tha, isiliye hum yahan aye, ab yahan bhi ... Kya Refugee hona gunah hain?*" (It had become difficult for us to live there. So we had to come here. Now here too ... Is it a crime to be refugee?) The army officer is dumbfounded.

A few months ago a group of Tibetans in New York, mostly youngsters, found themselves in a difficult situation. A Tibetan youth had died and nobody in the group knew the cremation rites. All of them stared at each other. Suddenly they found themselves too far away from home.

> ... and meanwhile through the years
> our unburied dead eat with us
> followed behind through bedroom doors.

Abena PA Busia

Tibetan refugees, like other immigrants from Asia to the West, work hard to earn a living in that highly mechanised and competitive environment. An old man was thus very happy when he got a job that would pay him enough so he wouldn't be a burden on his family's scarce resources. He was put in charge of pressing a button whenever there was a beep. He found it amusing doing that trivial thing throughout the day. He sat there all day with a rosary in his hand, softly murmuring his prayers. Of course, he pressed the button religiously whenever there was the beep (forgive him, oh lord, for he knew not what he was doing). A few days later, out of curiosity, he asked his co-worker what the button was for. He was told that every time he pressed the button, he cut the neck of a chicken. He immediately left the job.

In October 2000 the world was tuned in to the Sydney Olympics. In the hostel, on D-day we were all glued to the TV set eager for the opening ceremony to begin. Halfway into the event I realised that I couldn't see clearly anymore and my face felt wet. I was crying. No, it wasn't the fact that I dearly wished I was in Sydney, or the splendour of the atmosphere, or the spirit of the games. I tried hard to explain to those around me. But they couldn't understand, couldn't even begin to understand ... how could they? They belong to a nation. They have never had to conceive of its loss, they have never had to cry for their country. They belonged and had a space of their own, not only on the world map but also in the Olympic Games. Their countrymen could march proudly, confident of their nationality, in their national dress and with their national flag flying high. I was so happy for them.

"Night comes down, but your stars are missing"

Neruda spoke for me when I was silent, drowned in tears. Quietly watching the rest of the show I was heavy and breathless. They talked about borderlessness and building brotherhood through the spirit of sports. From the comfort of home they talked about coming together for one humanity and defying borders. What can I, a refugee, talk about except the wish to go back home?

Home for me is real. It is there, but I am very far from it. It is the home my grandparents and parents left behind in Tibet. It is the valley in which my Popo-la and Momo-la had their farm and lots of yaks, where my parents played when they were children. My parents now live in a refugee camp in Karnataka. They are given a house and land to till. They grow maize, their annual yield. I visit them once every couple of years for a short vacation. During my stay, I often ask them about our home in Tibet. They tell me of that fateful day, when they were playing in the lush green pastures of the Changthang, while grazing their yaks and sheep, how they had to pack up and flee the village. Everyone was leaving the village and there was hushed talk that the Chinese were killing everybody on their way in. Monasteries were being bombed, robbery rampant, everything was in chaos. Smoke could be seen from distant villages and there were screams in the mountains. When they actually left their village they had to trek through the Himalayas and then to India, and they were only children. It was exciting but it was fearful too.

In India, they worked as mountain road construction laborers in Masumari, Bir, Kullu, and Manali. The world's highest stretch of metalled road, running hundreds of kilometers from Manali to Ladakh, was built by the Tibetans. My parents tell me that hundreds of Tibetans who came across into India died in those first few months. They could not bear the heat of summer, and the monsoon caught them in poor health. But the camp lived on and had many shifts along the road. Somewhere along that journey, at a roadside, I was born in a makeshift tent. "Who had time to record a child's birth when everyone was tired and hungry?" my mother says when I ask for my birthday. It was only when I was admitted into a school that I was given a date of birth. At three different offices three different records were made, now I have three dates of birth. I have never celebrated my birthday.

The monsoon is welcome to our farm, but not to our house. The forty-year-old tiled roof drips, and in the house we get to work planting vessels and buckets, spoons and glasses, collecting the bounty of the rain gods, while Pa-la climbs onto the roof trying to fill the gaps and replace the broken tiles. Pa-la never thinks about revamping the whole roof using some good asbestos sheets. He says, "Soon we will go back to Tibet. There we have our own home." Our cowshed has seen some repairs; the thatch is re-laid annually and old worm-infested wooden poles and frames are replaced.

When the Tibetans first settled in Karnataka, they decided to grow only papayas and some vegetables. They said that, with the blessings of His Holiness the Dalai Lama, it wouldn't take more than ten years to return to Tibet. But now even the guava trees are old and withered. The mango seeds they dumped in the back yard are bearing fruits. Coconut trees are brushing shoulders with our exile house. Old folks bask in the sun drinking chang or butter tea, chatting about the good old days in Tibet with their prayer wheels in their hands, while the youngsters are scattered all over the world, studying, working. This waiting seems to be redefining eternity.

> money plants crept in through the window,
> our house seems to have grown roots,
> the fences have grown into a jungle,
> > now how can I tell my children
> > Where we came from?

I recently met a friend of mine, Dawa, in Dharamsala. He had escaped to India a couple of years ago after being freed from a Chinese prison. He spoke to me about his prison experiences. His brother, a monk, was arrested for putting up "Free Tibet" posters and, when tortured in prison, it was he who spilled the beans on Dawa. Dawa was imprisoned without trial for 422 days. He was then only 26. Dawa had been working under Chinese bureaucracy for quite some time. He was taken to Beijing from Tibet for formal education early in life and still he laughs at China's feeble efforts to indoctrinate their ideas and beliefs of Communism and its way of life on Tibetans. Thankfully, in his case the Chinese efforts didn't bear fruit.

Two years ago, a close school-friend received a letter that put him in the most difficult situation of his life. The letter, from his uncle, said that his parents, who were in Tibet, had got permission for a pilgrimage to Nepal for two months. Tashi, after collecting his brother from Dharamsala, went to Nepal to meet their parents whom they had not seen since their escape to India 20 years ago. Before leaving, Tashi wrote to me, "Tsundue, I don't know whether I should rejoice that I am finally going to meet my parents or cry because I can't remember how my parents looked … I was only a child when I was sent to India with my uncle, and it's twenty years now." Recently, he received another letter from his uncle in Nepal. It said that his mother had passed away in Tibet a month ago.

I saw the Germans shed tears of joy when broken families from the East and the West finally met and hugged each other over the broken wall. The Koreans are brimming with tears of joy as the border that divided their country into North and South is finally melting. I fear the broken families of Tibet will never rejoin. My grandparents' brothers and sisters were left behind in Tibet. My Popo-la passed away a few years ago; will my Momo-la ever get to see her brothers and sisters again? Will we be together there so that she can show me our home and our farm?

Questions for discussion

1 Garcilaso de la Vega is often regarded as a hopelessly colonized man who was overly generous in the *Royal Commentaries* in lavishing praise for Spanish institutions (including the Catholic Church). From this perspective, much of the text can be read as an apology for Incan backwardness and an attempt to demonstrate that the Inca have benefited from Spanish rule. More generous readings regard this as simple expediency— needing to have his message heard. It is possible, however, that Garcilaso was more subtle than either of these interpretations suggest. How might the excerpt above be read as an indictment of colonial conquest, and the Spanish conquest of Cuzco more particularly, as well as a call for a transcultural approach to governance in the New World?

2 The final sentence of the "London Manifesto" —"The answer is written in the stars"—is more than simply poetics. In what ways does it pose a critique of the "rationality" of existing democratic states and their economic systems, as well as of the "propaganda" of the *civilized* world?

3 Bernard Q. Nietschmann's essay on the Fourth World was written in 1985. In the decades since then, we have seen the international scene reshaped in a number of ways by indigenous peoples. In 1999, for example, under pressure from northern indigenous peoples the Canadian government redefined one-fifth of the country's landmass as the territory of Nunavut, and gave the resident population (85 percent Inuit) control over health and social services, education, and (critically) natural resources. In 2007 Maya land claims were recognized by the Chief Justice of Belize. In 2008 the Japanese government formally recognized the Ainu as a singularly distinct people in

an otherwise culturally homogeneous state. In 2009 indigenous peoples in Bolivia were given permanent seats in government and courts, and their own indigenous legal systems were recognized as legitimate. Does the Fourth World represent a possibility for an indigenized globalization or are these strides destined to remain peripheral to the global balance of power?

4   The ULIN Treaty expresses a global ethical vision for dealing with our contemporary world. How does it differ from a cosmopolitan ethic?

5   Makere Harawira's essay is evocative of Calhoun's argument in Section III. In it she asks us to reject a West vs. the rest viewpoint, or in this instance a division of the world into indigenous vs non-indigenous sectors. A dichotomy such as this will serve only to obscure the creative depth of local cultural and ethical frameworks for dealing with modernity. How does she further localize these critical frameworks?

6   How does the story of Maceo, as well as the history Sarduy learns from his great-grandmother and grandmother, speak to (i) the prevalent assumption that globalization is a post-WWII phenomenon and (ii) Western philosophical concepts (i.e. the Western notion of freedom) as universal?

7   The readings by Kofi Anyidoho and Tenzin Tsundue encapsulate many of the issues we have considered throughout this reader, and especially in this last section. They remind us that our global world is not defined merely by transnational migrations of people and cultures, capital, technology, and military apparatus—by the movement of people and matter across space. It is also defined by experiences and memories that shape contemporary life in ways that challenge not only a limited temporal view of globalization but also a notion of linear time so fundamental to Western modernity. Space is thus redefined by time.

As a last reflection, we might ask how religion offers us a view of globalization that is both heterotemporal[3] and bereft of reciprocity in the midst of unprecedented movements of people, commodities and information. What does such a view offer us in terms of understanding our late-modern world?

Suggestions for further reading

W.E.B. Du Bois, *The Souls of Black Folk*, Boston, MA: Paperview and the Boston Globe, 2005.

Charles H. Long (ed.), "Transculturalism and Religion," *Encyclopedia of Religion*, second edn, Lindsay Jones (editor-in-chief), vol. 14, Farmington Hills, MI: Macmillan Reference, 2005, 9292–9325.

George Manuel and Michael Posluns, *The Fourth World: An Indian Reality*, Don Mills, ON: Collier-Macmillan Canada, 1974.

David L. Schoenbrun, "Conjuring the Modern in Africa: Durability and Rupture in Histories of Public Healing between the Great Lakes of East Africa," *American Historical Review* 111, no. 5 (December 2006), 1403–39.

Suggestions for further reading

Notes

Introduction

1 Martensson, Bailey, Ringrose, and Dyrendal, 2011, vols 1 and 2; Armstrong, 2001; Esposito, 2003; Juergensmeyer, 2001; Gerges, 1999; Kepel, 2003; Herriot, 2008.

2 Stackhouse, 2009; Kurtz, 1995; Esposito, Fasching, and Lewis, 2008; Berger, 1999.

3 Wolfe and Gudorf, 1999; Ruland, 2002; Anceschi, Camilleri, Palapathwala, and Wicking 2011; Groody, 2007.

4 Gusdorf, 1956: 165.

5 Long, 1999: 7.

6 McQueeney, 2013.

7 Mauss, 1990: 12. See also page 82.

8 Mauss, 1990: 5.

Section I   Contextualizing globalization

1 Friedman, 1999.

Section II   Religion and globalization: A dialogue with prevailing wisdom

1 Fukuyama, 1989: 3–18.

2 Berger, 2010.

Section III   Cosmopolitanism

1 See Pojman, 2005: 62–71.

2 Harvey, 2000: 535.

3 This essay no longer represents Martha Nussbaum's views on the subject. For Professor Nussbaum's current view see Nussbaum 2013.

4 See Harvey, 2000.

5 Chakrabarty, 2000: 255.

Section IV   Before and beyond the discourse of globalization

1 Du Bois, 2005: 11.

2 Sahlins, 2005: 417.

3 Schoenbrun, 2006: 1410.

References

Published Sources

An Act for Continuing in The East India Company, for a further Term, The Possession of the British Territories in India, together with certain exclusive Privileges for establishing further Regulations for the Government of the said Territories, and the better Administration of Justice within the same; and for regulating the Trade to, and from, the Places within the Limits of the said Company's Charter. July 21, 1813. [or, *Papers Respecting the Negotiation with His Majesty's Ministers for a Renewal of the East-India Company's Exclusive Privileges, For a Further Term after the 1st March, 1814*, London: E. Cox and Son, 1813.]

Anceschi, L., Camilleri, J. A., Palapathwala, R., and Wicking, A. (eds), *Religion and Ethics in a Globalizing World*, New York: Palgrave Macmillan, 2011.

Anyidoho, Kofi, "Earthchild," in *Ancestrallogic and Caribbean Blues*, Trenton, NJ: African World Press, 1993, pp. 19–23.

Appadurai, Arjun, "Disjuncture and Difference in a Global Cultural Economy," *Public Culture* 2, no. 2 (spring 1990), 1–24.

Appiah, Kwame Anthony, "The Case for Contamination," *New York Times*, January 1, 2006.

—*Cosmopolitanism: Ethics in a World of Strangers*, New York: W. W. Norton and Co., 2006.

Aravamudan, Srinivas, "Guru English," *Social Text* 19, no. 1 (spring 2001), 19–44.

—*Guru English: South Asian Religion in a Cosmopolitan Language*, Princeton, NJ: Princeton University Press, 2005.

Armstrong, Karen, *The Battle for God*, New York: Ballantine Books, 2001.

Barber, Benjamin R., "Jihad vs. McWorld," *The Atlantic* (March 1992), 53–61.

—*Jihad vs. McWorld: Terrorism's Challenge to Democracy*, New York: Ballantine Books, 2001.

Barkawi, Tarak, *Globalization and War*, Lanham, MD: Rowman and Littlefield, 2005.

Berger, Peter L. (ed.), *The Desecularization of the World: Resurgent Religion and World Politics*, Grand Rapids, MI: Eerdmans, 1999.

—"Global Pluralism and Religion," *Estudios Públicas* 98 (autumn 2005), 1–13.

—'Wisdom From the East,' *The American Interest* (August 3, 2010), http://www.the-american-interest.com/berger/2010/08/03/wisdom-from-the-east/.

Beyer, Peter, *Religion and Globalization*, Thousand Oaks, CA: Sage, 2000.

Biggar, H.B. (ed.), *The Precursors of Jacques Cartier, 1497–1534, "Letters Patent granted by Henry VII to John Cabot, March 5, 1496,"* Ottawa, ON: Canadian Archives Publications, 1911.

Bohman, James and Lutz-Bachmann, Matthia (eds), *Perpetual Peace: Essays on Kant's Cosmopolitan Ideal*, Cambridge, MA: The MIT Press, 1997.

Calhoun, Craig, "Cosmopolitanism and Nationalism," *Nations and Nationalism* 14, no. 3 (2008), 427–48.

—"Secularism, Citizenship, and the Modern Social Imaginary," in C. Calhoun, M. Juergensmeyer, and J. Van Anterwerpen (eds), *Rethinking Secularism*, Oxford: Oxford University Press, 2011, pp. 75–91.

Castells, Manuel, *The Power of Identity, Vol. 2: "The Information Age: Economy, Society and Culture,"* Malden, MA: Blackwell, 2004.

Chakrabarty, Dipesh, *Provincializing Europe: Postcolonial Thought and Historical Difference*, Princeton, NJ: Princeton University Press, 2000.

Chidester, David, "Doing Cross-Cultural Religious Business: Globalization, Americanization, Cocacolonization, McDonaldization, Disneyization, Tupperization, and other Local Dilemmas of Global Signification in the Study of Religion," in Jennifer Reid (ed.), *Religion, and Global Culture: New Terrain in the Study of Religion and the Work of Charles H. Long*, Lanham, MD: Lexington Press, 2003, pp. 145–66.

—*Authentic Fakes: Religion and American Popular Culture*, Berkeley, CA: University of California Press, 2005.

Chomsky, Noam, *Profit over People: Neoliberalism and Global Order*, New York: Seven Stories Press, 2011.

Cox, Harvey, *Fire from Heaven: The Rise of Pentecostal Spirituality and the Reshaping of Religion in the 21st Century*, Cambridge, MA: DaCapo, 1995.

Csordas, Thomas J. (ed.), *Transnational Transcendence: Essays on Religion and Globalization*, Berkeley, CA: University of California Press, 2009.

Davenport, Frances Gardiner (ed.), *European Treaties Bearing on the History of the United States and Its Dependencies to 1648*, "Inter Caetera," Carnegie Institution of Washington, 1917.

Derrida, Jacques, *On Cosmopolitanism and Forgiveness*, New York: Routledge, 2001.

Du Bois, W.E.B., "Manifesto of the Second Pan-African Congress," *The Crisis* 23 (November 1921).

—*The Souls of Black Folk*, Boston, MA: Paperview and the Boston Globe, 2005.

Esposito, J. L., Fasching, D. J., and Lewis, T., *Religion and Globalization: World Religions in Historical Perspective*, New York: Oxford University Press, 2008.

Esposito, John, *Unholy War: Terror in the Name of Islam*, New York: Oxford University Press, 2003.

Friedman, Thomas L., *The Lexus and the Olive Tree: Understanding Globalization*, New York: Anchor, 1999.

Fukuyama, Francis, "The End of History," *The National Interest* (summer 1989), 3–18.

George, Bill, "Ethics Must be Global, Not Local," *Business Week* (February 12, 2008).

Gerges, Fawaz A., *America and Political Islam: Clash of Cultures or Clash of Interests?*, New York: Cambridge University Press, 1999.

Giddens, Anthony, *The Consequences of Modernity*, Cambridge: Polity Press, 1990.

—*Runaway World: How Globalization is Reshaping Our Lives*, New York: Routledge, 2000.

Groody, Daniel G., *Globalization, Spirituality, and Justice: Navigating the Path to Peace*, New York: Orbis Books, 2007.

Gusdorf, Georges, *Traité de Métaphysique*, Paris: Librairie Armand Colin, 1956.

Habermas, Jürgen, "The Kantian Project of the Constitutionalization of International Law: Does it Still Have a Chance?," in Omid A. Payrow Shabani (ed.), *Multiculturalism and Law: A Critical Debate*, Cardiff: University of Wales Press, 2007, pp. 205–18.

Hardt, M. and Negri, A., *Empire*, Cambridge, MA: Harvard University Press, 2001.

Harvey, David, "Cosmopolitanism and the Banality of Geographical Evils," *Public Culture* 12, no. 2 (2000), 529–64.

Held, D., McGrew, A., Goldblatt, D., and Perraton, J., *Global Transformations: Politics, Economics, and Culture*, Stanford, CA: Stanford University Press, 1999.

Held, David, "Cosmopolitan Democracy and the Global Order: A New Agenda," in James Bohman and Matthias Lutz-Bachmann (eds), *Perpetual Peace: Essays on Kant's Cosmopolitan Ideal*, Cambridge, MA: MIT Press, 1997, pp. 235–51.

Herriot, Peter, *Religious Fundamentalism: Global, Local and Personal*, New York: Routledge, 2008.

Huntington, Samuel P., "The Clash of Civilizations," *Foreign Affairs* 72, no. 3 (summer 1993), 22–49.

—*The Clash of Civilizations and the Remaking of World Order*, New York: Touchstone, 1996.

Juergensmeyer, Mark, *Terror in the Mind of God: The Global Rise of Religious Violence*, Berkeley, CA: University of California Press, 2001.

Kant, Immanuel, "Perpetual Peace: A Philosophical Essay," [1795] M. Campbell Smith (trans.), New York: The Macmillan Company, 1917.

Kepel, Gilles, *Jihad: The Trail of Political Islam*, Cambridge, MA: Belknap Press, 2003.

Kline, Naomi, *No Logo*, London: Falmango, 2000.

Küng, Hans, *A Global Ethic for Global Politics and Economics*, John Bowden (trans.), New York: Oxford University Press, 1998.

Kurtz, Lester, *Gods in the Global Village: The World's Religions in Sociological Perspective*, Thousand Oaks, CA: Pine Forge, 1995.

Lewis, Bernard, "The Roots of Muslim Rage," *The Atlantic* (September 1, 1990), 52–60.

Long, Charles H., *Significations: Signs, Symbols, and Images in the Interpretation of Religion*, Auroro, CO: The Davies Group, 1999.

Long, Charles H. (ed.), "Transculturalism and Religion," in *Encyclopedia of Religion*, second edn, Lindsay Jones (editor-in-chief), vol. 14, Farmington Hills, MI: Macmillan Reference, 2005.

Manuel, G. and Posluns, M., *The Fourth World: An Indian Reality*, Don Mills, ON: Collier-Macmillan Canada, 1974.

Martensson, U., Bailey, J., Ringrose, P., and Dyrendal, A., *Fundamentalism in the Modern World, Vol. 1: Fundamentalism, Politics and History: The State, Globalization and Political Ideologies*, and *Vol. 2: Fundamentalism and Communication: Culture, Media and the Public Sphere*, London: Tauris Academic Studies, 2011.

Matthews, Basil, *Young Islam on Trek: A Study in the Clash of Civilizations*,
    Whitefish, MT: Kessinger Publishing, 2007.
Mauss, Marcel, *The Gift: The Form and Reason for Exchange in Archaic
    Societies*, New York: W. W. Norton and Co., 1990.
Nandy, Ashis, "Defining a New Cosmopolitanism: Towards a Dialogue of Asian
    Civilizations," in Kuan-Hsing Chen (ed.), *Trajectories: Inter-Asia Cultural
    Studies*, London: Routledge, 1998, pp. 142–9.
Nelson, Benjamin, *The Idea of Usury: From Tribal Brotherhood to Universal
    Otherhood*, Chicago, IL: University of Chicago Press, 1969.
Nussbaum, Martha, "Patriotism and Cosmopolitanism," *Boston Review, vol. 14,
    no. 5* (October 1, 1994), pp. 3–16.
—*For Love of Country*, Boston, MA: Beacon Press, 2002.
—*Political Emotions: Why Love Matters for Justice*, Cambridge, MA: The
    Belknap Press of Harvard University Press, 2013.
Oman, Charles, "The Policy Challenges of Globalization and Regionalisation," The
    Organization for Economic Cooperation and Development Centre, Policy Brief
    No. 11, 1996.
Pojman, Louis P., "Kant's Perpetual Peace and Cosmopolitanism," *Journal of
    Social Philosophy* 36, no. 1 (spring 2005), 62–71.
Radhakrishnan, R., *Theory in an Uneven World*, Malden, MA: Wiley-Blackwell,
    2003.
Ritzer, George, *The McDonaldization of Society*, Thousand Oaks, CA: Pine Forge
    Press, Sage Publications, 2011.
Robertson, Roland, *Globalization: Social Theory and Global Culture*, London:
    Sage, 1992.
Ruland, Vernon, *Conscience across Borders: An Ethics of Global Rights and
    Religious Pluralism*, San Francisco, CA: University of San Francisco Press,
    2002.
Sahlins, Marshall, *Culture in Practice: Selected Essays*, New York: Zone Books,
    2005.
Said, Edward W., "Between Worlds," *London Review of Books* 20, no. 9 (May
    1998), 3–7.
—"The Clash of Ignorance," *The Nation* (October 4, 2001), 1–4.
Schaeffer, Robert K., *Understanding Globalization: The Social Consequences of
    Political, Economic, and Environmental Change*, second edn, Lanham, MD:
    Rowman and Littlefield, 2002.
Schoenbrun, David L., "Conjuring the Modern in Africa: Durability and Rupture
    in Histories of Public Healing between the Great Lakes of East Africa,"
    American Historical Review 111, no. 5 (December 2006), 1403–39.
Sen, Amartya, *Identity and Violence: The Illusion of Destiny*, New York: W. W.
    Norton and Co., 2007.
Stackhouse, Max, *God and Globalization*, London: Bloomsbury, 2009.
Thomas, Hugh, *The Slave Trade: The Story of the Atlantic Slave Trade 1440–1870*,
    New York: Simon and Schuster, 1997.
Tillich, Paul, *The Protestant Era*, Charleston, SC: Nabu Press, 2011.
Troulliot, Michel-Rolph, *Global Transformations: Anthropology and the Modern
    World*, New York: Palgrave Macmillan, 2003.
Tsundue, Tenzin, "My Kind of Exile," in *Kora: Stories and Poems*, Dharamshala,
    India: Tibet Writes, 2012, pp. 26–31.

de la Vega, Garcilaso, *Royal Commentaries of the Incas and General History of Peru*, Part One, chapters 15–17, Harold V. Livermore (ed.), Austin, TX: University of Texas Press, 1966, pp. 41–6.

Waghorne, Joanne Punzo, *Diaspora of the Gods: Modern Hindu Temples in an Urban Middle-Class World*, New York: Oxford University Press, 2004.

Wallerstein, Immanuel, *The Modern World System: Capitalist Agriculture and the Origins of the European World-Economy in the Sixteenth Century*, Berkeley, CA: University of California Press, 2011.

Waters, Malcolm, *Globalization*, New York: Routledge, 1995.

Weber, Max, *The Protestant Ethic and the Spirit of Capitalism*, New York: W. W. Norton and Co., 2009.

Wolfe, R.W. and Gudorf, C.E. (eds), *Ethics and World Religions: Cross-Cultural Case Studies*, Maryknoll, NY: Orbis, 1999.

Selected additional electronic resources

Films

A Day without a Mexican, 2004 (100 minutes). A humorous and critical consideration of the possible impact of the sudden disappearance of the Mexican American population.

Alambrista, 1977 and 2004 (110 minutes). Deals with the experience of illegal Mexican immigrants.

Darwin's Nightmare, 2004 (107 minutes). Deals with two Tanzanian nightmares: ecological destruction caused by the introduction of the Nile perch into Lake Victoria and the ravages of global capitalism.

Inch'Allah dimanche, 2001 (98 minutes). Considers the plight of Algerian women who have immigrated to France since WWII.

It's All True, 1993 (86 minutes). A compilation of unfinished film shot by Orson Wells in Brazil in 1942.

Manufactured Landscapes, 2006 (90 minutes). A documentary array of images (principally in China and Bangladesh) that spotlight environmental change created by globalization.

Mardi Gras: Made in China, 2005 (72 minutes). Explores the globalization of the Chinese economy through the lens of the trade in Mardi Gras beads.

The Phantom of the Operator, 2004 (65 minutes). An anthology of archived films made by Bell Telephone and Western Electric in the twentieth century that suggests that telephone operators were early and integral instruments of globalization.

The Shock Doctrine, 2009 (80 minutes). Raises the question of whether free markets and free societies are compatible with one another.

The Yes Men Fix the World, 2009 (90 minutes). A parody of global business culture.

War Redefined: Women, War, and Peace, 2011 (60 minutes). A documentary highlighting the ways in which women are indispensable for brokering peace initiatives on a global scale.

Internet articles, lectures and documentaries

Ashdown, Paddy, "The Global Power Shift," *TED*. www.ted.com/talks/paddy_ashdown_the_global_power_shift [accessed July 3, 2014].

Barkawi, Tarak, "Military Globalization is Nothing New," *Aljazeera* (June 11, 2011). www.aljazeera.com/indepth/opinion/2011/06/2011610134756341516.html [accessed September 15, 2013].

Berger, Peter. "Wisdom from the East," *The American Interest* (August 3, 2010). www.the-american-interest.com/berger/2010/08/03/wisdom-from-the-east/ [accessed May 2, 2014].

Chang, Leslie T., "The Voices of China's Workers," *TED*. www.ted.com/talks/leslie_t_chang_the_voices_of_china_s_workers [accessed July 3, 2014].

Freeland, Chrystia, "The Rise of the New Global Super-Rich," *TED*. https://www.ted.com/talks/chrystia_freeland_the_rise_of_the_new_global_super_rich [accessed July 3, 2014].

Frichner, Tonya Gonnella, "Impact on Indigenous Peoples of the International Legal Construct Known as the Doctrine of Discovery, Which has Served as the Foundation of the Violation of their Human Rights," section 7, New York, United Nations Economic and Social Council: 2010. http://www.google.com/url?sa=t&rct=j&q=&esrc=s&source=web&cd=2&ved=0CCgQFjAB&url=http%3A%2F%2Fwww.un.org%2Fesa%2Fsocdev%2Funpfii%2Fdocuments%2FE%2520C.19%25202010%252013.DOC&ei=j7C1U9S7GcmlqAa4r4GYAg&usg=AFQjCNHILAJtAiDeIRhbwGlHFDLEjSoNTg&sig2=ZKHVHYQmAvgtMAX1-fn4lg&bvm=bv.70138588,d.b2k [accessed July 3 2014].

Friedman, Thomas L., "A Manifesto for the Fast World," *New York Times* (March 28, 1999). www.globalpolicy.org/component/content/article/172/29945.html [accessed July 3, 2014].

Ghemawat, Pankaj, "Actually, the World Isn't Flat," *TED*, *TED*. https://www.ted.com/talks/pankaj_ghemawat_actually_the_world_isn_t_flat [accessed July 3, 2014].

Glenny, Misha, "How Global Crime Networks Work," *TED*. https://www.ted.com/talks/misha_glenny_investigates_global_crime_networks [accessed July 3, 2014].

Global Policy Forum. *Globalization*. www.globalpolicy.org/globalization.html [accessed July 3, 2014].

The Globalization Tapes, 2002, topdocumentaryfilms.com/the-globalization-tapes/ [accessed July 3, 2014].

Grandin, Greg, "History's Sinkhole." *The Nation*, October 22, 2013. www.thenation.com/article/176782/historys-sinkhole# [July 3, 2014].

—"Reading Melville in Post-9/11 America." *The Nation*, January 7, 2014. www.thenation.com/article/177825/reading-melville-post-911-america [accessed July 3, 2014].

Harawira, Makere, "Economic Globalization, Indigenous Peoples, and the Role of Indigenous Women', Presentation at The Hague Appeal for Peace Conference (May 1999). Organized by the Women's International League for Peace and Freedom. www.converge.org.nz/pma/Mak.htm [accessed September 30, 2013].

Hedges, Chris, "Empire of Illusion: The End of Literacy and the Triumph of Spectacle," Shipka Speakers Series (September 10, 2010). https://www.youtube.com/watch?v=PdxQ7fyBqV0 [accessed July 3, 2014].

International Monetary Fund, *Globalization*. www.imf.org/external/np/exr/key/global.htm [accessed July 3, 2014].

Legler,Gretchen, "The Happiness Index: Putting people before profit in Bhutan." *Orion*. January/February 2014. www.orionmagazine.org/index.php/articles/article/7968 [accessed July 3, 2014].

Mann, Charles C., "The Real Story of Globalization." *Wall Street Journal*. August 6, 2011. http://online.wsj.com/news/articles/SB100014240531119034545045764864213071710 28 [accessed July 3, 2014].

McQueeney, Kerry, "Disconnected: One Billion people still don't own a mobile phone, and a third of the world does not have access to the internet." *Daily Mail* online. September 10, 2013. www.dailymail.co.uk/news/article-2216625/Report-shows-1billion-people-dont-mobile-phone-half-world-access-internet.html [accessed July 3, 2014].

Nawaz, Maajid, "A Global Culture to Fight Extremism," *TED*. www.ted.com/talks/maajid_nawaz_a_global_culture_to_fight_extremism [accessed July 3, 2014].

Nietschmann, Bernard Q., "The Fourth World: Nations without a State," *Tamilnation.org*, Center for World Indigenous Studies (1985). www.tamilnation.co/selfdetermination/fourthworld/bernard.htm [accessed October 12, 2013].

Pan-African Congress, "London Manifesto, 1921." http://college.cengage.com/history/primary_sources/world/london_manifesto.htm [accessed August 25, 2013].

Pérez-Sarduy, Pedro, "In Living Memory," AfroCubaWeb, 2001. www.afrocubaweb.com/pedroperezsarduy/inlivingmemory.htm [accessed October 6, 2013].

Sen, Amartya, "What Clash of Civilization? Why Religious Identity Isn't Destiny," *Slate* (March 29, 2006). www.slate.com/articles/news_and_politics/politics/2006/03/what_clash_of_civilizations.single.html#pagebreak_anchor_2 [accessed August 26, 2013].

Unicef, "Millennium Development Goals." www.unicef.org/mdg/poverty.html [accessed October 9, 2013].

United League of Indigenous Nations, "Treaty, 2007." www.indigenousnationstreaty.org/wp-content/uploads/2012/05/SignedTreatyAug1.pdf [accessed September 4, 2013].

United Nations, "Everyone's a Delegate: 2005 World Summit." www.un.org/summit/poverty.html [accessed September 14, 2013].

van Heerden, Auret, "Making Global Labor Fair," *TED*. https://www.ted.com/talks/auret_van_heerden_making_global_labor_fair [accessed July 3, 2014].

Yousafzai, Malala, "Malala Yousafzai addresses United Nations Youth Assembly." www.youtube.com/watch?v=3rNhZu3ttlU [accessed July 3, 2014].

Websites

1. *Human Rights Education Associates*, www.hrea.org/index.php?doc_id=97 [accessed July 3, 2014].

An international non-governmental organization that supports human rights learning; the training of activists and professionals; the development of educational materials and programming; and community-building through on-line technologies. HREA is dedicated to quality education and training to promote understanding, attitudes and actions to protect human rights, and to foster the development of peaceable, free, and just communities.

HREA works with individuals, non-governmental organisations, intergovernmental organizations and governments interested in implementing human rights education programmes. The services provided by HREA are:

- assistance in curriculum and materials development;

- training of professional groups;

- research and evaluation;

- clearinghouse of education and training materials;

- networking human rights defenders and educators.

2. *Center for World Indigenous Studies*, http://cwis.org/ [accessed July 3, 2014].

The Center for World Indigenous Studies (CWIS) is an independent, non-profit [U.S. 501(c)(3)] research and education organization dedicated to wider understanding and appreciation of the ideas and knowledge of indigenous peoples and the social, economic, and political realities of indigenous nations.

The Center fosters better understanding between peoples through the publication and distribution of literature written and voiced by leading contributors from Fourth World Nations. An important goal of CWIS is to establish cooperation between nations and to democratize international relations between nations and between nations and states.

3. *Doctrine of Discovery Research Group*, www.doctrineofdiscovery.org/index.htm [accessed July 3, 2014].

A web-based public forum that works with indigenous peoples locally and internationally to discuss and educate a wider public audience about urgent issues relating to the legacy of the Doctrine of Discovery. Issues include climate change, the mistreatment of the earth, and social and economic exploitation.

4. *United Nations Permanent Forum on Indigenous Issues* [UNPFII], http://undesadspd.org/IndigenousPeoples.aspx [accessed July 3, 2014].
The United Nations Permanent Forum on Indigenous Issues (UNPFII) is an advisory body to the Economic and Social Council (ECOSOC), with a mandate to discuss indigenous issues related to economic and social development, culture, the environment, education, health, and human rights.

5. *United Nations Department of Economic and Social Affairs [DESA] Division for Social Policy and Development* (DSPD): http://undesadspd.org/ [accessed July 3, 2014].
The Division seeks to strengthen international cooperation for social development, particularly in the areas of poverty eradication, productive employment and decent work and the social inclusion of older persons, youth, family, persons with disabilities, indigenous peoples, persons in situations of conflict and other groups or persons marginalized from society and development.

6. *Material World: A Global Hub for Thinking about Things*, www.materialworldblog.com/about-us/ [accessed July 3, 2014].
Material World is an interactive, online hub for contemporary debates, discussion, thinking, and research centred on material and visual culture:

> We will use this digital framework to post exhibition, book and other reviews; discuss key topics; develop online reading groups and symposia; post links to images, objects and collections; highlight cutting edge research and fieldwork, conferences, meetings and other events; develop teaching resources and syllabi; and encourage student participation.

Material World believes in high quality debate and discussions in all areas of material and visual culture.

7. *United Nations Development Program* [UNDP], www.undp.org/content/undp/en/home/ourwork/povertyreduction/overview.html [accessed July 3, 2014].
Since 1966 UNDP partners with people at all levels of society to help build nations that can withstand crisis, and drive and sustain the kind of growth that improves the quality of life for everyone. On the ground in more than 170 countries and territories, we offer global perspective and local insight to help empower lives and build resilient nations.

Index

This index covers the principal topics of globalization, religion, cultures, cosmopolitanism, and economic issues, categorized further by different headings. Terms are indexed by their full name, not by their abbreviation, except where the abbreviation is in more common use.